The Girl in the Pink Shoes

Jessica Harrington

First Edition 2021

ISBN-13: 978-1-913822-14-9

Fortis Publishing
Kemp House
160 City Road
London
EC1V 2NX

Acknowledgements

Behind every story told there are always special people that need to be thanked.

To my partner, James Freeman.
You stood by my side and taught me that love exists.
You helped me heal and face my demons.
You gave me a life I didn't think was possible and the one thing I always wanted,
our family. I love you with all my heart. Xx

To my youngest brother.
Family means the world to me.
Even when we were separated, not a day went past that I didn't think of you.
I am so proud of the gentleman you have become. x

To Cathy.
You helped me more than you will ever know.
Just a simple hot chocolate or our days out made all the difference in the world.
I will never forget what you have done for me, it kept me going.
Thank you from the bottom of my heart for always being there. X

To my editor, Joan Elliott.
Thank you for doing an amazing job.
Your kind words gave me courage.
I will always be grateful for everything you have done. Xx

To my agent and mentor, Ken Scott (www.kenscottbooks.com).
Your delicate approach and encouragement

gave me the confidence to carry on with this difficult book. Thank you for guiding me on this journey to become the author I am today. X

To others going through similar situations.
Don't lose hope; you are stronger than you think.
Sometimes in life the hardest decisions you make are often the ones that lead you to happiness. X

To my readers.
Thank you for buying my book; please don't forget to review it on Amazon. x

Dedication

One day you will understand why I wrote my story; it was all
for you.
If I can give you the life I never had, then it will all be worth it.
From the first time I felt you move you became my world.
I love you with all my heart and I always will.
Love, Mummy xx

Prologue

My story never started as a book, I simply started to write one day. After years spent attempting to blot out my past, I needed to make sense of it all. I had tried to bury the horrific events that took place and ultimately what happened to me; I was mentally and sexually abused. Torture was inflicted upon me and my life was filled with lies. I had never been protected by the people who were meant to be there for me, I felt let down by everyone.

Everyone I have ever met has a story about coming into the world and how their childhood holds happy memories. Sadly for me, I didn't experience the same; my early days were fraught with unhappiness. I was abandoned by my biological father and I feared my mother most of the time.

This book details the events that took place, events that involved my stepfather and the sexual abuse he inflicted upon me. My mother was aware of what he was doing to me, but she did nothing. She buried herself at the bottom of a bottle and beat me instead.

Every decision I made led to horrendous consequences which involved many other abusers. They made threats to my life and a price would most certainly have to be paid if I were ever to speak out or disclose what they did to me. I was petrified. Bullied at school and assaulted at home, I eventually attempted suicide. Yet no one did anything to help me.

When I started to write, my demons came flooding back; the smells and memories still haunt me, taunting me while I sleep. This made me realise my story needed to be told. I hope that anyone else who or has gone through or is experiencing something similar will find some comfort knowing that life can get better. Mine eventually did.

I did not turn to drink and drugs to mask what happened and I do not see myself as a victim. The scars left behind have made me determined to be stronger.

Like a Lighthouse there is always light,
Even in the darkest depths and the scariest moments!
You just have to follow it.
Jessica Harrington.

No matter how hard life may seem, you only need to find the courage to speak up!

Due to legal reasons, all names, apart from my own, have been changed. Events that occurred are the truth formed from my memories and the scars left behind.

This is my story.

Chapter 1

Daddy

On the fifteenth of August, 1997, a bouncing baby girl named Jessica was born. She kicked and screamed as she searched for the loving arms of her mother. This is how I would like to believe it was, just as my son had searched for my arms when he fought his way into this world many years later. As he was cut from the comfort of the womb, he attempted to punch the doctor.

There are no happy photos of the first few moments of my life; none were taken. No proud mum or dad holding me. All I know is that I had to be dressed in dolls clothes for the first few weeks of my life. I was so tiny, nothing else would fit me. My early history has been made up of snippets of information pieced together from unreliable sources; even my surname was pulled from a hat.

My birth was registered in Malta where I was born. My mother gave me a surname that I never used nor never knew about until much later in life; I was almost deported when I applied for an English passport and it transpired that I had been using an unofficial surname all my life.

My father, I finally found out he was called Manuel, was Maltese and my mother, Susan, was English. I have three siblings. My older brother, Jack, and I have the same father. We have a half-sister, Laura, and a half-brother, Jacob. We moved to England from Malta, after my father attempted to throw me down a flight of stairs. To this day, I have no idea what could I have possibly done to deserve that. I was no more than a year old at the time.

After this incident, Susan hatched a plan to escape from Malta and my abusive father. She arranged a family holiday to England and, once we arrived, she told my dad he would be going back to Malta on his own. He could not do anything about this decision, she was now on UK soil and so were we. I wonder what the peanuts on the return flight home must have tasted like as he contemplated his future prospects. His visions must have painted a lonely picture when he realised he had been deceived by my mother.

I heard the story of my Maltese father from my older step-sister; I have no idea if it is true.

As a child and on my birthdays, I would wake up earlier than normal to wait for the post to arrive. I sat on the bottom step of our staircase and stared at the front door. It was the same each year; I waited patiently for the letterbox to open and hoped for a pile of letters popping through and onto the red carpet. I wished that, just once, my dad would remember me, even if it was only a birthday card. He was out there somewhere and I wanted him to acknowledge that I was his daughter. I didn't know anything about him; his name was never mentioned. No one talked about him and he was only ever referred to as *your father*. I wished my childhood was filled with love and protection, but it wasn't. Instead, I was brought up on lies and manipulated into believing everything was normal, even when that wasn't the case. I had to learn to accept it and often wished my life could have been different.

On my ninth birthday, I woke up and looked around at my purple painted walls and pulled back my *Sponge Bob Square Pants* bed cover. Everyone has something they love as a child and mine certainly wasn't that cut price bed cover. Sponge Bob is my mortification moment and I am dying with embarrassment describing my old bedroom to the world. However, I climbed down from my wooden cabin bed and ran out of my bedroom into Jack's room. I found his feet poking out of the bottom of the duvet while he snored loudly.

"It's my birthday Jack!" I yelled at the top of my voice.

"Fuck off, you little shit!" he shouted back, as a pillow hit me on the head.

Unfazed by my brother's reaction, I chuckled to myself as I dashed out of his bedroom and down the stairs. I took my place on the bottom step and patiently waited for the letterbox to open.

Finally, a pile of letters landed on the carpet; I jumped up to retrieve them. Four cards had arrived. I sat back down on the bottom step and stared at one of the cards that had arrived, it had a postmark from Malta. I had waited for years to receive this card. With butterflies in my belly, I turned the small pink envelope over and started to carefully open it. On the front of the card was a picture of a large bear and small white duck, surrounded by pink hearts and flowers.

For You Daughter was printed on the front of the card. Then a small, white piece of paper fell onto the floor. I didn't even attempt to pick it up, as I took a breath before opening the card.

To My Lovely Daughter Jessica

With lots of love on your Birthday

xxxx

Lots of love from Daddy

Hope that you have a nice day

love u always.

Then on the opposite page of the card, I found a second note.

Happy birthday

From Rosie xxx love you

Tears started to develop in my eyes, as I closed the card and looked down at the stupid bear.

Why was a small duck giving a present to a big bear? - I wondered.

It didn't make sense, shouldn't it have been the other way around? This card was meant to be for a small daughter from a big dad. I was angry at the word Daddy.

What right has he got to call himself Daddy? - my thoughts were confused.

He had never taken me to school, read me a story or kissed me good night.

Who is Rosie? - I suddenly thought.

I opened the card again and re-read the note from her.

My father must have another daughter? My half-sister, - things were swirling in my head

This made me angrier. She knew him and I didn't even have a clue what my own father's name was. He probably takes her to school and tucks her in at night before he reads her a bedtime story.

What did I do that was so wrong? Why had my first birthday card taken nine years to turn up? - my sad thoughts caused tears to trickle down my cheeks.

I picked up the white piece of paper that had fallen onto the floor and wiped away my tears.

Great, he's sent me some fake money! - I thought.

I continued to study the piece of paper and printed at the bottom was a name. I could read *Mr Manuel* but I couldn't make out the surname. This was followed by a messy signature. It was then that I discovered my father's name was Manuel. I had waited so long for this moment and I truly believed it would make me feel happy and wanted. But it didn't, instead, I felt upset and abandoned.

6

I sat for a few moments staring at my dad's name before I started to open the other three cards. Some £10 and £20 notes fell onto my lap from aunts and uncles. I had a very healthy stash of money. This changed my mood and I ran to the kitchen, where Susan had already started to make breakfast.

"Look, Mum, I'm rich!" I shouted at the top of my voice, as I waved the bundle of crisp notes at her.

I didn't hear from my father again until my tenth birthday when Susan handed me a small, pink, rectangular box marked Kirks Folly. In it was a small gold chain with gold hearts and teddy bear charms attached; there was a matching bracelet. Susan explained that my father had purchased this gift for me on the day I was born.

My dad must have wanted me at some point if he bought these gifts, - I smiled to myself.

Nothing more was said about my dad until, a few weeks later when Susan woke me one morning and told me she had a surprise.

Later that day, Jack and I climbed into Susan's car and we headed to Bristol. A few hours later, we arrived in the town centre and entered a large shopping mall. Susan seemed anxious, as she sat us down on a bench. She appeared to be searching for someone among the vast numbers of people who walked by.

"Hello Susan," a tall, stern-faced man with brown eyes said as he approached us.

He spoke with an unusual accent and was dressed in black. He was holding a small child by the hand; she was wearing a bright pink jumper. On his other side was a smartly dressed woman; she clutched at his hand and looked as nervous as Susan.

"Hello, Manuel," Susan replied.

"Do you remember me, Jack?" Manuel asked.

Jack didn't reply. He looked confused as he stared at him.

"You probably don't remember me, Jessica. You were far too young," he continued.

"Jack, Jessica. This is your father and his new family," Susan announced sarcastically.

I stood up, staring at him. I had waited my entire life to meet him but even although my mouth opened, no words came out.

"Well say hello then, don't be rude," Susan said, as she pulled at my hand.

"Hi," I said, as a strange shyness came over me.

What else could I say? Could I really have said what I was thinking? *Hi, Dad, where have you been all my life? Thanks for the card and money you sent. I would much rather you had been around. Where have you been for the past decade? Oh, why did you try to kick me down the stairs, when I was a baby?* - I let the questions swirl in my head.

My father was standing in front of me with his new family and I felt even more abandoned and rejected than ever before. Everyone seemed awkward and on edge. The woman holding my father's hand suggested that she would take us shopping. I guess this was to escape the situation and to give Susan and my father a chance to talk more freely. Manuel reached into his pocket and produced a large bundle of £50 notes. He stuffed money into each of our hands and we were ushered away to the nearest shoe shop. Using the money he had given me, I bought a pair of beautiful, black rocket-dog boots that I had my eye on for some time.

When we met up later that day, the atmosphere seemed more relaxed and we went ice skating. I managed to spend some time with my dad at the ice rink, he appeared nice and not like the person in the stories I had been told. As we left the rink, I thought that my time with him was over, until Susan invited him and his family back to our house for dinner. Before bedtime, he cuddled me and told me that he had missed me, I fell asleep that night happy that I had finally met my dad.

The next morning, I woke up early and jumped out of bed. I skipped as fast as I could down the stairs and stopped dead in my tracks when

I reached the lounge. They were gone. My dad was gone and I felt an emptiness growing inside me. This was the last time that I ever heard from my father, no more birthday cards arrived. He had vanished without an explanation. I wondered if I had scared him off, if I wasn't good enough or had done something wrong.

Years later, I managed to obtain his telephone number and after weeks of building up my courage, I called him. He told me to make an appointment if I wanted to talk to him. That broke my heart. I only wanted to tell him that I was going to have a family of my own. For some stupid reason, I wanted him to know.

Chapter 2

Lost at sea

Summer in Cornwall means one thing to most people; long hot days on the beach and eating every flavor of ice cream imaginable. Even though we lived close by, my family rarely visited the golden sands but I cherish memories of the chances we had to visit.

My eyes adjusted to the sunlight streaming through my bedroom window and I could feel its warmth in my room. I made my way downstairs for breakfast to find Susan and Jack already in the kitchen.

"Jessica, eat your breakfast, we're going to the beach today," Susan's cheerful voice announced.

"Woo hoo! I need my boat," Jack hollered.

He crashed out of the kitchen to look for his dingy, while I did a happy dance on my seat. I poured Coco Pops into a bowl as Susan started to make some sandwiches for our picnic.

* * *

After breakfast, I packed a few things for my day out. A pink towel, a bucket with a spade and a fizzy drink were packed neatly into my school bag. I was ready for a fun-packed day of building sandcastles. We travelled the short distance to Par beach and, full of anticipation, unloaded the car. Jack struggled to carry his inflatable dinghy as Laura led the way across the sand. She chose a perfect spot to sunbathe on the enchanting beach. After arranging the towels, Susan and Laura made a shaded area for three-year-old Jacob while Jack and I raced to see who could dig the deepest hole in the sand. After digging his way through to the darker part, Jack picked me and dumped me in the hole. I soon found myself covered up to my neck and stuck under the weight of the sand. Jack ran off laughing and by the time I had wriggled out of the hole, I resembled a sand monster, much to the amusement of the others. With our delicious picnic demolished, Jack attempted to blow up his inflatable dinghy.

I looked around at my family and smiled as the sun warmed my face and my hair blew in the wind. Susan and Laura were lying on their towels sunbathing, while Jacob played next to them. He was curiously studying the sand; picking it up and letting fall through his tiny fingers. Jack looked like a giant blowfish as he huffed and puffed to inflate his boat. There was no fighting, screaming or shouting today. Instead, we were a happy family.

I made some sandcastles and began to dig a moat around the best one.

"Jessica!" Susan yelled at me.

I turned around to see why I was being yelled at and saw Susan and Laura covered in sand.

"Oops!" I murmured under my breath.

They had just lubed themselves with suntan lotion and now the sand was stuck to every part of them.

"You've got the entire bloody beach! Go and build a sandcastle somewhere else," Susan was shouting as she tried to dust the sticky sand from her body.

"Jessica, do you fancy coming out with me on my boat?" Jack asked. He was standing proudly beside the inflated dinghy.

"Awesome!" I screamed.

I bounced to my feet and Jack handed me a paddle stick. Carrying the little boat between us, we half walked, half ran across the hot sand towards the ocean and full pelt into the sea where a giant wave of cold water washed over my body. I tossed and turned under its power until the ocean spat me back into shallow water. Dazed and disoriented, I saw Jack and the dingy appear next to me.

"Fuck me! It's cold!" Jack's high-pitched scream bellowed out.

We headed back to shore in an attempt to get warm and Jack placed the boat at the water's edge.

"Get in the boat Jess, I'll push us out," he instructed.

Jack steadied the dinghy by holding on to its side and I clambered in. Keeping it balanced, he waded out to deeper water until it started to float. He jumped in beside me and together we paddled our way out to sea. Once we passed the high waves, the water calmed and the sun became warmer as we floated along in the little boat.

Jack was 6 years older than me and was out with his mates a lot, so I rarely managed to spend time with him. I felt close to him when we were together and I was thoroughly enjoying the afternoon with him as we chilled and chatted on the sea. Half an hour must have passed before we looked back to the shore. Susan was standing at the water's edge waving her arms in the air but her voice was carried away by the wind.

"Hey, Mum!" we shouted back to her and waved.

Our fit of giggles disguised the predicament we were in. Suddenly, Jack stopped giggling.

"Oh shit!" he choked.

12

The penny finally dropped and he realised why Susan was waving and shouting at us.

"Shit! Shit! Shit!" Jack cursed, he looked frightened.

We had drifted out to sea. The current was pulling us out further with every second that passed. Susan became ant-like within a matter of minutes. Jack snatched his paddle and frantically tried to steer us back to shore.

"Grab your paddle, Jess!" Jack's worried voice rang out.

My brother normally acted like a tough guy so I knew we were in trouble. I picked up my paddle stick to help but Jack was bigger and stronger than me. I couldn't keep up with him; he paddled as fast as he could to no avail. We were going round in circles as the tide continued to carry us out further to the sea. Not surprisingly, I lost grip of my paddle and it dropped into the sea.

"Oops!" I muttered as I watched it float away.

Jack turned around to see it drifting in the opposite direction. I started with a short giggle which soon turned into an uncontrollable laugh as I cheekily waved goodbye to the paddle.

"Jess, this is not funny," Jack snapped.

He placed his hands on his head in frustration.

"What are we going to do?" I stammered.

"I'm going to have to swim us back," he announced.

Jack handed me his paddle before he jumped off the side of the boat and into the sea. He disappeared under the water and returned to the surface gasping for air.

"Holy shit, it's fucking cold," he cursed.

In a frantic attempt to grab the side of the oily boat he bobbed up and down. He looked like a bouncing, bug-eyed French bulldog trying to catch its reflection in a mirror. This made my fit of laughter emerge again but now tears of laughter streamed down my face. I watched Jack slip and slide while he continued bobbing. When he finally managed to grab hold of the boat, he wasn't smiling.

"Jess. For fuck's sake, stop laughing and paddle!" Jack barked.

Frustrated, he attempted to tow us back to shore but while Jack swam furiously towing the little boat I was barely able to breathe. I picked up the remaining paddle and tried my best to move it through the water. Immediately, I dropped it and watched it drift away before it could be rescued, just like its partner.

"Paddle, paddle, paddle!" Jack instructed me.

I stretched my arm over the boat to try with my hands while he was desperately swimming.

"Urm, I dropped it," I said calmly.

Jack stopped swimming and turned around to look at me.

"Dropped what?" he demanded breathlessly as he screwed up his eyes.

"The paddle!" my smile showing the gaps between my teeth.

"Where exactly did you drop it?" Jack demanded.

"Urm, in the water," I replied.

I gave Jack the cutest smile possible in the hope that he wouldn't shout at me.

"FuuuuuucccK!" he screamed, as he slapped the water with his hand.

Oh dear, Jack's mad at me, - I thought to myself.

He climbed back into the boat and cupped his hands over his face and shook his head.

"We're going to die out here," Jack cried into the palm of his hands.

"Don't be silly. Mum said she would buy us some ice cream, when we get back," I placed my arm around his shoulders to comfort him.

He looked down at me and chuckled to himself before he looked in the direction of land again. We were hardly able to see the beach; it was a thin line in the distance and I was becoming increasingly worried as we continued to drift further out to sea. The sun seemed even hotter than before and, with the sea being the only water around, I began to feel thirsty. We were well and truly up shit creek without a paddle.

14

Maybe Jack's right, we're going to die out here. Who'll look after my teddies? - I wondered.

The sound of the seawater lapping against the dinghy broke the silence between us. Minutes started to feel like hours as we sat in the little boat until I heard a faint chopping sound above. I looked up to see a small object that looked like an ant flying towards us. It drew closer and, as the noise increased, I could see it wasn't an insect but a helicopter.

"Awesome!" I shouted at the top of my voice.

We frantically waved our arms above our heads and finally, the helicopter arrived near our boat. As it hovered above us, the seawater splashed around, spraying us from head to foot. We waited for someone to drop out and rescue us but nobody appeared. Instead, we continued to get soaked and the noise from the rotating blades deafened us.

"Is he trying to blow us back to the bloody shore?" Jack shouted sarcastically.

I was distracted when I noticed what looked like another insect approaching us across the water.

"Look!" I shouted back at Jack above the noise of rotor blades.

I pointed at the new object heading our way, it was a lifeboat. As it pulled alongside Jack's little boat, we realised we were not going to have a helicopter ride. One of the lifeguards lifted me into the lifeboat and, only after Jack had been helped to safety too, did the helicopter fly away. Sadly, we watched Jack's boat disappeared out of sight as the lifeboat raced across the waves back to the beach. The shoreline drew closer until we noticed a worried-looking Susan standing at the edge of the water.

"Shit! I'm in trouble," Jack murmured under his breath.

He was sure he was going to get it in the neck from Susan. Once we were beached, she ran to the boat with her arms outstretched and lifted me out of the boat. I noticed Jack hop off the boat and try to hide behind one of the lifeguards while Susan was thanking the people that had saved us.

"Don't you ever do that again, you could have been lost at sea!" Susan cried.

Within seconds, she had pulled Jack into her arms and hugged him. He immediately pulled away with an expression of embarrassment on his face. The lifeguards left but not before they told Jack and me about the dangers of the sea. On the way back to Laura and Jacob, Susan stopped at the ice cream van and bought everyone ice cream, except Jack.. He solemnly sat looking out to sea while he threw pebbles at the beach. As we ate our ice creams, I tried to analyse his sad expression.

Jack had loved his dingy. But maybe he wanted ice cream? Was that the reason why he looked so upset? - I asked myself.

I offered him the sticky mess that was left of mine by way of compensation.

"No thanks, you have it. It looks gross now anyway," he muttered.

Our day finally ended and once we had gathered our belongings, we loaded up the car. The sun hadn't been the only thing that warmed me that day. It had been a family day with warm, happy feelings and a bit of excitement thrown in. Susan hadn't gone crazy the way Jack and I had thought, the only thing that was gone was Jack's little boat; it was lost at sea.

Chapter 3

Laura and Jack

I call my mother Susan, not mum or mummy, for a reason. She decided to have four children; nobody forced her to make this choice, but she wasn't a real mother to us. We often came across as an inconvenience to her; something that infiltrated into what should have been happy occasions.

If she didn't want us, why did she have us? - I often wondered.

Like any other child, Christmas was my favorite event of the year. I loved the time spent with family and of course, there was the excitement of presents. Rose was Susan's close friend so we referred to her as Auntie Rose. One Christmas day our family was invited to spend it with Auntie Rose, her daughter, Sophia, and the rest of her family. Once we opened presents that had lain around the oversized Christmas tree, Jacob, my four-year-old brother and I spent most of the day playing in Sophia's bedroom. Auntie Rose had made a special effort to welcome us and the smell of Christmas dinner being prepared downstairs drifted up the staircase to Sophia's bedroom.

"Dinner!" Susan finally called from the base of the stairs.

The three of us made our way down to where a beautifully decorated table, complete with a piping hot Christmas dinner and trimmings, waited for us. Jack, Laura and her new boyfriend, Ben, had already taken their places at the table. Auntie Rose served dinner and, as we read the jokes from the crackers, I felt part of a proper family.

During the meal, I noticed Susan filling her wine glass several times. She poured and gulped the contents until I lost count but, at ten years old I was determined to ignore her and enjoy the rest of Christmas. Unfortunately, when Susan drank a lot of alcohol, the night would go in one of two ways, good or bad, and, by the end of this particular night, she was not in a position to be in charge of a car. Ben kindly offered to drive us home so we soon found ourselves squashed into his red Peugeot 306. We waved goodbye to Auntie Rose and Sophia. A few minutes into the trip, Susan decided to vomit on my lap and over the back seat of Ben's car.

Brilliant! - I thought.

It had been such a nice day and I was now sitting covered in puke as Susan tried to mop up her mess with her jacket sleeve. Ben pulled over into a deserted Tesco's car park and managed to get Susan out of the car. He attempted to clean the mess inside the car while Susan, rather than helping, drunkenly offered advice on how best he should do it. After Ben's best efforts to try, we continued the journey home. Susan was paralytic by the time we reached the house; she needed help from Laura and Jack to negotiate her way up the garden path and get to the front door. I looked back to wave at Ben who was now surrounded by smeared vomit but he looked pissed off and drove away without a backwards glance. I can only imagine he regretted offering to give us a lift. I opened the front door and turned the hallway light on as Jack and Laura hauled Susan into the house. The moment the front door closed behind her, Susan suddenly had a burst of energy. This meant only one thing, the night was about to turn very bad indeed.

"Laura! Who the fuck do you think you are going after a married man? You're a useless, lazy slapper!" Susan yelled viciously.

The insults she screamed at my sister were not entirely true. At twenty years old, Laura not only worked at a local nightclub but also held a second job during the day. From her wages, she was able to pay rent to use the dining room at the rear of the house as her living quarters; she kept it immaculate. I was always slightly jealous of Laura's bedroom, expensive porcelain dolls sat neatly on her bedroom shelf and beautiful fairy lights lit up her bedroom at night. She was far from lazy but fought for acceptance from Susan by making time to help me with my homework, cooking, cleaning and babysitting Jacob and me when asked. The only part which held any truth was that Ben was still married and had to return to his wife and kids after he dropped us home.

"You're a fucking slapper, Laura!" Susan repeated.

She started to foam at the mouth.

Oh well, that was a good day, - I thought to myself as Jack, Jacob and I trudged upstairs.

In these situations, it was usually best for me to get out of Susan's way. Unfortunately, in doing that, Laura was left to deal with her. I turned at the top of the staircase to see Laura making her way to her living area leaving Susan standing alone in the hallway, looking as though she was about to explode.

"Don't fucking walk away from me!" she suddenly erupted.

Still shouting and slurring abuse, Susan followed Laura into the lounge. She picked up the salt and pepper pots from the table and threw them at Laura. The last pot hit Laura directly on the forehead. I could tell she was stunned and shaken; she stumbled and held her head trying to reach the safety of her bed. Susan was out of ammo and, full of rage, she breathed heavily and looked livid. She paused, obviously considering her next move. Running towards my sister's room, she disappeared until crashing and smashing noises echoed out from below and debris flew out of the bedroom door onto the lounge floor. I could only imagine the devastation that was taking place. I heard Laura scream out in pain and beg my mother to stop this violent attack.

"Stop! Mum, please!" Laura's pleadings fell on deaf ears.

Susan was out of control and on a mission to demolish Laura's room. "Mum! No, please that really hurts, please no!" a harrowing final plea reverberated from Laura's room.

Terrified of what my mother might have done to my sister, I cupped my hand over my mouth and nervously placed one foot on the top step. Susan reappeared in the lounge, her face filled with rage, she was dragging Laura by the hair towards the front door.

"Get out of my house, you fucking slag!" Susan bellowed.

She opened the front door and threw my sister outside. A gust of cold December air blew up the stairs; sending a shiver down my spine. The door slammed shut so I darted towards my bed and hid under the covers. Like a naughty child, Susan stomped her way up the stairs. Unrecognizable words slurred from her mouth as she walked past my room, then her bedroom door slammed.

I climbed out of bed and crept downstairs. Debris was strewn across the lounge floor. I stopped to look through Laura's open bedroom door; things were no better there. Her once beautiful bedroom had been smashed to pieces, total carnage. Without warning, Laura's face peered through the window and into her bedroom. Startled, I jumped and let out a scream. My hand automatically went to my mouth and I hoped Susan had not heard me. I made my way through the smashed possessions and opened the window for Laura. It seemed so unreal, amusing if truth be told. It felt like I was about to serve ice cream or play shops with her through the open window. I have no idea why this sprang to mind but I started to giggle; probably because I was only ten years old at the time. Exhausted and broken, she stared at the carnage of her once immaculate room; she looked confused as tears formed in her eyes.

"Jessica, can you please go and find my phone? It's on the floor somewhere. Can you meet me in the alley outside?" Laura choked as tears fell down her face.

I nodded and Laura disappeared from view. I closed the window and searched through the broken, porcelain dolls until I found the phone; it had survived. Seconds later, I heard Susan's bedroom door open. My heart raced and a cold chill gathered throughout my body; goosebumps rose on my skin. I daren't be caught downstairs so, in an attempt to hide, I dropped to the floor and pulled a blanket down from Laura's bed. Susan's shuffles and muttering reminded me that anybody could be her next target.

"Mum, fuck off! You're drunk," I heard Jack's voice.

This was probably not the best thing he could have yelled considering she was spoiling for another fight. There was every chance Jack would be her next victim.

"You lazy fucking shit! Look at the state of this room!" she roared at him.

Granted Jack was messy and lazy, but he didn't deserve this. No one did! I got to my feet and crept to the front door while they were randomly hurling abuse. Once outside, I ran as fast as my feet could carry me until I reached the alleyway.

"We need to call the police! We need to call the police!" I yelled frantically the moment I saw Laura.

"Calm down! You know what Mum's like when she has had a drink. Go back inside and just stay out of her way," Laura said in a surprisingly composed voice.

"But I'm scared," I cried.

I handed her the phone and tried to catch my breath.

"Jessica it will be ok, now go!"

I was taken aback that my sister was more interested in tapping on her phone keypad than my fear. I could sense her irritation; there was nothing I could do but leave her in the alleyway and slowly make my way back home.

Drunken nights with Susan are not uncommon; maybe the occasional object would be thrown. But this seems worse than normal. This is serious and scary, so why is Laura sending me back? - I was confused.

Pushing the front door open quietly, I could hear the argument still raging between Susan and Jack. This allowed me to get back to my bedroom without being caught. Once there, I had a clear view of Jack's room and could see and hear the entire argument.

I watched as Susan suddenly erupted again and pulled Jack from his top bunk; he landed on the floor with a thud. Winded, he clutched his chest in an attempt to breathe. Susan stepped back and looked down at him then calmly pushed his TV off his chest of drawers. It tumbled down and hit Jack's leg before smashing onto the floor. A smirk spread across her face; she was enjoying the devastation and pain she had caused.

Jack screamed out in pain and looked up at her in disbelief. Clutching his chest, he used his bed for support to get onto his feet. Susan's face suddenly changed and anger took hold again as she lunged towards him, throwing a windmill of punches that landed on his body. He unsuccessfully tried to shield himself while frantically grabbing at her flailing arms. He was losing but he managed one last powerful push; she lost her balance and landed on the floor by the doorway.

"Enough, Mum! For fuck's sake!" Jack screamed.

He clutched his chest once more but Susan was oblivious to him. She was down but not done. Her mouth formed an evil grin as she steadied herself; in her hand she held a kitchen knife. Months before, the doorknob had fallen off Laura's bedroom door; ever since, this kitchen knife had been used to open the door. Susan must have picked up the knife during the fight.

Why has she brought the knife? - I wondered

True evil took the place of my mum; her distorted smile focused on me.

"Jessica, get your teddies! You're moving into your brother's room," she said calmly.

No drunken slurring was evident but her dark eyes were evidence of intoxication. I let out a nervous chuckle. Jack glared at me but I couldn't say anything. He thought I was laughing at him but I wasn't, I was edgy and scared. Susan faced Jack again and pointed the knife towards him.

"Mum, what the fuck are you doing? Please put the knife down!" he pleaded.

Pure terror shot across my brother's face.

How has this escalated so much? – I asked myself.

A tremble was taking hold of my body as I feared what might unfold. Susan looked like a snake about to pounce on her prey as she swayed back and forth, holding the knife pointed at my brother. Jack was frozen to the spot. I could read his mind as he glanced around the room. He was weighing up his two options; the closed window or the open door. For sure Susan would reach him by the time he opened the window and she was blocking his exit through the door. He was trapped with no way out. Susan was unlikely to back down now that she was holding the only weapon. His only option was to face Susan. It was as though a starting pistol had rung out in his head and his mind was made up. I watched him sprint towards Susan as he tried to barge his way past but he wasn't fast enough. She lunged at him with the knife. I watched the blade run down his back and he let out a blood-curdling scream. He had enough strength to carry on running across the landing and down the stairs. Bang! The front door slammed behind him. At sixteen years of age, he was now homeless.

"Go on then, get the fuck out!" her voice full of venom.

Susan's turned to look directly at me; she still held the blade in her hand.

Shit, am I next on her list? - my head swirled.

The trembling spread throughout my whole body. But, without another word, she turned and walked back into her bedroom. The door closed quietly behind her and an eerie silence descended on the house.

Is Jack ok? Has Susan hurt him badly? When will they come back and will I ever see them again? - I pondered the questions quickly gathering in my head.

How did this happen? We were sitting around a Christmas table, as a family, just a few hours ago, - I recalled our day at Auntie Rose's.

I sat on my bed cold, frightened and alone with half my family gone and half the house trashed. I turned to look over at Jacob snoring softly in his bed.

How has he slept through all that? - I wondered.

I got under my blankets and pulled my favourite teddy close for comfort.

Everything will be ok in the morning! - I told myself.

Nevertheless, I cried myself to sleep.

A few weeks passed without word from Jack and Laura. Susan acted as though they had never existed; she never mentioned them. I found myself thrown into a strange new world where I didn't know if I was allowed to ask about them.

I came home one day after school and found Susan had moved all my belongings into Jack's bedroom. Jacob now had our room to himself. At four years old, he was very young and wasn't aware of what had happened. He was also upset that I was no longer in his room.

Months passed and there was still no word from Jack or Laura. It didn't take long to realise things were never going to be normal again. One day, Susan, Jacob and I came home from the supermarket to find that Jack and Laura had been to the house and removed most of their belongings. It was as though they had vanished. With an empty house and an empty heart, I knew they were both truly gone for good.

"How dare they!" Susan shouted.

She was furious while I felt sad and lonely. She slammed the shopping down on the kitchen worktop but I walked up the stairs into my new bedroom; Jack's bedroom. I sat on the bed and pulled my teddy close to my chest as I sobbed in silence.

I really miss Jack and Laura! – my heart was filled with loss.

Chapter 4

The Devil

Susan could be an amazing mum when sober, but she became an unrecognisable monster when drunk. The morning after an evening's drinking; she had no recollection of the carnage she had caused. If I alluded to her behaviour in any way, she would tell me I'd had a nightmare. I was confused and this led me to question my sanity.

Since the horrific night when Laura and Jack were kicked out, I became Susan's new punch bag. Her wicked behaviour escalated. Many times I was pulled from my bed at night and given some form of verbal abuse, slapped, punched or kicked to the floor. I became Susan's new house-elf. After a day at primary school, I had to cook and clean at home. Laura's chores became my chores. If I hadn't cooked a decent dinner or cleaned properly, there would be hell to pay. Only when my chores were complete, was I allowed out to play. Susan's drinking had become completely out of control and I found myself concentrating on how much she drank. I noticed a pattern. If three glasses of wine lasted her for the evening, she was an amusing, entertaining person; there would be no drama. The times when she drank fast and was on her fourth glass early on, were when things would change. Her top lip would curl back to reveal her teeth; in a slurred voice; she would talk from the side of her mouth and her facial features warped. She looked like Susan, but at the same time, she didn't. Then the aggressive side came out. On her fourth glass of wine night, I knew it was time to run and protect myself, I had to find cover in the hope that someone else took the brunt of whatever was about to come.

The next morning, and in an unbelievable good mood, she acted as though nothing had happened. She would play the part of Super Mum; breakfast would be on the table early. When I asked about the night before and told her what had gone on, there was a standard response.

"Don't be so silly! That didn't happen, you must have dreamt it," she would snort.

'You have a very overactive imagination."

That was when confusion set in for me.

Am I going mad? Did I really dream about what happened? - I wondered. While I revisited the events of the night before, Susan had an excuse for everything and said my imagination had got the better of me. She told me these were only scary dreams. Eventually, I believed her lies, but I was mixed up because dreams don't leave bruises. Walking into a room to witness the devastation from the previous night made my head spin.

Did my imagination really get the better of me when Laura & Jack disappeared from my life? The new bruises littering my body - are they there or am I imagining them too? – I questioned myself.

It was a total head fuck, of epic proportions. Susan lied to mask the truth and made lame excuses about what happened. But for the better part of a sober Susan, she did her best to be a mother and I cherished these moments. Jacob and I had no-one else to guide us through life. Months passed, and Laura eventually made contact. After being turfed out, both Jack and Laura had spent their nights either sofa surfing or sleeping in Ben's car. Laura had fallen pregnant with Ben's baby and he had left his wife to be with her. They had rented a house together and Jack had lived with them until he managed to find his own place. The knife Susan had cut Jack with had scarred him but luckily not too seriously. I was so pleased to hear that they were ok.

After Susan heard about the baby news, almost overnight, everything changed. All seemed to be forgiven and forgotten and an entirely new relationship blossomed between Susan and Laura. They were no longer mother and daughter, they became best friends. Susan was at Laura's beck and call, it was almost like she wanted to win a Super Granny of the Year award. Trips to the shops for baby clothes, cots and prams became the norm.

Baby madness was upon us as Susan became Super Granny by day and a heavy drinker by night. The contrast in her life went further; she took Laura to breakfast every morning but disappeared to parties in the evenings. At ten years old I was left in charge of Jacob while she frequented bars and nightclubs located around Truro and Newquay. Occasionally, a strange man would arrive with her but he would be gone the next day. Susan's nightclub of choice was called Shout where Laura worked behind the bar.

Ben regularly visited Shout with his mates. One night, Ben introduced Susan to one of his friends, Shawn. Shawn had grown up on the wealthier side of the village and had attended the same school as Ben; they remained friends into their twenties. After Susan met Shawn, she spent even more time away from home. This left Jacob and me to fend for ourselves but, I didn't mind the time she spent away from the house, life was peaceful without her drama.

Susan's mood improved once Shawn became part of her life and, after a few weeks, it was time for Jacob and me to meet her new flavour of the month.

"I would like you to meet someone special," she had announced.

The next day, Laura and Ben came over to our house for tea. Thinking back, this was probably for moral support while we met Shawn. Laura, her pregnancy showing, and Ben played with Jacob downstairs; I sorted out bits and pieces in my room.

"Mummy's home! Mummy's home!" four-year-old Jacob screeched.

I popped out of my room to get a better view from Susan's bedroom window. A dark purple Cherokee Jeep was parked outside our house.

I wonder how long this one will last, - I thought to myself.

The driver's door opened and a dark-haired man stepped out, he walked around and opened the passenger door for Susan. Laura, Ben and Jacob made their way outside to greet and chat in the front garden. Susan locked hands with the man and they walked towards the house.

Here we go again, - my mind raced as I wandered out of Susan's bedroom and made my way downstairs.

"Jessica, come down and meet Shawn," Susan said from the hallway. She looked like a giddy school girl, clutching the hand of a strange and, to me, ugly man.

"How's it going? I'm Shawn," he introduced himself attempting to hug me.

What the fuck, - I thought to myself as my ten-year-old body automatically stepped back to avoid his embrace.

Susan glared at me while Shawn looked put out by my quick dodge.

Shawn was nothing special to look at. He was overweight with an unfortunate mole on his chubby-faced cheek and he did not have the best dress sense in the world either. His long, dark hair and deep-set, brown eyes didn't appear endearing to me.

What on earth does Susan see in him? - I asked myself.

He seemed like a weirdo; his stance, his gaze and his body language didn't sit well with me. However, Susan ushered everyone into the lounge and asked Shawn if he would like a drink. Her perfect hostess role was strange to see; normally I would have been asked to make the drinks. When Susan left the room, I noticed Shawn's stare fixed on me; his dark eyes glanced in my direction at every opportunity. Even when he was talking to someone else, he was looking over at me. And so, during my first encounter with Shawn, I made up my mind; I didn't like him. His presence creeped me out and my gut told me to stay clear of him.

Susan didn't drink as much over the next few months. As her love relationship developed, her mood and demeanour improved even more. She acted like a caring mother and, although I didn't like Shawn, I liked the effect he had on her. For Susan's sake, I made the effort to be polite to him because he made her happy and when she was happy, our lives became less stressful. She spent her time split between our house and his then eventually, during the week, we would receive random visits from him.

I hated when he stayed over at our house because, even to my ten-year-old mind, he was oddly attentive. Whenever I walked into a room where he was, his eyes followed me. That's when Susan would find an excuse to remove me from his presence. I was sure she had noticed Shawn watching me so, if I was given a job to do elsewhere, she could regain his attention.

Even though I found Shawn strange, I saw he was doing his best to blend in with the family dynamics. He would often sit and play with Jacob or ask me about my day. I would only give him three-word answers before I made a hasty escape.

Susan wasn't wealthy; she could never afford holidays and I rarely went on school trips, My school holidays were normally spent at home so, when my school friends talked about the amazing places they had visited, I was jealous. There came a time when Shawn booked us a family holiday to Butlins. I couldn't wait to go, but even this kind gesture didn't make me warm to him; I could never quite put my finger on why I didn't like him. In general, he seemed kind and harmless enough. I thought I needed to give him a chance because Susan and Shawn's relationship had other positive effects.

The bad air between Laura and Susan had gone completely; she and Ben came around a lot more. Susan attended some of the baby scans and always returned as the proud grandmother to be. I had my sister back in my life and, when Jack made his peace with Susan, our lives had improved. I believed the positive changes in our family were mainly down to having Shawn in our lives.

The happiness was written all over Susan's face when she left for another weekend away with Shawn. That night, Jacob and I settled down to watch a film with some comfort snacks and drinks. Eventually, Jacob's head began to rock forward and he fell asleep, snoring softly in my arms. I carried him to bed in the certainty that, once he was asleep, he would be as quiet as a mouse for the rest of the night.

The film wasn't as entertaining as I had thought so I decided to go to bed. I was drifting off to sleep when I heard banging at the front door followed by the sound of the letterbox clicking open. I sat up in bed and hoped whoever it was would just go away. Anyway, I had been told never to answer the door when home alone.

"Hello, is there anyone home? It's the police!" a strong male voice bellowed through the letterbox.

The police, what do they want? Jacob and I have done what we were told and only watched a film, are we in trouble? - I asked myself.

I climbed down from my cabin bed and grabbed my pink, fluffy dressing gown. After rushing down the stairs, I reached for the letterbox, took a breath and peeked through the gap. A face appeared. I screamed and let the flap fall. It reopened.

"Hello, I'm Jim, is your mum home?" a policeman asked in a much softer voice than before.

"Hello, I'm Jess," I replied.

We had a polite conversation through the letterbox but, when he asked about my mum, I gave vague answers. Our letterbox conversation went on for about ten minutes until I heard a car pull up outside. I was surprised that Susan's voice was audible; she was supposed to be with Shawn. Jim started to talk to her instead. I kept peering through the letterbox while listening to their conversation. I gathered that an argument had erupted between Shawn and Susan at his flat. Susan claimed that he had pushed her off the balcony but Shawn claimed that she had jumped.

Either scenario could be plausible when Susan drinks, - I thought.

The policeman left so I closed the letterbox and ran to my bedroom, jumped under my covers and pretended to be asleep.

Susan was in an extremely bad mood the next day. She told us she had broken up with Shawn and the holiday was off.

It was no surprise that, over the following weeks, her excessive drinking started. Once again, I found myself being used as Susan's punch bag for inexcusable reasons. If, for example, she couldn't find her jeans, somehow it was my fault and I was slapped and punched to the floor. I had momentarily forgotten how bad Susan could be but, as bruises appeared on my body again, I longed for the peaceful life I had glimpsed.

But, Shawn was gone and the holiday we had been so looking forward to was not going to happen. For the most part, he had made our world better because, when he was around, Susan acted as a mother should and didn't drink as much. I found myself wishing for his return. But, as the old saying goes, be careful what you wish for.

Chapter 5

Embarrassment

Certain films remind me of one specific school sports day. The kind of film that tugs at heartstrings. A young boy in a playing field holds his baseball bat while looking nervously between the slightly older pitcher and the spectators. His mum is clapping and cheering him on but glances towards the car park. Both mum and boy look disappointed. Without a word being spoken, the viewer can tell the boy's dad was too busy to turn up for his game again. In this heartfelt moment, the viewer feels his pain.

Cornwall had been blanketed by thick fog and heavy rain for weeks. In the last week before the school holidays, beautiful sunshine replaced the rain. The warm sun looked set to stay so my school decided to hold a sports event on our last day of term. Parents were invited to come and join in but, as I stepped out onto the playing field, I realized nobody had turned up to watch me. The only difference between me and the boy in the film was that I had no one to cheer me on. I imagined Susan at home, raiding my piggy bank for money to buy another bottle of wine.

I loved sports and I had entered every event, including the egg and spoon. Even although I was incredibly short, I had fast legs. By the end of the day, I had managed to do well and held tightly on to my Sports Day 2008 - Junior Girls' Winner's plaque. I had enjoyed the day and felt proud of myself. I rushed home to face my chores; I had to put dinner in the oven, vacuum and then do the washing up after we had eaten. After dinner, I would be allowed outside to play with my friends to play football in the park behind our house. I had been out for about thirty minutes when Susan called me in; it was 6.30 pm. She was on the phone but, to my disappointment, I heard her slurred speech and saw an empty wine bottle nearby.

"Get in the shower!" she yelled at me.

For fuck sake, it's going to be a long night, - I thought,

I made my way upstairs and, in my bedroom, I stripped down to my knickers then, in the bathroom, I turned the shower on. Thump, thump, thump. I heard the familiar sound of Susan's feet stomping up the stairs telling me she was annoyed and I was in trouble.

"Jessica, why are you so late and why are you naked?" she slurred.

The rank smell of alcohol wafted across my face.

"I'm not late, Mum, I'm having a shower as you asked me," I replied while stepping further into the bathroom.

"Are you some sort of a slut? Look at you with your tits out, your bedroom curtains are wide open. Do you want the entire world to fucking see you?" she snapped, pointing her finger in my face then at my developing body

"No, Mum, honest, I didn't realise ...," I choked.

I watched the rage build up in her eyes.

"Well, you little slag! If you want to show your tits off to the entire fucking world, let's fucking show them!" she screamed and lunged towards me.

She pulled me by the ear, naked except for my knickers, from the bathroom into my bedroom. She slammed my head hard against my bedroom window then held my face against the glass. From that position, I could see my friends were still playing football and now my exposed breasts were squashed against the window. I wanted to die and prayed no one would look up.

As if from another world, I could hear Jacob laughing in his bedroom, unaware of what was going on and, thank God, my friends were at the other side of the park and quite far away. Nobody noticed what was going on, but this meant Susan had not achieved the desired outcome; this angered her more.

"Right, you want to be a little slut, go be a little slut on the street," she screamed viciously.

I found myself being dragged by the hair from my bedroom.

"Mum, please!" I cried.

Some hair ripped from my scalp and my feet hardly touched the ground as she pulled me down the stairs and across the hallway. The front door opened and I had hit the ground outside before I heard the door slam shut behind me. I was in the front garden, practically naked. The shock and embarrassment immediately set in so I stumbled to my feet and banged on the front door.

"Mum, let me in!" I pleaded.

I heard the click of the lock as I stood there for the world to view my not-so-new knickers. Not knowing what to do next, I folded my arms across my chest in a feeble attempt to cover my top half. With tears streaming down my face, I turned to look up and down the street to see if anyone had witnessed my dilemma. The street was empty. It was a hot day and the smells of BBQ's were in the air. I was thankful that people must have been chilling in their gardens or at the park. Then I noticed a plastic bag at the bottom of our front garden.

Maybe there's something in that bag that I could use to cover myself up, - I hoped.

36

When I opened the bag, I found unopened beer bottles.

Why is this in our garden? - I asked myself.

I reached into the bag and picked up a bottle.

Maybe if I drink one, I will understand why Susan acts the way she does, - I sniffed.

At that precise moment, I heard a familiar voice.

"Oi, Jessica, what are you doing?"

I looked up to see my brother, Jack, with six of his mates walking towards me. I covered my breasts again.

"Why are you naked?" Jack asked.

His mates started to snigger.

"I was trying to have a shower when mum kicked me out," I said, trying to keep my voice low.

I could feel myself blush with embarrassment as I wrapped my arms tighter around my body.

"Go back inside, it will be ok," Jack tried to reassure me.

"I can't, she's locked the door. She's raging, you know what she's like," I protested.

Jack's mates reminded me of animals about to pounce on their prey. They stared at my exposed body, making me even more uncomfortable.

"I don't know, you will sort something out. See you later, come on lads," Jack beckoned to his mates and left without a care in the world.

Fucking asshole! - I said to myself as I watched them leave. Jack didn't even offer me a shirt. Same as usual, he's only interested in getting pissed! He knows what Susan's like. There's no reasoning with her when she's drinking. Why has he left me in this state?'

While I watched that group of spectators disappear out of view, I saw other neighbours at their windows. Here I was, naked in the front garden and the only real comfort I had left was the warmth from the sun; I wondered what to do next.

My only other lifeline was Laura but she lived about an hour away. Strange as it may sound, I started to walk to her house. With my arms folded across my chest and my little knickers, I started out but quickly realised it was going to be a very long and painful journey. The hot pavements burned my bare feet and every so often I stepped on a sharp stone. But these were not my only problems. If I heard a car coming, I had to dash for cover behind bushes and trees. Stinging nettles attacked my exposed skin adding to the pain of my gruelling walk.

I reached a long stretch where barbed wire separated the road from a sprawling field which meant I had no cover if a car passed. My heart pounded when I heard a loud exhaust roaring behind me. I turned around to see a sporty-looking car approaching. It drove towards me at speed but I couldn't hide. I prayed that the driver would not pay me any attention so I tried to walk normally and cover my breasts. The car zoomed by and I breathed a sigh of relief. Suddenly, red brake lights shone and the car skidded to a stop. I panicked. Running was not an option; I could hardly walk let alone run because by then, my feet were practically torn to shreds. The car sat in the middle of the road then reverse lights twinkled through the tyre smoke; the loud exhaust started to burble and the car backed up. Visions of being abducted flashed across my mind as the car screeched to a halt beside me. The sound of loud bass music kept playing as two lads leaned out of the passenger windows of the car.

"Hello, sexy! Do you need a lift?" the lad in the front asked.

His sneer worried me.

"No! I'm fine thanks," I retorted, continuing to hobble with the car creeping alongside me.

"Are you sure? We could all go and have some fun," the lad in the back suggested.

He gave me a wink and a smile.

I need to get out of this situation, fast,- I thought to myself.

I was in a vulnerable situation, alone and wearing nothing but a pair of knickers while three lads in a car perved at me. An inner strength took over.

"Fuck off! Leave me alone!" I screamed at them a couple of times.

Suddenly, the car exhaust made a loud noise, the tyres started to spin and, thankfully, the car sped away.

Could my day get any worse? - I wondered - Just a bit further, keep going. I walked with feet that were burning until Laura's house eventually came into view. Laura and Ben lived in a farm cottage near the main farmhouse. The last few steps were the hardest of all because I had to make my way up the gravel driveway that led to their front door. Like a thousand paper cuts, the sharp stones ripped at the already damaged flesh on my feet. I slumped down onto their doorstep and lifted each of my legs to pull the stones from the cuts that peppered my feet.

Tears welled up in my eyes as I knocked on the door. No sound came from within. I knocked again and burst into tears when I realised they weren't home.

What am I meant to do now? - I questioned myself.

I saw the sun was disappearing fast; the evening chill was giving me goosebumps and making the hairs on my arms stand on end.

"They've gone out," a voice with a strong Cornish accent rang out.

State the fucking obvious, - I replied inwardly.

I wondered if I was dreaming but someone was definitely shouting to me. I wearily looked up to see Mary, the farmer's wife, standing at the garden gate of her farmhouse.

"Do you know where she has gone, or when she will be back?" I called back wiping my tears away with my bare arm.

"Plymouth. You're welcome to wait here if you like, it's a bit warmer inside," Mary offered.

I slowly got to my feet and started the painful walk back across the gravel.

39

"My God, what has happened to you?" Mary enquired with a horrified expression on her face.

"You don't want to know," I answered quietly.

"Quick, let's get you inside and fix you up," she smiled and gestured to her front door.

Once inside her house, Mary sat me down at her oversized kitchen table.

"I'll be back in a minute. I'll see if I can rustle you up some clothes," she mothered me and hurried out of the kitchen.

Mary's house was a typical farmhouse. Upside down wellies piled up by the front door, stone tiles on the floor and low ceilings with wooden beams that most people would have to bend down to avoid bashing their foreheads.

"Here you go, my love. Pop these on," Mary said, handing me a large shirt that reached my knees and a pair of sandals.

"Thank you," my bottom lip quivered as I took the clothes from her. This was the first act of kindness I had been shown since my ordeal had started. I put the shirt over my cold, battered body; pain ricocheted from my head to my toes. The adrenaline had worn off and I began to cry.

"Let me make you a cuppa, it might help," Mary offered as she rested her hand on my shoulder before walking over to the kettle. "I've rung your sister, she's on her way."

A hot mug of tea was placed in front of me.

"It looks like you've had a tough day," she said by way of a question. I explained how the argument between Susan and me had erupted and how I had ultimately been kicked out of my home. I didn't go into the dynamics of my mum's drunken rages.

"It's all part of growing up; mums will always argue with their daughters. Unfortunately, it's just the way of life," Mary ventured with her hand on top of mine.

I got the impression she didn't know what else to say or do. I felt Mary was doing her best; she had brought me in and made me comfortable, but maybe she didn't want to too step over the mark. It's a risky thing to get involved in other people's business even that of a child in tears. She could have closed the curtains and shut me out like those who walk past homeless kids; it takes a lot of courage to ask what is going on behind the scenes. Mary had just seen me crying on my sister's doorstep and she was good enough to let me into her home. That was enough for me and I will always be grateful for her kind act of kindness.

When Laura and Ben arrived home it was late and moonlight had replaced the sun. I thanked Mary as I left and made my way across to where Ben was unloading the car.

"Nice shirt!" Ben joked.

"Yeah, it's a new fashion statement," I retorted as I lifted my arms to show how baggy it was.

"Hey, Sis, do you fancy a Mcdonald's?" Laura asked.

"Yes please," I smiled.

I didn't realise how hungry I was until food had been mentioned. We climbed into the Peugeot and made our way to McDonald's at Newquay. I tried to explain to Laura and Ben what had happened between Susan and me, however, Laura didn't seem shocked by what I told her. It was easy for me to forget that Laura knew exactly what Susan could be like.

I felt a lot better with food in my belly. We sat in the car, chatting and eating burgers until Laura's phone rang.

"It's Jack," Laura announced as she put the phone on loudspeaker.

"What the fuck is going on? Mums going fucking mental. She's at your house!" Jack's voice bellowed out of the tiny speaker.

"Well, we're not there," Laura piped up.

"Is Jessica with you?" he asked.

Laura turned to look at me; I shook my head from side to side.

"Please, no!" I mouthed.

"Yes, she is." Laura spilled the beans.

My fingers clenched into the palms of my hands and I could feel a cold sweat gather across my forehead.

Why did she just betray me? - I screamed inwardly.

My breathing became erratic.

"You'd better get back quick, she is going fucking mental!" he finished.

I heard the phone cut off and the car fell into silence. My heart thumped like a drum in my chest and I started to panic. I knew my sister was going to send me back.

"Jessica, I can't have this in my life and at my house. I'll soon have a little one to think about now," she spoke quietly without looking at me.

I could feel rage build inside me as Ben pulled out of the car park.

Great! So you have a new family and I'm left to deal with the fucking drunk, - I voiced inwardly.

My heart sank. No one was going to help me; I was on my own and afraid. Tears streamed down my face.

A short time later, the car headlights lit up the driveway and we pulled up outside the cottage. I took a deep breath in anticipation of what might be in store for me.

What abuse was I going to get from Susan? - I wondered.

The hair on the back of my neck was rising, everything seemed too still. Susan and Jack were nowhere to be seen. I looked around at the bushes and trees and expected one of them to suddenly jump out. Ben killed the engine and a deathly silence filled the air.

"They must have gone," Ben broke the silence,

Both Laura and I jumped at the sound of his voice.

"Yes, let's get inside quickly," Laura whispered.

We crept towards the house; we were three mice trying to sneak past a sleeping cat. Ben unlocked the front door and we carefully made our way to the kitchen in complete darkness. Laura closed each curtain she walked past before she switched the kitchen light on. It took a moment for my eyes to adjust to the brightness.

"Cuppa?" Ben asked turning to fill the kettle.

"Yes please," Laura and I replied in unison.

Breathing a sigh of relief, we felt brave enough to go through to the semi-dark lounge. Everyone seemed to avoid the elephant in the room. Where did Susan go? We knew she was unpredictable so, over our cups of tea, Laura tried to call Jack but his phone was off. I could tell by her huffs and puffs that this annoyed her. This was so typical of Jack. He rarely wanted to get involved, instead, he disappeared. Suddenly, the lounge lit up. I moved over to the window to peek out and saw a tall policeman stepping into view and walking towards the cottage.

"It's the police," I whispered to Laura and Ben.

I dropped to the floor but I have no idea why I felt had to hide.

Bang! Bang! The policeman knocked then the house fell back into silence again.

"What does he want?" Laura whispered to Ben.

Ben had his crystal ball with him and of course, had all the answers, - I thought to myself. Ben shrugged his shoulders.

"Go and open the bloody door!" she ordered him and gave him a shove.

He didn't have a choice.

"Sorry to disturb you, Sir. We have had a report of a runaway. She goes by the name of Jessica and is possibly at this address," the policeman said.

"Yes, she's here," Ben replied and invited the policeman inside.

I made my way back to the kitchen.

"Hello, you must be Jessica?" the policeman asked as he walked in and took a black notebook from his pocket.

"I didn't run away, she kicked me out without any clothes on! Look at the bruises she gave me," I blurted out, lifting my shirt.

"Now, now, Jessica, your mother has been very concerned about you. She has been frantic and sick with worry," he replied in a patronising way.

Has he not just seen the damage to my body? How can she be frantic? She was the one who caused this horrible night in the first place. - I thought.

My anger grew and I couldn't help myself. I blurted out the entire story as the policeman jotted down notes in his notebook.

"It's probably best if you stay with your sister tonight. But you will have to return to your mum's in the morning when things have cooled down," he announced.

Laura nodded in agreement.

Is that it! So, as far as the police are concerned, I've been found and their job is done. Case closed! Did he not listen to what I told him? Did he not believe me or see my bruises? Isn't it his job to protect me? - I thought over as he left the cottage.

I had always believed the police were meant to catch criminals and protect those who needed protection. Where was my protection from the person who beats me? The policeman was happy to send me back to the very one who kicked me out, naked, for the entire world to see. What about the next round of abuse? Perhaps he was late for his doughnut break and didn't want to get involved. I had been let down by everyone and none of what had happened seemed right or normal. What had I done wrong? I only went for a bloody shower, but somehow the whole thing was my fault.

Ben and Laura drove me back to the house the next day. We turned into the street and it seemed like the whole world was outside; playing football, cutting grass or just generally chatting to their neighbours. The lady who lived next door was in the garden with Susan who, to a certain extent, looked distraught. We drew up at the curb. Laura was first out of the car and went mental at Susan.

"What the hell, you kicked Jess out, naked! You really have reached an all-time low ...," she shrieked.

"Jessica, where have you been?" Susan interrupted using a concerned voice.

I had only just stepped out of the car when she ran over to me; I was scooped up into a tight cuddle, so much so I could hardly breathe. This sudden burst of affection felt false and theatrical, I was sure her actions were for the benefit of the onlookers. When Laura had yelled at Susan, I noticed that everyone in the street had stopped what they were doing, staring in our direction. Susan released me, pulled back and placed her hands on my shoulders.

"I've been so worried, why did you run away like that?" she bawled as though she could cry.

Her shout was loud and melodramatic, confirming what I thought. I looked into her eyes; the vagueness I used to see when she was drunk was no longer there.

Does she have no recollection of what she did? Does she believe I ran away? - I asked myself.

I stood on the lawn looking at Susan, my mother, my mum, the drama queen, while everyone else looked at me. I had no option but to apologise.

"I'm sorry, Mum. I didn't mean to worry you, it won't happen again."

Chapter 6

Happy birthday to me

My actions in front of the neighbours would have confirmed in their minds that I was a runaway child. No one would have been blamed for thinking Susan was a caring mother with problem children. No one questioned what had happened; the police never returned to see if I was safe in Susan's care. Life continued.

When my sister went into labour, baby madness went into overdrive. Susan rushed backwards and forwards to the hospital and even helped with the birth of my niece. I could never understand why, but Laura decided to name her daughter Susan. Susan, the grandmother, was over the moon with the baby's name; she turned a corner and became a mum again; life got better. I wondered why there was a sudden change in her and at first thought it was due to the baby; then I realized that Shawn was back in our lives. During visits to the hospital, Susan and Shawn had patched things up. I still found him creepy, but I wanted to make an effort with him. No doubt about it, life was better when he was around; he had a positive effect on Susan. The Butlins holiday was back on and I felt excited again.

I was overjoyed when, on my eleventh birthday, Susan and Laura filled the room with balloons and a birthday banner. They had made an effort and that meant a lot to me. I opened my cards but it was yet another year without a card from my biological dad. Susan gave me a Nintendo DS which she probably struggled to afford. I hugged her. She also wanted to prepare a special birthday meal for me so Laura took me to Plymouth for a girly day out. We met friends of mine at the ice rink and afterwards Laura and I spent some time in Drakes Circus. I don't know why, but we ended up in Primark and bought some silly frog pyjamas.

When we arrived home, I spied an opened bottle of wine on the table and Susan's mood had changed slightly. Ben and Laura looked at each other.

I hope it's just one glass, - I thought.

After dinner, Susan brought in a princess cake with a candy necklace on top; she lit the candles. Two years previously, I had mentioned to Susan that I liked this cake so I was delighted to finally have one.

That Mum will never drink again. - I wished as I blew out the candles.

But unfortunately, Susan drank her fourth glass of wine and started to slur her words. As a result, the atmosphere rapidly changed. She poured her fifth glass and her lip started to curl up, showing her teeth; a sign that all was not well.

"So, what did you buy today?" she asked before she gulped another mouthful of wine.

"Frog pyjamas," Laura replied looking nervously at Ben.

"Really! Well, I've got to see this!" Susan pointed me in the direction of Laura's old bedroom and took another swig from her glass.

"Go try them on, Jessica," she insisted, swaying around in her chair.

I wished Shawn had been there to deal with her.

Actually, where is he? - I wondered.

In the bedroom, I pulled the clothes from the bag and noticed the size on the hanger didn't match the size of the silly pajamas; they were two sizes too big. This made them look even more ridiculous.

Oh well, this should make everyone laugh, - I mused.

Ben, Laura and Jacob burst out laughing when they saw me.

"Well. I think you picked up the wrong size, Sis," I laughed waving my arms around.

Susan didn't laugh; her face changed and the monster within erupted.

"You stupid idiot! You can't even buy a pair of fucking pyjamas, can you?" Susan garbled her words.

The wine spilled from her glass as she waved it around uncontrollably. If you could have cut the air in the room with a knife, this would have been that moment. Susan glared at Laura who stared back in disbelief.

"Mum, it's an easy mistake, anyone could have made it," Laura reacted in an attempt to calm the situation down.

"Really! Well it would seem you make a lot of fucking mistakes, doesn't it?" her face became more distorted.

"We should get home, it's late," Ben said.

He handed the baby to Laura then, without warning, Susan leapt from her seat and punched Laura in the face. As fist and face collided, baby Susan fell from Laura's arms. Ben dived to catch her before she hit the ground. He stood up, his daughter clutched to his chest and his eyes firmly fixed on Susan. Susan sat calmly back in her seat, picked up her wine glass and took a gulp as though nothing had happened.

"Jessica, Jacob! Get your things, we're leaving!" Ben said icily.

Still dazed from the assault, Laura picked Jacob up and frog marched us outside. Before I knew it, we were next to Ben's car. I turned to watch Ben hurrying down the garden path towards us; he was still holding his daughter while Susan shouted abuse at him from the doorstep. The people in the street turned to see a screaming, drunken woman and me in my oversized frog pajama's. I felt mortified as people started to stare.

Well at least, I am clothed this time, - I breathed a sigh of relief.

We stayed at Ben and Laura's house that night and all I could think about for the rest of the evening was my unanswered birthday wish when I blew out the candles.

The next day, Ben drove Jacob and me back to our house and tried to talk to Susan about her outburst. She had forgotten everything and suggested he had made up the entire story. The expression on his face told me he was confused, he might have been questioning his sanity too.

Is it even possible to forget and lose time the way Susan seems to or is it all just an act? - I wondered

Shortly after Ben left, Shawn arrived.

"Are we all excited about the holiday?" Shawn looked at me.

He hardly waited for a reply before he whisked Susan away for the weekend.

That night, Jacob and I packed for our holiday; not surprisingly, the topic of conversation was focused on Butlins. I stayed up but Jacob had just fallen asleep when the front door burst open. Susan stormed into the house and picked up the phone. She rang my sister.

"Laura, it's Mum, I've split up with Shawn! Would you like a free holiday? Can you take Jessica and Jacob? It's all paid for, so you may as well use it," she suggested.

I sat quietly in the lounge watching TV. When the phone call ended, Susan sat staring at the wall for a while, she seemed lost in her thoughts and her pale face made me think she had seen a ghost.

"Laura will take you and your brother to Butlins," she announced.

Her voice sounded robotic. She got up and wandered off to her bedroom without another word. I had never seen Susan like that before, her entire body seemed almost mechanical and, for the rest of the weekend, she spent most of the time in her bedroom.

We said goodbye to Susan the next day and set off on our first-ever holiday. As we drove, the conversation turned to Susan and Shawn and why they had split up. Laura wanted to find out the juicy gossip, but I knew as much as she did. Susan had barely spoken the entire weekend and the situation seemed rather unusual. Normally the wine would have been out and a bad night would follow. Something wasn't right and it had affected her in a very unusual way. She had locked herself in her bedroom without a drink; that was extremely unlike her.

At Butlins, Jacob and I chose to race down the water slides before exploring the multitude of other activities and I was able to be a kid for a change. A few days into the holiday, Laura got word that Susan was on the phone at reception. At least thirty minutes passed before Laura came back.

"Mum just rang," Laura announced. "She's just told me why she broke up with Shawn. Apparently, he is a convicted paedophile!"

Having never heard of a paedophile before, I was surprised when Ben's hand flew to his mouth.

"He's been caught with pornographic images of children on his computer!" Laura continued.

She paused and looked at Ben to gauge his reaction.

"Fuck me!" Ben sounded shocked.

I didn't know why they were shocked.

"He's on the sex offenders register and isn't allowed to be near kids. But I think Susan was with him when she rang, she denied he was there though," she added.

My sister looked between Jacob and me while Ben stared at her in disbelief. Jacob wasn't interested, he continued watching TV. Even although paedophile wasn't a word I had heard before, their reactions told me it wasn't good.

50

"So what does pedowild mean?" I asked.

"It means an adult who likes children and enjoys photos of them and it's paedophile not pedowild." Laura explained.

What's wrong with that? Lots of people take pictures of their kids - I thought.

Still confused by her explanation, it was left like that. Throughout the remaining few days of the holiday, we tried to have a good time but on the last day my heart sank; I knew I had to go back home.

Will Susan be hitting the bottle again? Will her anger be taken out on me? - I wondered. We said goodbye to Butlins and started the long drive home. My life was about to change and not for the better.

Parking nearby, we looked through the thick, grey, Cornish fog at our house with no lights on; it looked abandoned through the gloom. Laura knocked on the door but there was no answer. Previously, we would have been able to tell if Susan was at home; her car would have been there, but she didn't have a vehicle now. While out at a party a few months before, Susan decided to drive home drunk. She crashed her Renault Megane into a garden wall and wrote it off. Without her licence, she had to rely on buses. So, where was Susan?

"Where the fuck is she? Jessica, have you got your key?" Laura couldn't hide her frustration.

"No!" I replied.

"For fuck sake!"

Laura pulled her phone out and called Susan. It rang but she didn't answer.

"What the hell! We take her kids on holiday and she can't even be bothered to be home when we return. Fucking typical!" Laura yelled. "It's freezing. We'll just have to go back to ours, the baby will need feeding soon."

Immediately we pulled onto the gravel drive of their cottage, Laura's phone rang.

"Where the hell are you?" Laura shouted.

"I'm on the bus, on my way back," I heard Susan reply casually.

"Well, it sounds like you're in a car, not on a bus. Are you with him?" Laura questioned sarcastically.

She knew that she had just caught Susan out in a lie, this angered her more.

"No!" Susan quickly denied the accusation.

"You're a liar! I can tell," Laura screamed.

"Well, what can I say? I love him and people can change," Susan muttered.

"You're fucking stupid! Your kids will be at home," and with that, Laura ended the call.

Why is my sister about to send us back if kids aren't allowed to be around him? Why is Susan also ok with this? Granted she's a shit mum, but would she really put us in danger like that? - my thoughts went round in circles.

Chapter 7

Moving house

Shawn may well have been dangerous, the boogie man, but Susan was back in a relationship with him. Jacob was scared at the thought of moving to an unknown house; for me, it was all about being with an unknown man. We didn't like to be around him and Laura stopped talking to Susan, nobody was happy. As the weeks went by, the holiday fiasco and the announcement about what Shawn had done was simply brushed under the carpet and Susan desperately tried to make Jacob and I call Shawn, Dad.

"Go and ask your dad," or "Where has your dad gone?" she would spout out at every opportunity.

The creepy, dangerous man was our new dad, or so we were told. We were confused to begin with. However, I wanted and needed Susan to be our mum again and for that single reason, I tried my best to accept Shawn. He appeared to love his new title and played the role of our father. He would pick us up from school and take us to the park. Shawn around all the time; there was no escaping him. At the weekend, the four of us spent time as a family, Susan and Shawn no longer disappeared for last-minute breaks. Shawn became a big part of our lives and eventually, we were brainwashed, we started to call him Dad.

Two months after we returned from Butlins, Susan and our new dad informed us that we were about to move into a new house together. Shawn's grandmother owned a sizable bungalow near Truro but, unfortunately, a burst pipe had caused a major flood and most of the house had been destroyed. Shawn took it upon himself to supervise the contractors involved with the rebuild and redecoration. Inevitably, because Shawn was overseeing the project, the entire house was completed to his taste rather than his grandmother's.

"A modern monstrosity!" his grandmother protested.

The house had lost its original charm and she was devastated at the dramatic change. She moved into Shawn's flat rather than spend time and money restoring her house to what it once was. Delighted with his grandmother's decision, Shawn immediately invited Susan to move in with him. She threw all caution to the wind and accepted his offer. Her decision ultimately meant that Jacob and I, without having a say, would be moving house with them. I had had a lot of unhappy memories from when we lived in our small, council house but I also had good memories. It had been our home so we were not happy when they told us the news. This was a massive change; Shawn had the house keys so it was a done deal.

A few days later, with boxes filled and bags packed, we found ourselves in Shawn's Jeep ready to go. We waved goodbye to our old friends, our old house and our old lives; we were off to begin a new life in a new house with a new dad. We arrived at the entrance to our new abode to see apple trees growing either side of a long, bumpy, gravel driveway. A large field made its way up the hill to two double stables. There was a waterfall and a stream that curved its way around the edge of the field to the mouth of a river. It was a splendid view that could be seen from the main road. We were greeted by a large double garage and a newly installed trampoline.

"Jessica, we can get you a horse to fill the stables and Jacob, you will love the trampoline," Shawn boasted.

No doubt he was buying us; it was his way of getting us to like him.

As we made our way further along the driveway, a large, L-shaped bungalow came into view. In this fairytale location with panoramic views, I was mesmerised at the beauty of the place, it was worlds away from our humble council house. I could tell the house had been built a long time ago, but it was far from being derelict. Its white paint and glass that sparkled in the sunlight was fresh and welcoming.

Once inside we were greeted by newly painted white walls and a huge mirror that hung from the wall in the hallway. A brand new kitchen and breakfast area intrigued us further into the house, with its modern worktops and a tiled floor, it was straight out of a magazine.

Another hallway branched off from the kitchen and led to a utility room and toilet, some steps led to an attic. The kitchen was open plan and incorporated one of the largest lounges I had ever seen. At the opposite end, daylight flooded in through French doors which opened out to an enormous balcony. From there, breathtaking views of the Cornish countryside with its rolling hills and rivers were revealed. The vision took my breath away.

This can't be our new house, surely not? - I thought to myself.

"So what do you think then?" Shawn asked.

My eyes struggled to take in the beauty of the place.

"It's really beautiful," I whispered in awe.

"Do you want to see the rest of the house?" he asked and ushered us back inside.

We walked back to the hallway, where the bungalow turned to the right and another corridor with four doors waited to greet us. Behind the doors we found, three bedrooms and the main bathroom. The bathroom was ridiculously big; it had a double walk-in shower and a bath with jets to fire from all directions. Shawn's and Susan's bedroom was the next room along, then Shawn's office. We were shown the last room which Jacob and I were to share. I found this a bit odd given the number of bedrooms in the house; however, it had two single beds and smelt fresh and airy. It was a bright room with a walk-in wardrobe. It was also filled with Jacob's favourite toys, monkeys. Jacob had a massive thing for monkeys and his collection had filled our room back in the council house. The idea of sharing with my brother again wasn't so bad because the changes had happened so fast. I needed something or someone familiar. I felt safe that first night in this strange new house with our beds pushed together. Neither Jacob nor I liked change so being together, helped us to adjust and get used to the new house.

The next day, Jacob and I were surprised to find our beds separated and in their original positions. We were even more surprised to find a woman, Crystal, cleaning the house. Even though Shawn didn't work, he preferred someone else doing the laundry and cleaning. Crystal whizzed around the house and after she had finished, she handed Shawn a large envelope, it wasn't sealed and clearly full of money. It was only when I discovered Crystal was not only Shawn's mum, but also supporting him financially by giving him thousands of pounds on a regular basis, that I understood why the exchange of money was not the other way around. After she left, Jacob and I pushed the beds back together, we reinvented our haven.

This was like a fairytale coming to life: a new house, trampolines, stables and a cleaner. However, like many things in life, after a few months, the novelty wore off. My guard dropped and I accepted Shawn as my new dad. In fairness to him, he hadn't done anything wrong. I was part of a real family and I became increasingly happy as time went on. But, nothing lasts forever and, if I had known what was about to happen to me because of moving to this house, a cardboard box would have been the preferable option.

It was late November and everyone agreed that it would be a nice idea to decorate the house early this year. After all, Christmas was just around the corner. Shawn asked me to join him in the attic to hunt for decorations and we laughed and joked together as we rummaged through a mountain of boxes.

"Jessica, I think I found them," Shawn called from the other side of the room.

He was standing beside a pile of opened boxes and as I looked over, his creepy eyes fixed on mine. Whenever I was around Shawn had a peculiar air about him. The expression on his face, the look in his eye, the set of his mouth or his attempt to invade my personal space, made me uncomfortable. I convinced myself that his strange manner was part of who he was.

"You have hair covering your face," he scolded jokingly.

I stood still while he reached out and used his finger to tuck my hair behind my ear but his hand seemed to linger a moment too long as it brushed lightly against my face. The way he looked at me and touched me seemed wrong. His hand then moved down to my chin and, without warning, he leant forward and kissed me on the lips. I was like a stunned rabbit in the headlights.

What the fuck! Did he just do that? I need to escape, I need to get outta here fast! - my head was swirling at a million miles an hour and I was no longer able to focus.

Shawn's eyes were still firmly locked on mine; his head started to move towards me again.

"Can I come up and help?" Jacob's voice broke my frozen state.

Run! - my head screamed.

I turned and, almost tripping over, got out of the attic. I stumbled past Jacob on the stairs then ran to our monkey-filled bedroom and burst through the door. I was surprised to find Susan there.

"Mum!" I skidded to a stop.

Susan looked startled at my dramatic entrance.

"What is it, Jessica? I thought you were helping your father?" she said holding a monkey in her hand.

"Urm," I had lost the ability to speak.

Susan stared at me and waited for me to reply. What could I say? *Hey mum! We found the decorations. Oh, by the way, your creepy boyfriend has just tried to kiss me! Is that normal or is he just being friendly? -* thoughts rather than words were all I could come up with.

"What is it, Jessica!" Susan said again with irritation in her voice.

Click! Click! I could hear the sound of Shawn's shoes on the tiled floor before he appeared at the bedroom doorway. His dark eyes locked firmly on mine.

"Urm. I can't remember, I need a shower," was all I could come up with.

How could I tell her what had happened, with him standing there?

"Ok," she shook her head in confusion.

She was probably wondering why I had burst into the room only to announce I needed a shower. I pushed past Shawn and made my way to the bathroom. Once I had locked the door behind me, I got undressed and turned the shower on. The hot water rained down on me but I sat on the ceramic shower tray huddled up into a ball.

"It was just a kiss! It was just a kiss," I muttered quietly.

Dads kiss their kids all the time, don't they? But the way he kissed me, the way he moved my hair and looked at me with his scary dark eyes. It just didn't feel right. Do dads really kiss their children like that? What should I do, should I tell Mum? If I was to tell her, would it ruin everything? I can't risk that, we are finally a family. I am just being silly? - I tearfully asked myself.

No matter how hard I tried to make up excuses for what Shawn did, everything felt wrong. The next day at breakfast, I glanced at Shawn a couple of times but he kept his head down while he ate and avoided any eye contact with me.

Does he know what he's done is wrong? - I wondered when I glanced at him before I left for school.

I needed to talk to someone, so I looked for my friend, Naomi, as soon as I arrived at school.

"Does your dad still kiss you?" I asked.

"Yes, of course, that's what dads do and he gives me cuddles too," she smiled.

"Isn't it a bit weird though?" I asked as I tried to probe a little deeper.

"It's what parents do, Jess, it's normal. You have a family now; you're just not used to it, that's all,' she reassured me.

Naomi understood why this all seemed so strange and weird to me, I had told her bits about my life so she knew I wasn't used to any form of affection; she also knew that I didn't have a real dad either. The conversation helped ease my mind and I started to feel much better, as I came to the conclusion that I had overreacted.

It was just a kiss, it's just what dads do! - I unconvincingly told myself.

Chapter 8

Drugged

The house was beautiful; a Christmas grotto in November. Looking forward to Christmas always made me feel better, and I needed a distraction from Shawn's inappropriate attempt to kiss me. I still felt that I should say something to Susan but I was worried my revelations might cause her to turn to drink again. My talk with Naomi had helped to a certain extent until Shawn took on his peculiar, creepy air around me again. He would lower his head and avoid any eye contact with me, like a naughty school boy. This caused an argument to erupt in my head.

If Shawn knew what he had done was wrong, then the way I felt must have been right. The kiss was wrong and he should not have done it, it was definitely not what dads do. However, if I was to open my mouth, what would the consequences be? Susan had been much more of a sober mum since we had moved to this house; I didn't want to risk things deteriorating.

One night, Shawn was doing his usual. His creepy eyes were up to their old tricks again. He had a peculiar expression on his face and his eyes followed me around the kitchen, while I made dinner.

"Jessica should have her own bedroom. She's older now and it's not fair she has to share a room with her brother," he announced to Susan.

I put a plate of food in front of him.

"I think that's a good idea," Susan smiled.

"I'll move my office into the lounge and she can have that room," he continued.

"Can I really have my own room?" I asked excitedly.

I had become a young woman; twelve on my next birthday. I was conscious of my developing body so it was awkward sharing a room with six-year-old Jacob.

"Why don't you take Jessica to the shops after school tomorrow and buy some furniture for her new room?" he pointed his fork at Susan before tucking into his dinner again.

I loved this new idea but Jacob looked upset.

"Don't worry Jacob. I'll see if I can find you another monkey, while we are out," Susan pacified him.

Jacob's face lit up. I love my brother but not his monkeys not and I couldn't wait to have a room more to my taste.

Susan took me shopping the next day. I found a big, fluffy, pink bean bag with a dark pink heart imprinted on it. I just had to have it along with some nic nacs. I was allowed to choose a new duvet bed set and a large chest of drawers. I think Susan enjoyed our girls' day out as much as I did. It gave us a chance to bond and forget problems from the past. After lunch, Shawn came to pick us up and, once home, I found he had moved his office paraphernalia to a corner of the lounge.

While Shawn went to collect Jacob's friend Jack who was going to stay the night with us, Susan and I started the task of assembling the flat-packed furniture. A few hours later, my bedroom was finished; all that was needed was for me to close the door on the world and claim it. I leapt onto my freshly made bed and did a starfish, I finally had my own room and every detail looked perfect.

As I got ready for school the next day, Crystal dropped her dog, Gemma, off at our house; she was a large dog and always in the way. After Crystal left, Gemma decided to wander into Jacob's bedroom where Jack and my brother were boys being boys. Gemma didn't like what they were doing so she barked at them.

"Come on Gemma!" I said and tugged at her collar.

She was the size of a mini horse and refused to budge, so I grabbed at her collar once again only this time with more force.

Ping! A sound echoed out as an excruciating pain shot up my spine and I fell to the floor, screaming in agony.

"What's happened," Susan called out.

She rushed from the kitchen when she heard the screams. Gemma was trying to lick my face as I lay there. After having a look at me, Susan decided I couldn't go to school. I was sent back to bed for the day and slept for hours. The house was quiet when I woke up. Jacob was at school, Susan was at work and I had no idea where Shawn was; he did whatever he wanted. My back felt slightly better and I was able to stand again.

Six months beforehand, I had tried smoking. The popular kids at school did it so it was not only cool to smoke but also a comfort to me when things had been going downhill with Susan. I decided to go for a cigarette and tottered into the kitchen, rolled a cigarette then walked towards the balcony. The minute I opened the French doors, the cold air hit me I stepped outside and hugged my gown tightly around my body. I lit my cigarette and took a long drag before I took in the breathtaking view.

"What the fuck!" I screamed out as I felt a sharp pain stabbing my neck.

I moved my hand to my neck; a small cold object was embedded in my skin. The next thing I knew, the entire world was moving in slow motion. The fields in front of me twisted and distorted when I tried to turn my head. My vision was cloudy and I felt my body go rigid; I had no control. I started to fall but I didn't hit the floor hard. Instead, I seemed to float for a few seconds before I felt the damp wood of the balcony floor. Darkness descended over me and I drifted in and out of consciousness before I was fully consumed. I was petrified and could barely make out the silhouette of a large figure standing over me.

Vague, muffled noises were coming and going and a ghostly figure moved around in front of me. I drifted in and out of the darkness with no perception of time. The cold winter wind was no longer on my skin; my body felt like a dead weight and not like mine anymore. I struggled to open my eyes and could almost make out a dimly lit ceiling; I was no longer outside. Pain suddenly ripped across my skull and my head started to throb; my throat was parched and my body had the sensation of swaying around on a boat. The motion only added to my dizzy and disoriented state. The ghostly figure came into focus and rocked back and forth in front of me.

What the fuck is going on? - It was impossible to vocalise my question. I was terrified, there aren't strong enough words to describe how I felt in that moment.

Is it the damage to my back that has caused me to pass out? Have I fallen off the balcony? Is that why everything has gone black? Oh crap! Why can't I move? - chilling questions gathered in my head,

My mind raced faster than I could follow. I felt vomit building in my throat and I tried to turn, but my body was completely immovable.

Please no, am I paralysed for life? – more terrifying thoughts.

I tried to move again. Nothing worked yet my body still seemed to sway around. memories from before I passed out slowly filtered back into my head.

There was a stab to my neck, I saw a large figure. Has someone done this to me? But who? - I wondered as I struggled to see.

The effort involved to open my eyes one more time took every last bit of strength I had. A fuzzy, silhouetted figure continued to move around in front of me but the movement was too fast for my eyes to keep up with. The darkness quickly clawed away at me again, as I fell back into an unconscious state. My head was tilted to the side when I finally came to and my eyes finally focused on something brightly coloured, my pink, fluffy bean bag in the corner of my room.

I'm in my room, I must have had a bad dream. - I took some comfort in knowing where I was.

I felt a stinging in my right arm, a bit like pins and needles but a much sharper pain. I brushed my hand across my belly; the sensation confused me. I had expected to feel my night shirt but all I felt was my skin, soaked with sweat.

What the fuck! Where is my top? - I wondered.

My hand moved to my legs. It wasn't only my top that had been removed, I was on my bed completely naked and dripping wet. A numb pain gathered within my belly but that wasn't the only thing hurting. It felt as though a hot poker had been shoved up inside me; my insides were on fire! My vagina felt like it had been torn and ripped apart.

"What the hell!" I muttered not quite under my breath.

When I felt fluid run down the inside of my leg, I began to think that something more sinister may have happened to me. I lifted my hand back up and blinked until I could see clearer; a white creamy liquid mixed with blood was covering my fingers,

This is not real, it must be a dream! I will wake up in a minute. I must be on the balcony still smoking my cigarette. - I supposed I had fainted.

I lay for a few minutes and waited for the nightmare to be over.

What's happened to me? – my head whirled.

I didn't have a clue what had been done to me or what covered my hand. A cold chill made me shiver; my body was returning to me. I tried to sit up and placed my hand on the bed to steady myself. My vision was still cloudy and the bedroom started to spin.

My tiny body seemed to glisten in the light that streamed through my half pulled curtains. I knew someone else had closed them like this; I could never sleep if there were any gaps in them. My fluffy gown was on the floor next to my bed along with my night shirt and pyjama bottoms. Both were screwed up into a ball; I figured that someone had removed my clothes. I bent down to pick up my gown, lost my balance and fell over. Luckily my bean bag broke my fall. I was weak and my body felt foreign. After what seemed like an age, I gathered all my strength and pulled my gown tight. I managed to stand up then, tentatively, made my way to the door.

My steps to the bathroom echoed in the now silent house. I slumped onto the floor and, fumbling to find the bolt, I slid it along and breathed a sigh of relief. I felt a little safer in my room but my stomach churned and I vomited. The haze in my head started to lift after my stomach had emptied; I felt a bit better as I groped my way to the shower. The hot water rained down on my body. I scrubbed myself clean before collapsing onto the ceramic shower tray. I pulled my knees close to my chest and huddled up into a little ball, sobbing my heart out.

What happened to me? What was that creamy stuff that leaked out of me? Who was the ghost figure I saw? - my thoughts were never-ending.

I tried to deal with the questions that invaded my mind as numbness from the cold water invaded my body; pins and needles stabbed away at my wrinkled skin. My body was rebooting. After unbuckling myself, I clumsily hoisted my body up and staggered to my bedroom. I thanked God that the house was quiet. I needed to be alone with time to gather my thoughts. The chaos in my head subsided when I grabbed a blanket and curled up on my bean bag.

During the evening, Susan came into my room to check on me and bring some food but I pretended to be asleep. I was still huddled up the next morning and had not moved the entire night. By morning, the others were gathered at the breakfast table.

"Morning sleepy head, are you feeling any better today?" Susan enquired.

"Morning. Yes, much better thanks," I replied politely.

I looked towards Shawn but he didn't look up; he continued tucking into his breakfast. The only chair available was beside him but there was no way I was going to sit next to him.

"Move over, Monkey," I gave Jacob a light shove and thankfully, he did not argue with me.

Shawn looked up and caught my eye; he immediately dropped his head and looked back down at his breakfast. He was acting weird, the same scenario as when he'd tried to kiss me in the attic.

"I've bought you some riding gear and guess what? I've got you a trainer. You can learn to ride horses!" Shawn blurted out as he continued focusing on his breakfast.

Hang on, what? Why is he being so nice? - this spun my head out.

"Sorry. Riding lessons?" I almost choked.

"Yes. I've got you riding lessons; I thought you would like some," he went on.

He lifted his head and looked me directly in the eye. As his dark eyes searched for my reaction, I clocked Susan staring at me.

"Well are you going to thank your father?" she quizzed, agitated.

"Oh wow, thank you," I said while all eyes turned to me.

After this, I found myself stuck in my thoughts and I no longer wanted to interact with anyone. I needed time to piece the puzzle of that day together. Weeks passed by and I just tried to avoid people. Even my friends at school began to disappear.

It was obvious to me that someone had drugged on the balcony that day. The cold object that I felt in my neck must have been a needle,

66

not that I could ever prove it; I never found one. When I had come round and was left with the aftermath, I was only partly aware of what had happened to me. This scared the shit out of me. I had no idea what had happened while I was unconscious. A smell seemed to follow me around wherever I went and I felt dirty all the time. In the shower, it didn't matter how hard I scrubbed my skin, I was haunted by the smell. I hadn't paid attention to what I had smelt that day but now someone else's sweaty scent was on me.

Can other people smell what I can? - I began to wonder.

I wanted to tell someone, I needed to talk over what happened but I didn't know what to say.

Urm. Someone put a needle in my neck, I think. I then passed out and a ghostly figure appeared. I think I was also on a boat, but then I was in my bedroom. I was in a lot of pain and covered in sweat when I woke up and I was naked. Then some creamy looking blood leaked out of me. Am I broken? Did someone do something to me? – mixed up thoughts haunted me.

I was eleven years old at the time.

Chapter 9

I should have kept my mouth shut

A thin ray of light streamed through a small crack in my bedroom curtains as I watched the dust particles dance in the light. It was the end of spring and everything was colourful and bright. Outside, the trees grew and flowers blossomed while I seemed to wither and die. My life was dark and gloomy. I felt locked inside my head and wished I could forget about what had happened. No matter how hard I tried, the memory of that day ate me up. It invaded my every thought and nothing seemed to make sense to me anymore, I needed to talk to someone. But who? I had alienated myself from everyone I knew and trusted; I was left with one person, Susan. Thinking over my options caused me to reflect on what I knew of her. Susan as a child, Susan the mother and Susan and her wine. Then there was Susan as Shawn's partner.

I knew Susan had had issues that stemmed from childhood. My aunt had spoken about the horrific upbringing they experienced in a strict children's home where punishment was commonplace.

"That home had no business being involved with children," my aunt declared.

She told me a story of when Susan was whipped with a leather belt and then tied to a bed for hours on end. She had no choice but to soil herself, despite a plea to be released. The person in charge was furious so Susan was stripped naked and pushed up against the glass of a window for the entire world to see.

My mind flashed back to what Susan had done to me, as she told me this story. When I passed a comment, my aunt stopped telling her tale. Maybe she had noticed a change in my expression or my voice or realised I was too young to be hearing about such barbaric treatment of children. With the story only partly told, she refilled her wine glass and then acted as though she had simply forgotten what she was talking about. My aunt, unfortunately, liked to drink too. I never knew why the story stopped so abruptly but she appeared sad afterwards. Susan and her sister were adopted, eventually ending up with a family in St Austell, The story helped me to understand Susan a little better and, to a certain extent, explained some of her bizarre actions.

She could be an amazing mum and cool to be with. I loved her in the role of mother. I remembered the many times she had played with me, she let me help when Jacob was a baby, taught me to make cakes and we had fun filled karaoke nights together. I loved our shopping trips and the closeness we had once had.

These pleasant times were interspersed with Susan and wine. Now and again she became locked in her inner battle, trapped by her demons. She didn't know how to express herself when sober and would return to drink when she could no longer contain her emotions. I suppose it was her way of hitting the red button when things got too much. The only problem was when Susan hit that bloody red button, heaven help anyone that stood in her way. The gloves would be off and like a bare-knuckle fighter, she would come out swinging.

Susan had searched for years for someone to love her completely, someone to be her rock and soulmate. The problem was she seemed to hate herself and she only ever attracted the bad boys. Shawn seemed different from a lot of the guys she would normally end up with and he gave her something that no one else had; stability and hope. He had provided a beautiful family home with the promise of a future that would last. Susan grabbed at this chance with both hands. She wanted a sanctuary for her family and threw her life and soul into this relationship. She even gave up the security of her home to be with him. She needed this to work for her sake and well as ours. Although all Susan's eggs had been neatly placed into Shawn's basket, he now seemed more interested in me than in her. I had watched the pressure cooker inside Susan reach its limit as she tried to contain her anger. There was only so much she could take before the red button would be pushed and she would turn to the drink again. I would then be blamed for Shawn's behaviour towards me. However, I needed to tell someone about what I thought Shawn may have done to me. It was killing me, I had to tell Susan the mum and hope that not only the wine cork was kept firmly on but also her anger stayed under control.

But before I went down that road, I needed proof to back up my story, a story that didn't make any sense to me, never mind to someone else. I searched for clues and evidence that could somehow prove what happened to me, but I never found anything. I didn't have any leads to go on. I only had my suspicions about who the ghostly figure was in my room that day. There was no evidence of a break-in at the house and I was grateful for this. The thought of a stranger in my room only terrified me more; this left one person as a possible suspect.

70

Since that day, Shawn became child-like around me, his voice would change and his body language was more akin to a young boy than a grown man. Lots of gifts for me kept coming, new riding gear or more lessons, whereas Jacob only got a few. That triggered questions. Why would he only be so generous towards me and not Jacob? Was it his guilty conscience? His behaviour convinced me he was the ghostly figure that haunted me. Susan became frustrated the more she saw Shawn giving me the attention she craved. I chose not to say anything at that point but the old Susan resurfaced anyway; she became increasingly angry at the attention I was getting.

Now and again I rehearsed what I might say but it sounded wrong and mixed up.

"Hey, Mum. I think I was drugged, I can't really say I'm 100% sure. I was kinda in La La Land when it happened. I didn't see a face, but I think your boyfriend did it. My so-called dad! He did something to me, but I'm not sure what. I think I am also broken, as a strange liquid leaked out of me from down there!" I formed the dialogue then shook my head.

I mean really, what the fuck? How could I ever have that conversation, knowing that it could ruin everything? I knew the damage and devastation this could potentially cause but life with my secret seemed so dark; it made me sick. Like a broken record, I relived that day over and over again in my mind. I didn't know how to break the chain and was locked in the prison of my thoughts. It affected my entire world, even to get out of bed in the morning had become a struggle.

One morning during breakfast, Shawn said that the garden needed some attention. The weeds and grass had grown so quickly, due to the sudden changes in temperature and everyone was given a job to do. My job was to strim the high grass. I enjoyed it; my mind was released from its torture. I was mesmerized as I watched the bits of cut grass fly about.

After lunch. Susan said that they had run out of baccy. They both smoked heavily and, by that time, she knew I smoked too. She never seemed to have a problem with me smoking, even though I was only eleven years old.

"Do you fancy a walk to the garage with me?' Susan asked.

The garage was about a mile away. We would have to walk because she still wasn't allowed to drive.

"I'll drive you if you like?" Shawn said, as he suddenly appeared from behind a bush.

"No, it's fine we'll walk, it's a nice day,' Susan chirped.

I got the impression she was bored of the work in the garden and she wanted to get out of it. We got into a nice conversation on our walk; Susan seemed relaxed and calm. We bought a pouch of tobacco and some cold drinks and Susan bought me some strawberry laces.

"Don't tell your brother," Susan chuckled as she accepted one of my strawberry laces.

I felt comfortable in Susan's company and managed to pluck some courage up.

"Mum, a few months back something happened," I blurted out.

"What's that Jess?" Susan enquired.

She couldn't have imagined what I was about to say.

"Well, I'm not really sure but I think Shawn did something to me," I said nervously.

Goosebumps rose on my arms as I searched for words, but I didn't get the chance to expand further.

"Don't be so silly, he is your father and loves you," Susan answered angrily.

The conversation ended as quickly as it had started and I felt stupid for opening my mouth. Susan's mood and body language changed, she became locked deep in her thoughts and she marched on ahead of me. She was annoyed.

I had finally managed to pluck up the courage to talk to her after weeks of mental torture and I had just fucked it up big time. I felt so stupid, why did I open my big mouth?

The rest of the way home Susan remained silent; I chased her footsteps. She disappeared into the house without a glance back at me. I didn't know if I should stay outside or go inside. I felt awkward and confused standing on the driveway alone then plucked up the courage to go in.

I spent an hour in the bathroom having a shower then a further hour drying my hair. I was wasting time because I was anxious and worried about Susan's reaction.

Probably for the best if I just to try and stay away from everyone, - I told myself, but I badly needed a cigarette to calm me down.

Crystal was normally the only person who used the utility room, so I escaped there. It should have been empty but as I opened the door I saw Susan sitting on the worktop smoking a cigarette. Fuck! The utility room was the last place I would have expected her to be. Susan stared at me as if she was waiting to see if I had the balls to stay in the room with her. Stupidly, I lit the cigarette and looked down at the tiled floor.

"Mum, about earlier. I'm certain Shawn did something to me, on my bed," I spouted out.

Like verbal diarrhea, the words flowed.

What the actual fuck! - I thought.

My mouth had taken over my brain. With my eyes fixed firmly on a floor tile, I took another long drag from my cigarette and waited for her reaction. The intensity seemed to grow in the room. Smoke dissipated from my nostrils and Susan still didn't say a word. Finally, I lifted my head and looked over to where she sat; her dark eyes stared directly at me. She picked up a large glass of wine and downed the lot; all the time, her eyes locked on to mine. Without a word, she continually refilled her glass from the nearby bottle.

Oh fuck! This meant that she was on her fourth glass. Susan's gloves were about to come off now that the bottle was almost finished.

I was petrified. I watched Susan take another large gulp from the newly filled glass.

"You're a lying slut," she hissed.

That was the signal, the shit was about to hit the fan.

"Look at you prancing around with your makeup on and your slutty clothes, your tits hanging out for everyone to see!" Susan's words cut through me like a knife. "You're just jealous of what I have, you want my boyfriend!"

This made no sense. She bought my clothes and why was I jealous? Wine spilled out of her glass as she tried to light another cigarette.

"Mum, please! I'm trying to tell you."

Before I even had a chance to finish my sentence, she jumped off the countertop and punched me square in the face. I lost my balance and hit the tiled floor hard. The impact was just as painful as the punch.

"Get out, you little slag!' she spat out.

I lay dazed on the floor from the sudden attack. I tried to get back up on my feet while my eyes filled with tears. My face throbbed and my knee felt broken but none of this mattered. The pain that gathered in my chest was what hurt the most; my heart shattered into thousands of pieces.

I was back on my feet and, without another word, I walked out of the utility room.

"Get the fuck out!" she screamed after me.

That final dagger ripped me to shreds. I heard a glass explode against the wall and I dropped to the floor. The glass had narrowly missed my head before fragments splintered off in every direction. I turned to face Susan once more; her dark eyes were full of hate.

Why can she not just be my mum and protect me? - I asked myself.

That was never going to happen. My mother hated me!

74

Tears tumbled down my face but I made it to the front door and stepped outside. With nowhere to go or no-one to turn to, I didn't look back. I started to run as fast as I could. My eyes were blinded by my tears as I ran. Large stones and raised roots tripped me up, I was broken inside; my worst fears had just come true.

My mother hates me! How could I have been so stupid? Why couldn't I have just kept my mouth shut? - my mind screamed at me.

The battle that had raged on inside me for so long, had just been lost. I hunched over and tried to gasp for air at the end of the driveway. I took my phone out; there was only one person I could call.

"Laura. Please help me!" I tried to get the simplest of words out but I was sobbing.

The phone dropped out of my hand; I was hysterical but I could do no more than sit huddled up on the ground. A set of headlights suddenly blinded me, as a car pulled up to the curb.

"Jessica, Are you ok?" Ben asked in a soft voice.

He stepped out of his car and he helped me to my feet.

"I'll take you to your sister," Ben's words were what I needed to hear!

Chapter 10

Give me a break

History had repeated itself. I was no longer welcome at the family home. I had been beaten and kicked to the curb just like my brother and sister before me. I had only ever seen that expression of pure hatred on Susan's face once before and that was the night she attacked Jack and Laura. I caused this to happen through my stupidity; I had believed my mum would protect me but she didn't. Someone in the role of a mother is meant to protect you and a dad isn't allowed to abuse.

I had felt so dirty and ashamed since the day I was drugged, I wasn't 100% sure it was Shawn who was responsible. But I was 99.9% sure. Either way, I thought Susan would believe me. This was a serious error in my judgment. I knew sober Susan would bury her head in the sand and drunk Susan would always be a catalyst for disaster. My brain felt like a little hamster running on his wheel inside my head; there was no end in sight. Why did I open my stupid mouth!

Wow, we got here fast, - I thought as I snapped out of a deep trance-like state.

Ben pulled to a stop on the gravel drive outside the little cottage. I don't think we even exchanged one word the entire journey, instead music played quietly whilst we drove through the night.

Ben is a very chilled out sort of guy, he's always around when you need him. He's like a butler who looks after a big house and sweeps up behind everyone. Here he was, sweeping up the carnage of this family. He was always very interested but in a way where he doesn't get involved. Most people would have probed me about what had happened, trying to get the gossip. Real-life entertainment, real-life Eastenders. But Ben just got me where I needed to be and allowed me to think. I felt safe in his company.

"Are you ok?" Ben asked, as he switched off the engine and killed the lights.

"Yeah, I think so, thanks for the lift. I appreciate it, I'm just going to have a fag then I'll come in," I said quietly.

I needed some time to myself to gather my thoughts before Laura questioned me about what had happened.

"I'll leave the door off the latch. You do know smoking stunts your growth?" Ben chuckled to himself

He walked towards the house.

"Bit late don't ya think?" I called after him.

The calm, cloudless night and the beautiful, bright moon were in stark contrast to the storm I had come from.

What happens now? I can't stay with Laura forever, - I said to myself.

My future seemed uncertain but I took a breath and made my way to the front door. Baby Susan beamed from ear to ear, she let out a loud screech when she saw me. This made me smile. She was in the middle of her dinner and looked a sticky mess. She flicked mushed up food around while Ben desperately tried to get it in her mouth. Laura appeared with a dessert pot.

"Hay, Sis, are you ok?" she asked.

"I'm fine, it's just Mum, you know how it is," I answered.

I couldn't look at Laura, tears were welling up in my eyes again as I spoke. Whilst outside, I had already decided if I was to tell Laura the full story it would just cause more trouble. She would march over to Susan's and have it out with her; I didn't want another bad reaction. No doubt it would probably become my fault anyway and I would be branded a liar because I had no proof that Shawn was the culprit. If Laura thought it was all a lie, who else did I have to turn to for help? Jack had disappeared from the face of the planet and my real dad lived in Malta, I wasn't exactly at the top of his list when it came to parental priorities. If I told Laura, I would risk jeopardising the only sanctuary I had left, the streets and sleeping rough would be my only other option. I needed to keep my mouth shut.

I watched my sister, now part of a happy family and felt scared. I was young and vulnerable and, unlike Laura, I had nowhere to call home. Being with her and Ben was my last hope and probably only for a few nights or a few weeks at best. Laura couldn't put me up forever. I could only see a very long and dark road in front of me, with no idea where it would lead.

A horrible thought rushed into my head, what if Laura said I couldn't stay? I looked up so she could see the tears in my eyes and hoped she would realise I needed help.

"Can I stay with you and Ben for a while, just till things settle down at home?" I asked.

"Sure, are you ok, Sis? Ben, make a cuppa," my sister interjected.

I felt a weight lift from my shoulders and started to calm down, I was safe but for how long? I needed some clothes for school but Laura didn't want to risk retrieving them from the house. She didn't want any conflict with Susan.

The next morning, Laura took me to buy school clothes. I had been wearing my school shoes when I ran from the house but I badly needed some new ones and I chose a cheap pair of plain shoes. Laura found a pair that she liked instead, velcro strapped shoes with pink flowers that lit up when you walked. I was nearly twelve years old, I wasn't five. She would not back down about these bloody shoes. People could hear us arguing in the shop so I gave in to Laura and let her buy me these awful shoes.

My face had swelled where Susan had punched me so I stayed away from school for the rest of the week while they healed. My entire time off was spent with my niece when all I wanted to do was sleep. Laura kept me constantly busy with baby Susan while she rested or did her own thing. By the time my bruises were fading, I could cover the remaining marks with some makeup; I was looking forward to school. I needed the break, babies are hard work.

I had to wake up earlier than usual the next day, as school was over an hour's walk away. Ben had already left for work, so he could not give me a lift and Laura didn't drive. I enjoyed the walk to school, it gave me some peace and time to think. I had hidden the velcro light-up shoes in the house and wore my old battered school shoes instead. There was no way I would be seen dead in light-up shoes.

At primary school I had always been a very popular kid, in secondary school, my life seemed harder. I was the youngest and shortest in my year and probably the skinniest too, born practically deaf in one ear. I wore a hearing aid and used my thick bushy brown hair to hide it. Most people mistook my age and thought I was only about nine years old; I still had very childlike facial features.

The only part of me that made me look a bit older was my breasts, they had developed fast. Tiny in weight and build with double D bra cups. This trait ran in my family; small framed but top-heavy. I would wear a baggy jumper where possible to cover myself. Unfortunately, my breasts attracted unwanted attention at school. My bra would be unhooked in class or as I walked along a corridor, a great game for the boys. It was a total humiliation for me.

I went from being a popular kid to a total loner in less than a year. I was the one who attempted to get through the day in the hope no one would notice me. The kid that people liked to pick on. Take a breath, count to ten, walk into class, take a seat, pray no one will notice me; that had become my daily routine.

A boy in my year called Johnny decided that I would be the butt of all his jokes. He had walked into class and sat behind me.

"Alright small fry?" Johnny asked sarcastically.

Small fry, apparently this was my new nickname.

"How are your tits today? I see you pumped them up. Did you have a puncture last week?" he continued laughing as he nudged his mate Paul

My breasts have been likened to some kind of a tyre and apparently, this was funny.

"You are such a dick," I retorted.

Most of the class had turned in their seats to listen to what was going on.

"Alright hard of hearing Harry, no need to shout," he replied with an evil grin on his face.

The entire class erupted into laughter; in the minute he had been in class he had managed to humiliate me. He had focused on what I was most self-conscious about and to add insult to injury the entire class laughed along with him. The teacher walked into the room.

"Quiet please, settle down!" he yelled.

The room fell silent.

"Jessica, can you come to the front please," the teacher beckoned me.

Oh fuck! My heart sank to the pit of my stomach. The teacher held a clear plastic bag with Shoe Zone written on it. I knew exactly what the contents were; the worst shoes I have ever seen in my life. Light up, velcro strapped shoes with fucking pink flowers!

"Jessica. I haven't got all day. Please can you come and get your shoes," he called out again.

80

The entire class looked at me; part of me died. I collected the bag while everyone else sniggered and stared.

"Nice shoes, Harry!" Johnny shouted out, as I reached my chair.

The entire class erupted into laughter as I stuffed the plastic bag and the shoes as deep as I could into my school bag. I swivelled around in my chair to face him.

"Fuck off, you twat!" I screamed at him as I tried to fight back the tears of humiliation.

He had a stupid grin on his face and was playing with a small pair of scissors.

"Snip, snip!" he chuckled and waved the scissors in my face.

"Just leave me alone," I said coldly.

I swivelled back around to face the front of the room. I folded my arms on the desk and rested my head upon them and soon after the bell rang. The classroom erupted into a bustle of noise again, as everyone went to class.

"Snip!" I heard Johnny say one more time.

A large chunk of cut hair fell onto my desk and an object hit the back of my head. Whatever had hit me didn't bounce off. I stared in disbelief at my hair strewn across my desk.

Oh my God, oh my God! - my head screamed.

I reached around to the back of my head and my fingers touched something wet and sticky.

"Have fun, small fry," Johnny spat at me and walked out of the classroom.

Something sticky had entangled itself to my hair and the more I tried to pull it out, the more it embedded itself. I ran out of the classroom to the next block and burst into the girls' toilets. At the top of my scalp, a large chunk of hair had been cut, the hair that remained stuck up in a peculiar way and looked awful.

"No, no, no!" I said over and over again, staring into the mirror.

I reached around and pulled my hair over my shoulder; there it was, a large lump of sticky pink bubble gum. It was hard and tangled in a large chunk of my hair. It wouldn't come out no matter what I did. I walked into one of the toilet cubicles, sat down on the toilet seat and burst into tears and thought about the past two weeks. Enough was enough!

Nowhere was safe. I had been punched, slapped and drugged at home then ridiculed and bullied at school. I felt loved by no one and hated by everyone and now I was reduced to hide out in a dirty school toilet with gum in my hair. I had no real friends anymore and no one to talk to or trust. I had become the loner at school and I was sure this made me a target. Laura had her problems and her own family. I was just in the way and had become an annoyance; I wasn't part of her world anymore. Somehow I knew my life was going to get worse, without anyone to protect me. I wondered how any other girl, not even twelve years old, would have felt in that position. Here I was, once again, sitting in grubby toilets. To make matters worse, my hair, the security blanket that concealed my hearing aid from the world, had been cut away in less than a few seconds. In that depressing moment, I knew new depths of despair. I stayed in the toilet for the rest of the day, people came and went but no one bothered me. They would simply use one of the other cubicles while I hid, huddled up, in mine.

Shit! What will Laura do or say when she sees my hair? - I thought.

If she went to the school about this or confronted the bullies, this would only make things worse for me.

The final bell rang out and I could hear the school erupt into a mass of noise, as everyone started to leave for the day. The school fell silent and I needed to leave, hiding in a toilet all day had a weird effect on my mental state. I kind of expected a large crowd of people to be gathered outside the cubicle with balloons and a banner. We knew you were there all along! written on it.

I took a deep breath and stepped out, thankfully the toilets were empty. There was not a soul in sight when I peeked out to the corridor either. I took my chance and ran to the exit. The school grounds were nearly deserted, just a few kids talking by the fields. My path seemed clear to the gates so I ran across the grounds as fast as my feet would carry me and out of the gates. A purple Cherokee Jeep was parked outside the school gates. The driver's door opened and Shawn stepped out as I skidded to a stop.

Why is he here? Where is Susan? Should I run and hide? - I thought.

I was scared of Shawn, but as I looked at him an overwhelming sense of relief came over me. It had been a very hard day and I needed someone to take me away from it all.

"Jessica, can we talk please," Shawn called out.

I didn't say a word, instead, I walked over to the car and got in. I wanted to go home.

"What on earth has happened to you?" Shawn asked and nodded towards my hair.

A blob of gum and a large patch of cut hair stood up in a strange way, it wasn't that hard to miss.

"Please. Can you just drive? I want to go home," I replied quietly.

He started up and we pulled away.

"Your mum is not well, Jess. She doesn't mean to act the way she does. You know that, right? She really didn't mean to lash out at you the other night; she's devastated and wants you home," he told me.

I wanted to go home, back to my room and fluffy bean bag but I was still unsure if Susan would beat me again. However, I didn't have other options. Laura had caused me so many problems at school earlier and I was mad at her. My life was hard enough without adding the velcro shoes to my list of problems. I didn't fit into Laura's world either. It was never going to last so where else could I go? Tired and upset, all I wanted was my bed; I made my decision.

"I'll try with her." I quietly relented.

Chapter 11

It was never a dream

Shawn pulled onto the gravel drive and the garage soon came into view. Jacob bounced up and down on the trampoline and waved at us as we drove past. I smiled and waved back, I had missed him. We pulled up outside the house and I took a deep breath before we walked in.

"Jessica what on earth! Who did this to you?" Susan asked with panic in her voice.

She pulled me into her arms and, horrified, she started to frantically look through my hair.

Well, that was an ice breaker! - I thought.

She pulled out her phone and rang the hairdressers. I hoped they could squeeze me in for a late appointment.

"Brilliant! We'll come straight away," she smiled as she rang off.

Maybe she felt she had fixed something, maybe she felt like a mum at that moment; whatever it was, my hair had saved a difficult conversation.

Later that day we returned from *Toni & Guy*: my beautiful long brown hair had been cut into a bob. The stylist had done her best to save as much as she could but a lot of damage had been done. I hated my hair this short because my hearing aid showed; my armour had been cut off and swept away. After I had taken a shower and closed the door on the world, I got under my covers and cried myself to sleep. It had been a terrible day.

The next day, Susan woke me to go to school. I didn't want to go so I pleaded for the day off. I could not face any comments about my hair or my hearing aid today.

What if Johnny does it again, I'll end up bald! - I thought to myself.

Shawn agreed it was probably for the best, as I had been through so much. I was pleased that he had sided with me on this occasion, but I still didn't like him.

"I suppose, just for today," Susan gave in.

Thankfully, a day off meant I didn't have to deal with Johnny and the rest of the school for at least another day, a little weight had been lifted from my shoulders. I returned to my nice warm bed, as I heard Shawn's car disappear from the drive and I was finally alone. I could sleep and relax under the warmth of my duvet.

I heard Shawn's car return about an hour later and my stomach began to churn. I forgot that he might come back home and I certainly didn't want to be home alone with him. The front door opened and slammed shut then I heard the click from his shoes on the floor as he walked towards my bedroom door.

"Please leave me be," I whispered under my breath.

He stopped outside my door. I could hear the handle moving and the door creaking open.

"Jessica are you awake?" Shawn asked softly as he stood at the threshold of the door.

Should I pretend to be asleep? Will he go away? What does he want?' - I wondered.

"Urm, yeah," I replied in a fake sleepy voice.

I added a yawn just to try and get him to leave, I hoped maybe he would get the hint and go away. No such luck! He walked into my room and sat on my bed. What the fuck! I didn't like Shawn around me at the best of times, least of all in my room and on my bed.

"I have missed you so much, Jessica," he looked directly into my eyes.

I had already seen the look that was creeping over his face and I started to feel uneasy.

"Urm, I've missed everyone too," nervously I pulled my bed covers higher.

The strange smile, a half-grin, appeared; the creepy side of Shawn I had never gotten used to. His dark eyes stared at me and, as I turned away, his hand reached out, held my chin and he forced me to look into his face. He bent down to kiss me.

"What the fuck are you doing?" I shouted and pushed him away.

He took me by surprise and grabbed both of my wrists. I tried to wriggle out of his grip but he squeezed even tighter.

"Let me go, what are you doing?" I pleaded with him.

His eyes darkened and an evil grin replaced his strange smile; it made him look sinister.

"Jessica, why do you resist me?" the evil in his voice matched the look on his face.

"It hurts, get off!" I demanded as the devil looked back at me and laughed. With all my strength, I tried to tug my arms free but he just applied more pressure and continued to laugh at me.

"Please leave me alone!" my plea was ignored.

He tried to kiss me again and I furiously shook my head to stop him as his weight pushed down on me. His vile breath was all I could smell and his lips touched mine. I was powerless and pinned to my pillow with his lips on mine. Somehow, I managed to move my head to the side.

"Get off me. What the fuck are you doing?" I screamed frantically.

"You will enjoy this Jessica, it's what dads do!" Shawn replied in his creepy, quiet voice.

The more I struggled the more he seemed to enjoy the thrill of what he was doing; I was powerless against a man of his size. My arms were forced above my head and my wrists pinned down with one of his hands as he leaned in again and attempted to kiss me. I felt the bed covers between us rip away; my only barrier and protection against him had been removed.

"Be a good girl, Jessica, play nice for daddy," his disgusting breath blew over my face as he panted with excitement.

Play fucking nice! I don't want to play this fucking game! - I screamed out in my head, as I continued to try and wriggle my way free.

What chance did I have against this overweight, fully grown man? I was tiny in comparison. The more I struggled the more weight he pushed down on me. I felt my chest being crushed under the pressure. It was impossible to breathe and I gasped for air when he suddenly released some of his weight. He watched me get weaker and weaker, he was like a cat that taunts a mouse caught and trapped under its paws. In my last bid to break free, I ran out of energy and became completely helpless. He watched in amusement while I gasped for air. Then he unbuckled his belt.

"Have you finished now?" he grunted.

Before I could even reply or spit in his face, my knickers were pulled aside and I felt his skin touch mine as he used his legs to prise mine apart.

"No, no, no! Please no!" my final desperate plea to Shawn fell on deaf ears.

I screamed out in pain and tears tumbled down my face, as what felt like a dagger ripped my insides apart.

I need to wake up! I need to wake up! This is just a dream, - I prayed, but this wasn't a dream.

I felt this dirty man inside me, his flesh on mine as he lifted my nightie to expose my breasts. Powerless, I tried to catch my breath and turned my head turned towards the door.

Please someone walk in and save me, - I prayed, but no one did!

He started to thrust himself inside me harder and faster; I was awake and aware of every painful moment. A tiny voice inside my head told me to fight again, so I started to struggle.

"Be a good girl, Jessica, the more you struggle the more it hurts!" his quiet tone was pure evil as his sweat dripped down on me.

It was him all along; the smell that had haunted me for weeks, he stank of it. He was the one who had drugged me and done something to me and now he was doing it again. With no fight left in me, my tiny body was forced up and down. I lay limp and tried to go somewhere else desperately in my mind. Anywhere but here.

Suddenly, he juddered and I felt him pulsate. His grip loosened and a remaining tear ran down my face.

"Go clean yourself up and I'll order some food," he calmly told me.

He got off of me and casually wandered out of the room. Confused by what had just happened, I lay frozen in the same position as he had left me.

Please wake up, please wake up! - I prayed over and over under my breath. Somewhere in the depths of my soul, I wished this was just all a bad dream.

I didn't understand what had happened to me. I was still only eleven years old. My head danced around from one thought to the next as the stench of him covered my body. Vomit rose from my stomach and suddenly my body took over; I grabbed my gown and ran to the bathroom. My stomach was wracked with pain and my insides felt like they were on fire. The contents of my stomach filled the toilet and I wiped the sweat from my forehead. In shock, I watched a thin line of sticky blood leak from me and make a trail down my leg.

Apparently, this is what dads do! - I thought to myself as the smell of the liquid overwhelmed me.

I needed to wash it off so I headed to the shower to get rid of his horrendous smell. No matter how hard I scrubbed, I reeked of it. His smell would not leave me. I returned to my bedroom and, on autopilot, I stripped the bedclothes from my bed. After I had replaced them with clean sheets, I got dressed and started to tidy my bedroom. I cleaned every item in my bedroom, over and over again in a trance-like state. My mind was blank and I felt weak, I didn't notice my door open.

"Eat this. You must be hungry. Our little secret, right?" Shawn stared at me.

He stood with a plate of Chinese food in his hand. He put it down and walked back out of my room closing the door behind him.

Our little secret! Did he mean the food or what he had just done? - I wondered.

The plate of food was stacked with all my favourites but I didn't want to accept anything from him. It felt wrong, everything felt wrong. I curled up on my bean bag.

Should I tell? Who is there to tell? - I wondered as I silently rocked back and forth and stared at a bed that no longer felt like my own.

Chapter 12

I give up

The school summer holidays had just started. Most kids would be happy to have the time off away from school. Sadly for me, the school break meant time alone in the house and more opportunities for Shawn to attack me. By this time, he had forced himself upon me on numerous occasions; the abuse had escalated. The assaults started to happen when other people were around. He seemed to get a thrill out of the possibility that he might get caught. Strength-wise, I was no match against him but, at every attack, I would put up a fight. He seemed to like the power he had over me and would watch until I became weak then he would take his prize. It was almost like he liked to watch the pain he put me through when I struggled to fend him off.

Shawn liked to manipulate everything to his advantage, even the house we lived in; he had manipulated his way into it. I watched him encouraging Susan to drink again, almost like he was moving another pawn from his chessboard. He supplied the alcohol to feed

Susan's addiction and, knowing she would find it hard to resist, he would keep filling her glass until she passed out. If Susan got into one of her many fits of rage while she drank, Shawn would instantly jump to my defence and a massive argument would erupt between them. This allowed me to escape the situation and run to my room. I would feel grateful that he had stepped in to protect me. My abuser had, ironically, become my defender.

However, he may have saved me from another night filled with kicks, punches and pain, but this was only to create an opportunity to abuse me. Shawn would deal with Susan until she passed out, then he would visit my bedroom. After he had finished with me, he would casually return to his bedroom to sleep with Susan.

The next day he would act like the entire world was normal and some form of a gift would appear; a new phone or riding lessons, there would always be a gift. I didn't want his gifts and I certainly didn't want him to visit me at night. Susan noticed the extra attention he was giving me again and she grew increasingly annoyed and very jealous. She argued with him about the money he spent on me because it was more than obvious that Shawn never gave Jacob the same. If Shawn bought me a new BMX bike, for example, Susan felt she had to find the money to buy Jacob a new bike too. If he bought a gift for me that Susan wanted, she would get very jealous and make it clear that she wanted whatever it was. I would just hand it over to her.

He attempted to buy my silence but he already had my silence because I was too terrified to speak up. I knew there would be horrendous consequences to be paid if I told someone but I felt dirty and too ashamed to say anything anyway. Shawn also acted differently around me in other ways too; he gave compliments and similar forms of affection. It was as though he thought we were in some kind of secret relationship, I hated it and so did Susan.

91

By way of punishment, the chores started to pile on me and I soon became Susan's house-elf again. I paid the price for Shawn's actions. Raped by Shawn then beaten by Susan while wearing my elf's hat became the new theme.

If Susan found out what he had done, would her rage be directed at me? Would she protect me or would she choose him instead? - these questions plagued my mind.

Every day, I was a scared and lonely child; I had no one to trust. The girls' toilets at school became my refuge so I became invisible. I had mastered the art of avoiding people, I didn't want to talk to anyone or get involved anymore at school. It was just easier to hide; no one could hurt me when I was hidden. However deep down, I desperately wanted to tell someone about what was happening to me. But who would listen? Would anyone be able to put themselves in my shoes?

I had tried to talk to the police before; I even showed them the bruises that littered my body. Yet, I was ignored and sent back home. I had also told Susan that I believed Shawn had drugged me, that outcome was horrendous. I was scared to tell anyone anything.

On my twelfth birthday. I was given a lot of presents from Shawn but Susan was not pleased with the amount he had spent on me. She drank herself well past the fifth glass and needless to say, it was yet again another birthday ruined. By the end of the summer holidays, all I wanted to do was go back to school. Back to my safe place in the girls' toilets; it had been a difficult summer at home.

In the first week back at school, I decided to make an effort and attend classes. I would turn up early and take a seat at the back of the classroom, that way no one could sit behind me and I simply kept my head down. No one seemed to notice or even bother with me; it was as though people had forgotten about me. I started to look forward to school; it became my haven but it was quite lonely. I watched

92

everyone else with their friends but it was worth it to enjoy the peace away from the stresses at home.

At the end of the third week back, my belly started to hurt and the pain was excruciating. My stomach felt like it was going to explode and I looked as white as a ghost.

"Are you ok?" Shawn asked when I walked through the door.

"No, my belly really hurts," I muttered.

Sweat dripped from my forehead.

Shawn quickly Googled my symptoms and decided that I was constipated. He left to buy some fruit and laxatives. Unfortunately, Dr Google's diagnosis was wrong and after a bad visit to the toilet, the pain got worse. When Susan arrived home, she immediately decided to take me to hospital. I was rushed in to have my appendix removed moments after we arrived. I finally had some peace as I spent the next five days in hospital. It was bliss there. Laura and Ben visited with baby Susan who had grown so fast. Shawn also turned up to visit me and handed me a teddy bear holding a plaque that read Get Well Soon. After he left, I gave the bear to a little boy who was also on my ward.

"You're going to be discharged today," a nurse announced one morning.

These were the dreaded words I didn't want to hear. My heart sank; it meant my holiday away from the house was over. I could hardly put one foot in front of the other when Shawn came to pick me up that afternoon but I was thankful to cling to his arm to get to the car. This was probably the only time I can ever remember that I didn't mind him touching me. I spent the rest of the evening in bed; food was brought in, empty plates were taken away and I was left alone. I heard Susan and Shawn argue during the night but thankfully it seemed to settle down and my bedroom door remained closed.

The next morning I was awakened by the sound of a car door slamming shut. I tried to sit up but I found that I was in a lot of pain.

The drugs that I had been given at the hospital had worn off and the wound from the operation was on fire. I heard Shawn's car start up then drive away. I knew he would be taking Susan to work and Jacob to school. When he returned, I would be home alone with him once again.

Surely he'll leave me alone given my condition? - I hoped.

No such luck. The sound made by the click of his shoes told me he was on his way to my bedroom. My door was flung open and he headed over to my bedside.

"How are you feeling?" he asked as he sat down.

"I'm in so much pain," I grimaced, hoping he would leave me alone.

"That's not good," he said, sounding as though he cared.

"I've really missed you," he continued as he reached out and stroked my face.

"Please, don't!" I replied quietly.

I knew that I was in too much pain to fight him.

"Jessica, you know it makes us happy," the devil glint in his eyes told their own story.

Us! There is no us, only you, - I thought.

"It's only normal, every dad does it with his daughter. It's natural and special," his creepy voice reminded me.

Why would any dad wish to hurt his daughter in this way and why would he call it special, when it feels so wrong? - I cried inside.

To be honest, I had no idea. I could remember having a dad in my life for one day, no more. I only knew what my friend, Naomi, had told me. Apparently, her dad kissed and hugged her and she said that was normal but had he also done what Shawn did to me? I had no idea; I couldn't ask her because we didn't speak anymore. With regards to Susan, I had witnessed Laura and Jack take regular abuse for years, yet no one stepped in and said that it was wrong. I had no idea what a normal family looked like, my entire childhood had been warped. Shawn could have been right and this was normal and part of life.

Perhaps I am broken in some way? Was that why I didn't find it special? But why does my gut still tell me this is wrong? - I had so many questions to vocalise.

Shawn started to run his hand up and down my leg and it took me by surprise, it tickled slightly. He seemed different from normal and was gentle, he didn't try to pin me to the bed.

"It's ok, Jessica, see it can be nice too," he said softly.

The horrible half grin appeared.

My head was a total mess; I had been out of the hospital for less than 24 hours. I didn't want to be pinned to the bed again, to move hurt and there was no way I could fight him off. The only control I had over this situation was to decide if it was going to be rough or gentle. It was as simple as that. I gave up and a part of my soul died, I had no fight left in me and opted for the lesser of two evils, the gentle option. I had taken the easy road and hated myself for it. Shawn had managed to break me down into submission and he knew it, like a fragile glass I had broken. I leaned back against my pillow. The half-grin became a smile that flitted across Shawn's face: I turned my head to face the bedroom door.

"That's a good girl, I knew you would see it my way," he whispered. I felt him pull back the bed covers and pry my legs apart and his hand started to work his way up my leg. My nightshirt was lifted while he tugged my knickers down. I closed my eyes tightly to hide my shame and embarrassment. I was disgusted that my very young private parts were exposed. Tears brimmed over as I desperately searched for my secret place.

After weeks of sexual assaults, I had learned to escape in my mundane thoughts about the washing up or dinner. My mind went into a kind of trance and shut down until the ordeal had ended. I had surrendered without a fight this time, but my soul punished me. I was locked out of my thoughts, the only haven I had left. My body lifted up and down like a rag doll with each of his movements, his sweaty skin sliding against mine. There was no violence to go with the violation this time. Even although he was gentle, I was never under the illusion I ever had a choice.

When the pain became too much and I pleaded with him to stop, he carried on regardless. Either way, he was going to take what he wanted. Finally, the disgusting judder arrived which normally marked the end of my ordeal. My stomach hurt and my scars burned. I waited for him to move but he didn't. Instead, he lay there, still inside me, with his weight pushing down on me.

Normally he gets up and leaves, why hasn't he left? - I wondered.

I opened my eyes in time to see Shawn's creepy eyes locking on mine. There was a different expression on his face this time.

What the fuck! What the hell does he want now? Does he want a conversation or a cuddle? - the pain swelling in my stomach blurring my thoughts.

His sweat dripped down on me. An attacker would normally leave once he had what he wanted but not Shawn, this was an entirely new level of craziness. He lowered his head and kissed me, before he slowly rolled off and lay next to me.

What the actual fuck! - I cringed as he pulled me tight for a cuddle.

This was a serious head fuck. My brain went from overload to total meltdown as we lay in bed together. I had no idea what to do; I couldn't move. I could barely walk never mind run and I was trapped under the weight of his hairy arms.

"We had better get cleaned up," Shawn said softly.

It was an eternity before he left my bedroom and by that time, I felt sick. I hated him and everything he had done to me.

I went through my normal ritual and scrubbed myself in an unsuccessful attempt to wash his stench off me. The smell made me feel sick and often took me by surprise.

Could anyone else smell what I could? Maybe they could, maybe this is why I got bullied? - I started to wonder.

The first time I woke up naked in bed after Shawn had abused me, things changed in every walk of my life. At school, I had been a popular kid but I became distant from my friends and the bullies singled me out. At home, Susan got annoyed with me because of Shawn's attention and she drank more and her anger increased.

Maybe she knows what's was going on? - My trail of thought led to a million new questions that continued to flood my mind, they all sought an answer.

Does Susan already know what Shawn is doing to me? - was by far the most harrowing question in my head.

Chapter 13

Under the spotlight

I was absent from school for a further three weeks while I recovered from my operation. During this time, I found myself lost in a world of my own; everything seemed distorted and muted as though I was trapped inside a bubble. When people talked to me they sounded muffled and I couldn't understand them. I quickly drifted off to the safe place in my head that I had created. Most of my time was spent lost in my own thoughts about Jacob or the outstanding chores at home, my safe place where no one could harm me.

"Jessica, Jessica, Jessica!' Susan shouted, awakening me from my dream world.

"Urm, yeah?" I replied.

I had no idea how long she had been talking to me.

"Are you ready for school tomorrow?" she went on.

Is it really time to go back? - I wondered.

The past three weeks of my life had vanished.

"Earth calling Jessica, Jessica!' Susan shouted again and regained my attention.

"Sorry, what?" I choked.

"School, Jessica, are you ready?" Susan repeated.

"Yes," I answered.

"I need to talk to you. The police have been in touch and want to meet you at school tomorrow," she announced.

I found myself suddenly fully focused on what she had just said. The policeman who had visited me when I was thrown outside naked had made me feel as though my predicament was my fault. So, my feelings towards the police weren't very good.

"They are going to try and tell you lies about your dad." Susan continued.

"Why?" I asked.

"They want to break our family apart and they will say some nasty things about him, it's all rubbish, they are liars!" she protested reaching out to take my hand.

I immediately flinched; a reaction that happened a lot since Shawn had started his bedroom visits. I hated when people touched me.

"Jessica, if you say anything you'll never see your brother again. You'll be taken away and put in some horrible place by yourself. Do you understand?" she looked into my eyes and squeezed my hand.

A horrible place didn't sound ideal and she had just used my biggest fear as a threat, being separated from Jacob.

"Yes, Mum, I won't say anything. Don't worry." I reassured her.

"That's a good girl. I knew you would see how important this is," she sounded more upbeat by the time she let go of my hand.

Another sleepless night followed the conversation with Susan and war broke out in my head that night.

What will I say to the police and why do they want to talk about Shawn? Will everybody at school see me talking to them? - I wondered as I tossed and turned in my bed.

After a few minutes, I was back to the questions.

Maybe I should tell them about what he does to me. If what he does is just normal and natural, what does it matter anyway? Why should I protect him? - I thought.

But then there were the threats Susan had made.

A horrible place, a police cell perhaps? Will I ever see Jacob again, if I tell them? - my thoughts were a mess.

I loved Jacob so much, he was my best friend. Jack and Laura had already been torn from me, I couldn't lose him too. Once in a blue moon, I got to see my brother and sister but we didn't know each other anymore. Jacob and Susan were all I had left. Susan made my life incredibly hard but she was still my mum and Jekyll and Hyde Shawn was all I had by way of a dad. He protected me from Susan and made an effort in lots of other ways.

I need to protect my family, what will happen to Jacob if I'm taken away? Will Mum beat him instead of me and what will Shawn do to him if I'm not around? - my stomach churned at the thought.

I had decisions to make and only a very short time to make them. I was back on the hamster wheel of thought and I desperately needed sleep. I don't know what time it was when I finally drifted off to sleep that night. Night turned into day and I was rudely awakened by my alarm. I considered bunking off school but I knew that would only delay the conversation with the police. I arrived at school and took my normal seat at the back of the classroom.

"Jessica!" the teacher's voice startled me from my thoughts.

"Urm, yes," I answered automatically.

Mrs Woodhouse, the head of school, was standing with my teacher. She was smartly dressed wearing a coloured scarf around her neck. She was the go-to person at school if you needed to talk to somebody. "Jessica, can you come with me, please?" Mrs Woodhouse said beckoning with her hand.

"What's Harry done, is small fry in trouble?" Johnny shouted and the entire class erupted into laughter.

In less than a minute, my invisibility had been taken away; everyone was looking at me. My cheeks flushed with embarrassment. I rushed past Mrs Woodhouse and fled from the classroom. The corridor was surprisingly empty; I had expected a policeman to be there.

"Follow me, please," Mrs Woodhouse said when she joined me in the corridor.

We headed over to the Bywwva Centre. I had shaken hands with Prince Charles and Camila Parker Bowles when they had opened it a short while before. Mrs Woodhouse pulled the door open.

"Two policewomen would like to talk to you today," Mrs Woodhouse told me.

"Yes, Mum mentioned it," I replied.

Mrs Woodhouse knocked on one of the meeting room doors where a woman, probably in her mid-thirties, was waiting. She was smartly dressed, athletic, with long brown flowing hair. She gestured for me to come into the room.

"Hi, I'm Racheal and this is Sharon. Come in and pull up a chair," Racheal said. "Thank you, Mrs Woodhouse, we will call you if we need you."

The door closed behind the head and I took a seat on a large, red chair while Racheal took her seat opposite me and next to Sharon.

"Your mother, Susan, has given us permission to talk to you today in her absence, We felt you might be more comfortable talking to us here rather than at home," Racheal said.

"Mum mentioned it," I replied,

"Do you know why you are here today?" Sharon asked.

She was older than Racheal and looked quite stern-faced with grey hair; she peered over her notepad when she spoke.

"No, not really," I placed my school bag on my lap.

"How are things at home?" Sharon queried.

"Yeah, good. Why?" I replied playing with the buckle on my bag.

"How are you getting along with Shawn?" Sarah asked.

"He's ok. What's this all about?" I could feel my body heat rising.

"Has he ever done anything to make you scared or anything that feels out of the ordinary?" Racheal took over the questioning

Well he comes into my room and pins me to a bed and does whatever he likes, then he buys me gifts for being his good girl, - this is what was in my head.

I should have blown the whistle on him. It was amazing the things in my head that I wanted to say but none of it came out of my mouth when I was put under a spotlight.

"No. What do you mean?" I said instead.

"Shawn isn't a very nice man, Jessica. Do you know what paedophile means?" Sharon looked directly into my eyes.

She made it very obvious; I'm sure was looking for changes in my body language. I was nervous and could feel my hands shaking but I knew I had to remain calm.

"No, not really, something to do with pictures I think," I answered.

I remembered Laura making a feeble attempt to explain the word paedophile when we had been at Butlins. I knew it had something to do with pictures.

"Yes, that is part of it. Before your mum got involved with Shawn, he had images of children on his computer. We took an incredible amount of evidence from Shawn's house at that time and he was convicted." Sharon explained.

Is that what they're concerned about? Shawn had never actually taken any photos of me, - I reassured myself.

"We could only charge Shawn with having pornographic imagery in his possession. There was never any proof or evidence that he had been involved in the sexual acts that had been committed by individuals in the photos," Rachael explained.

"Jessica, has he ever taken any photos of you?" Sharon was direct.

"Only family photos, like when we have all been together," I replied truthfully.

"Are you sure, Jessica? Has he ever taken any photos that made you feel uncomfortable?" Sharon leaned towards me.

Her questioning became more aggressive.

Does she think I'm lying?' – I wondered as my mouth went dry.

"No! Look I don't really understand what all this is about," I snapped back.

"We are very concerned about you and we're sorry we have to ask these difficult questions. Shawn is technically not allowed to be around vulnerable children and young adults under the age of eighteen, unless supervised, due to his conviction," Sharon explained trying to change her tactics and get me on her side.

If what she has just said is true and Shawn is so dangerous that we are not allowed to be around him, why are we still allowed to live with him? Why isn't he in prison and why are they questioning me?' - I wondered.

I was confused by what she had just said, it didn't make any sense. On one hand, they were telling me it was illegal for Shawn to be near me but, on the other hand, they were not unduly concerned that I was living in the same house as him, a convicted paedophile.

I looked up from the buckle on my bag and Sharon and Racheal were both staring at me, waiting for me to respond. Susan's warnings from the conversation we had the previous night still echoed in my head

"We need to know the truth, Jessica, we can't help you without it. Has Shawn ever touched you or taken photos of you? It's very important that you tell us, we can take you to a safe place away from him and protect you. But we need to know the truth," Racheal said almost pleadingly.

Take me to a safe place, - Susan's warning suddenly shouted out in my head.

They want to take me away from Jacob, away to a horrible place. Mum was right, police lie, - I thought.

Tears welled up in my eyes and my body started to shake.

"Why are you trying to break my family up? I have a good life and a good family, so just leave me alone!" I shouted angrily.

I didn't know where my sudden burst of confidence had come from but I needed to protect Jacob and myself from the horrible place everyone kept talking about. It scared the shit out of me.

"Jessica, look we know this is difficult but we are only trying to help," Racheal said calmly.

"I want to go now, can I go?" I asked angrily.

I had heard enough, all I wanted to do was get out of that room.

"You can go wherever you like. We can't hold you here this is just a conversation. We are just trying to make sure you are safe," Sharon's quiet voice was strangely comforting.

I stood up and made my way to the door.

"Jessica, take this," Racheal handed me a card.

"My mobile number is on this. If you need me or if you change your mind ...," her sentence trailed away.

I took the card.

Maybe I should have told them what was going on, then it would have been the job of the adults to decide what was wrong or right, - I wondered as I left the room.

Chapter 14

Dark thoughts

Months had passed since the visit from the police, Rachael and Sharon didn't contact me again. Susan drank practically every night and Shawn didn't seem to care if he was caught with me; his advances became more frequent. I had protected him and he thought he was untouchable. Shawn acted like a lost puppy around me and this annoyed Susan.

My chores piled up and more nasty comments were directed at me, it was as though she hated me. I couldn't see how she was unaware of Shawn's abuse but, instead of protecting me, she became jealous and angry; she probably thought I was stealing her boyfriend from her. It was a vicious circle, the more jealous she became, the more attentive Shawn became towards me and that triggered her jealousy again. He had Susan wrapped around his little finger. She wanted his attention and blamed me for stealing it; the worse she got the more blatant he got. It became a game to him.

Susan changed her tactics and changed her appearance, she became like a porn star. The noises that came from their bedroom at night, while they had sex, were horrendous.

Thank God you've got him tonight, - I smiled to myself covering my head with my pillow.

The entire situation was very fucked up. Shawn had somehow managed to get Susan to fight for his attention while he raped me behind her back. The twist was I felt I was to blame for his attacks and he also managed to make me believe that every dad on the planet raped their daughters; he told me it was a normal part of life, apparently. It was difficult to get my messed up head around his logic.

As if things weren't bad enough, a sad situation at school emotionally affected me. A girl committed suicide and, since her death, my thoughts regularly turned to the option of maybe taking my own life. She had been well-liked and appeared to have had a good family.

Maybe she found the normality of life hard too? Maybe it'll get too much for me one day and will I also opt for the same option as she had? - I wondered. If I went down that road, I would be gone and forgotten. I questioned the meaning of my life because I hadn't achieved anything spectacular.

RIP Jessica - the house-elf, would probably be written on my gravestone. Dwelling on this made me sad. I felt ugly inside and outside. I hated myself and I craved friends but my dilemma was, I also wanted to be alone. I hoped one day someone would save me from my life and love me; I still believe in Disney. But how could anyone love me, when I didn't even love myself anymore?

My thirteenth birthday came and went and Christmas was looming. The long, cold nights were back and I had spent a few months bunking off school. After the police had visited, the invisibility I had worked so hard to master, had been removed. The endless bullying had started again, my legs would be kicked away while I walked along the corridor and I was given nasty nicknames like minger or geek, while my bra continued to be pulled and unclicked. This left me clutching my breasts in embarrassment.

Johnny and Paul targeted me every time my guard was down; this made me feel lower than ever before. I was hiding in the girls' grubby toilets again. I even ate my lunch sitting in the cubicle. One day, I mulled over why I bothered going to school. No one had noticed that I wasn't in class, so I just stopped going.

On days I knew no one was at home, I would simply sneak back into the house once everyone had left and on other days I spent my time in town. It was easy in the summer to find things to do, but the cold weather was back and I couldn't sit in a park all day. My life became one of avoiding people but like everything in life that had to end.

Susan was pulled into my headteacher's office and told that I had been absent from school. When I arrived home later that day, I took the full force of her rage. I was punched to the floor and she kicked my ribs until I struggled to breathe. She targeted areas of my body where marks could be hidden; no one else would ever see the bruises she left behind that night. Susan also ripped into Shawn, she was convinced it had been his idea and accused him of having a secret relationship with me behind her back. After that night there was no doubt in my mind, she knew what he was doing. She didn't even see how wrong this all was and seemed more concerned about her own relationship, rather than the obvious; he was sexually abusing her child.

Maybe if I hadn't bunked school my grades would have been better, maybe what happened next would never have happened.

Chapter 15

Pages written in hell

I never thought things could get worse. I shake my head as I dredge up the past and become shocked at the amount I had buried. It's unbelievable that I didn't say anything or run away from my situation. But, I was young and this was my life. I knew no different. I likened it to parents who might tell their child the sky is pink; a son or daughter would accept this without question. Then a stranger tells them the sky is blue. What confusion for the child.

This was what my life was like, guided by people who were meant to protect me but instead took advantage. Strangers were telling me what my parents were doing was wrong. I faced confusion. Every decision I made, led to life-changing consequences that never had a happy ending for me. The following is about one of the hardest days of my life. This part has been buried deep however, I don't want my skeletons to have any more power.

The half-term before the Christmas break was time off to heal from the beating Susan had given me for bunking off and then I had to go back to school. Arguments had been going into the early hours of the morning between Susan and Shawn and I had heard them shouting at each other for most of the night. When Susan woke me in the morning, I was told to pack a bag so, having no idea what was happening, I packed some clothes into my school bag.

A short time later we piled into Shawn's Jeep. Everyone seemed locked in their thoughts, as we drove along. We travelled for hours before Shawn and Susan started to make some light conversation and Shawn told us we were going on holiday. Eventually, we pulled up outside a modern house that looked big enough to have four bedrooms. It was on a council estate but the surrounding houses had boarded up windows; this was not an attractive area.

"We're here," Shawn announced.

I didn't have a clue where we were but we gathered our belongings and walked toward the white, front door. A man opened it almost immediately and I had to look up at him. His arms had a few snakes and demon tattoos. He wasn't an old man but he appeared scruffy and wasn't particularly well built. He stood as though he carried two imaginary carpets under his arms.

"Alright geezer," he spoke in a gruff east London accent.

"Hi, Steve," Shawn replied with a half-wave.

Steve pulled Shawn into what can only be called a man hug before Susan, Jacob then myself were introduced. Steve's looked me up and down and lingered on my body. He had a familiar half-grin on his face that made me feel uneasy and I instantly took a dislike to him.

The house looked modern on the outside but inside it gave the impression of being worn and tired. There was a kitchen to the left and a large lounge to the right with a staircase in the middle. Dirty handprints peppered the walls and the carpets had a trail of dirt and debris imprinted onto their well-worn pile. There was a stale odor in the air, damp mixed with the smell of cigarettes.

Why have we been brought to this place? - I wondered.

A woman appeared from the kitchen, it looked like she had tidied herself up to look pretty. Badly dyed blond hair and a low-cut leopard print top, her squashed-up breasts were about to make an appearance at any point. She had also chosen to wear every item of jewellery she had ever been given in her life. Bracelets dangled from her wrists and gold chains filled her neck, her ears looked stretched from the massive gold hoops that hung from her ears.

I knew her name before she spoke, one of her many chains spelt Angie in gold letters.

"Hi, I'm Angie," she spoke, in a high-pitched, east London accent.

This house had a bad vibe to it and the entire situation just seemed odd. I could tell these people were strangers to Susan and Shawn the way they introduced themselves.

Why have we travelled so far to see them? - I thought, standing awkwardly in the hallway.

"Paul, Louise get your arses down here!" Steve bellowed out.

"Why?" A boy's voice called from upstairs.

"Don't fucking why me! Get your fucking arse down here!" Steve shouted back.

Lovely, - I thought.

Steve grinned and nodded at Shawn. The way Steve spoke, walked and puffed out his chest and arms, it was clear he thought of himself as an alpha male. Maybe he wanted everyone to think he was a hardman. However, like his wife's bad hair colouring skills, he failed dismally. He looked and sounded more like a twat!

A boy of about six and a girl of about twelve appeared at the top of the stairs. They started to sheepishly make their way down the staircase and, being roughly the same ages and Jacob and me, I thought at least we'd have some company.

"This is Paul and Louise," Angie said by way of an introduction.

"Well! Say fucking hello then," Steve yelled and slapped Paul round the back of the head as he reached the bottom step.

110

Paul's winced from the impact and his messy hair did a dance. The cold look he gave Paul told me he didn't like him. Louise walked and moved like an old lady as though someone had sucked the life out of her. Her dull eyes were vacant almost dead. She positioned herself into a corner and hid behind her brother. I had done the same, I had positioned myself in the opposite corner to her and attempted to hide behind everyone else.

"Beer?" Steve offered Shawn.

He was obviously bored with the formalities of the introductions.

"Take Jessica and Jacob up to the bedrooms," Angie ordered, maybe she sensed Steve was agitated.

We didn't come downstairs again until much later when someone called on us for food.

By the early hours of the morning, singing and shouting could be heard from downstairs. They sounded drunk and I was worried because Susan was already pissed off with me about bunking off school and I had in my mind what her drinking could lead to. Thankfully, we were left to our own devices.

Jacob easily made friends with Paul and they spent most of the night on the PlayStation. It took a while longer for me and Louise to make friends. We cautiously tried to find some common ground. We eventually found things that we could talk about and spent most of the evening chatting.

Louise was a few months younger than me and. She was petite and slim, with long honey blonde hair. She was shy like me and very careful about what and how she made conversation. She didn't give away too much about herself but, that was ok. I finally had someone who I could sit and chat with, like a normal teenager. Other than the noises that came from below and the particularly bad singing, I had quite an enjoyable relaxed night.

The next day we were woken by a surprisingly alert-looking Angie. She was in good spirits considering their party had gone on until around 4 o'clock in the morning. We made our way downstairs and saw Shawn and Steve, neither of them looked alert. They whispered to each other as Louise and I walked into the kitchen; they burst out laughing but whatever they found funny was lost on us.

Angie walked into the kitchen wearing something that looked like an 80s leotard; she linked arms with Susan.

"We're off to the Spa now, see you later boys," Angie's squeaky voice filled the room.

"Mum, please can I come too?" I asked quickly, I did not want to be left there alone.

"No, Jessica! I'm having a girls' day out for a change," was Susan's curt reply.

There was aggression in her voice; I could tell she was still mad at me.

"But, Mum ...," I started.

"Us girls need time away from you little brats, we need a pamper day! Isn't that right Susan?" Angie interrupted.

"Yes, that's right," Susan agreed, glaring directly at me.

"But ...," I began only to be interrupted again, this time by Steve.

"We have lots of things planned for today, don't you worry, Princess," he laughed and clinked his beer bottle against Shawn's.

Something seemed odd about this situation and I didn't feel comfortable.

"Right get your bag. Bye babes," Angie continued.

She blew a kiss towards Steve and strutted out of the kitchen. Susan walked over to Shawn and gave him an over-dramatic kiss before she swaggered out of the kitchen with her eyes fixed on me as she went. I heard the front door open and slam shut; they were gone.

What the fuck! While they fuck off for a pamper day, I have just been left in this house with this creepy bloke and Shawn, - I thought.

Louise and I returned to her bedroom to spend some time alone. Jacob and Paul had already locked themselves away and were back on the PlayStation when the call came.

"Jessica, Louise, can you come here?" Shawn shouted out from downstairs.

I looked at Louise and she went pale.

"We'd better go," her voice trembled.

"What's wrong?" I asked when I saw her body shake.

"Nothing, it's just easier if we just go," Louise muttered, staring at her bedroom door.

Without saying any more, I followed her out of the room and down the stairs into the lounge.

"Come into our office, ladies," Steve attempted a bow when we entered the room.

Steve closed the door behind us and locked it.

What the fuck is going on? - I wondered.

"How experienced is your girl?" Steve asked Shawn.

I looked over at Louise and I could see her eyes were full of tears.

"I'm still breaking her in," Shawn replied with a smug look on his face.

"Why don't you take Louise for a spin and I'll have a go on yours?" Steve suggested before he took a swig of his beer.

"Go easy, I don't want her broken," Shawn replied, with his eyes fixed on Louise.

Horses, they're talking about horses! - the words made sense now.

"Do you have a horse, Louise?" I asked.

She looked blankly at me as if to say what the fuck are you going on about?

At that moment the terrifying realisation of what was about to happen dawned on me. Shawn and Steve were laughing and this only confirmed my worst fears. I started to shake violently and tears welled in my eyes.

"Jessica, the quicker you give in to them, it will be over," Louise whispered.

Shawn suddenly pulled her by the hand and started to strip her naked and she didn't put up a fight. I watched in horror. Steve looked on as his daughter stood shaking like a leaf and naked in the middle of the room, Shawn unbuckled his trousers and pushed her down to her knees. He placed his hand on the back of her head and he inserted himself deep inside her mouth. Louise attempted to push herself off him. She was gagging. But he would not let go. Silent tears streamed down her face and her eyes started to bulge from her head. Shawn suddenly loosened his grip and she dropped to the floor gasping for air. The reprieve lasted for a few seconds before he repeated what he had just done. She was barely able to breathe and started to choke but these evil bastards only laughed.

In total shock and with my eyes fixed on the scene before me, I did not see Steve approach me. He had already stripped naked and his disgusting tattooed body towered above me. Without a word, he ripped my top from my body and forced me down to my knees. He grabbed my jaw and held my nose to force my mouth open, I knew then I was in for the same fate as Louise. I felt his skin touch my tongue; I could taste this disgusting man and I wanted to die.

His hand cupped around the back of my head, forcefully pulling me towards him. He let out a grunt as he forced himself down my throat. I couldn't escape and I couldn't breathe. He laughed at me while I choked and gasped. I was going to black out and, with tears streaming down my face, I punched at his legs. He suddenly let go but within seconds, my head was yanked back onto him again and he continued. He forced himself deep inside my mouth and grunted with every movement.

Suddenly, he stopped and I was tossed to the ground. I fell facedown onto my stomach but, the next thing I knew, my legs were being pulled and my leggings and knickers were savagely ripped away; I was totally exposed. Louise landed by my side and we were both huddled up naked on the floor. Both men drained their cans as they watched us struggling to breathe, naked on the floor.

"Louise, you need to break Jessica in," Steve sniggered, handing Shawn another can.

What the fuck does that mean? - I wondered, looking over to Louise.

She looked as scared as I felt.

"Well get the fuck on with it, we want a fucking show!" Steve shouted aggressively.

Louise slowly got to her feet, then suddenly turned and ran towards the door. She didn't even reach it, a massive punch to her face knocked her clean off her feet and she landed with a thud on the floor. Steve stood over her limp body; she twitched and let out a groan. A thin trickle of blood appeared from her head.

Oh my God, has he killed her? - I wondered, as I looked over to her small body.

Louise let out another groan and tried to sit up. She turned to face Steve as she wiped her blood away. The look of hatred on her face told me how she was feeling.

"What? Do you want another one? It can be arranged," Steve asked sarcastically.

He did a strange chicken dance towards her, maybe his way of showing some bravado. She didn't move a muscle or even blink. Steve turned to click his can against Shawn's.

"I think you should play with Jessica, Louise," Shawn announced.

"Yes hurry the fuck up, we haven't got all day," Steve added impatiently.

I was still huddled on my knees in tears as Louise pulled me gently to my feet and she kissed me on the lips.

"Put some fucking effort into it, or you will get another slap!" Steve snarled, as Louise pulled me close.

"Close your eyes just go with it, I will be gentle and it will be over soon. I promise," she whispered in my ear.

She kissed me and, without any resistance, I kissed her back.

"This is fucking kids' stuff, we want a show," Shawn yelled.

Shawn had been quiet up to this point but now he seemed to take on some of Steve's mannerisms. Louise slowly pushed me back onto the sofa and I felt her hand slide up my leg, I had never been touched by a female before. I opened my eyes briefly and glanced towards the staring, disgusting men.

"Now girls if you're good you will be rewarded, if you're bad you will be punished. I don't really give a fuck what option you take," Steve snapped.

Who the fuck is this muppet? - I questioned myself.

It was like he was attempting to recall a line from a film or something. Suddenly, Louise was pulled away from me and placed into a kneeling position. Her face now pushed onto my lap, Shawn was staring down at her bottom.

"Put it in her arse mate, she doesn't care," Steve said casually.

"Don't mind if I do," Shawn's smile rippled across his face.

The scream Louise cried out has always haunted me. I felt her fingernails digging hard into my legs and her eyes told the story of the pain she had just experienced.

"Can I do yours in the arse too?" Steve asked as he looked down at me.

What the fuck! No No No! - I had just witnessed the pain Louise had experienced.

Terrified, I started to shake uncontrollably.

"No! I've not done that yet and until I do, no one does," Shawn insisted.

"Well, fucking hell, mate, you're currently having a right fucking go there ain't you? How the fuck does that work?" Steve retorted.

"Do you want a go, or not?" Shawn came back at him.

While these two animals argued over the fate of my bum, I sat there shitting myself.

116

"Well mate you are currently fucking little Louise in the arse, I want my turn on Jessica," Steve looked at me.

"Fine!" Shawn said angrily.

He withdrew from Louise and reinserted himself into her vagina. She dug her fingernails into my legs again and screamed out in pain.

"Fair enough," Steve replied with a disappointed tone in his voice.

I was pulled onto my knees by my hair. My legs were yanked apart and Steve brutally sank his penis deep inside me. I screamed in pain and pleaded with him to stop! This only made him worse. He rammed himself in and out of me so hard and violently that my insides ripped apart. I wanted someone to end my life then and there. I was in agony as this man was inside me, violating me.

"I want to finish off inside, Jessica," Shawn said suddenly.

It appeared that we were only bits of meat to be passed about however they pleased.

"Ok, Gezza," Steve replied calmly.

We were pulled from the sofa and made to bend over on a large bean bag. Louise and I found ourselves face to face. I thought Shawn had saved me from Steve and his brutality but, I thought wrong. With one violent thrust, Shawn ripped my bottom apart. The air was sucked from my lungs; I gasped for air and the most excruciating pain tore through my body.

Louise, who was going through her own ordeal, tried to hold my hand as I was forced to watch Steve bury himself in Louise. They wanted us to witness what was happening to the other. I felt Shawn judder and I hoped the ordeal was over. Steve then grunted and pulled Louise tightly onto himself. He stared at me as he came and I felt like I was about to vomit.

"Now that wasn't so bad, was it girls?" Steve commented, continuing to stare at me.

What the fuck! Is he really asking us how we feel about what they had just done? - my head reeled.

117

"Well, fucking answer me," he spoke with familiar aggression in his voice.

"No, it wasn't," we both replied with croaky voices, terrified of what would happen if we didn't reply.

"Right, you had better go and get cleaned up," Shawn ordered but in a softer tone as he pulled himself out from me.

"That's my girl," Steve said to Louise.

I could see Louise wince as he slapped her on the backside and let her go from his grip. This wasn't the first time this had happened to her.

We got to our feet and a tissue box hit me as I gathered my clothes.

"Clean yourself, you're dripping on my carpet," Steve's angry voice rang.

Is he seriously going to make me clean myself here, while they're watching?
- I looked down at the tissue box.

"Well, fucking pick it up then!" Steve shouted.

I realised my last bit of dignity was about to be taken away. I reached down and picked up the box. I pulled out a few tissues and started to wipe myself off.

"Don't forget the fucking carpet, look at the mess you have made," Steve pointed to the floor.

I bent down and cleaned the small patch of cum mixed with blood that had landed on the dirty carpet. He burst out laughing and so did Shawn. I had just finished cleaning it when my jaw was grabbed violently and my head was turned to face Steve. I nearly vomited there and then when I saw his bad teeth and smelled his bad breath.

"If you ever fucking say anything, or tell anyone, I will hunt you down and fucking kill you. Do you understand?" Steve's evil eyes fixed on mine.

"Yes," I managed to get out despite his tight grip.

"Yes fucking what?" Steve growled gripping my jaw harder.

"I understand," I tried to shout through my tears.

118

Steve's face quickly returned to normal and he released me from his grip.

"That's a good girl. Now get dressed and off you pop. Fancy another beer, mate?" he asked Shawn.

"Yes, mate, why not," Shawn replied casually.

They both dressed and Steve unlocked the door. They wandered out into the kitchen as though nothing had happened. Louise looked at me and we both sprinted out of the room, carrying our clothes. We reached the bottom of the stairs only to be interrupted.

"Girls, girls, girls. Where's the fire?" Steve said stopping us in our tracks.

Please no, not again, - ran through my mind, I was petrified.

"No rush, Dad, can we go? Please?" Louise answered calmly.

"Yes, Princess, of course, you can. Go and have a shower. But you and Jessica have one together, water costs money. Make sure you both clean each other up good and proper," he laughed, as he moved out of the way and let us pass.

We ran to the bathroom and I immediately vomited.

"Are you ok?" Louise was holding my hair back while I was being sick.

"No, not really," I managed once I had finished.

"I'm so sorry for what I did to you," this poor girl was apologising to me and none of it was her fault.

"It's ok, you had no choice," I tried to reassure her.

"Has this ever happened to you before?" I asked.

"Yes," Louise looked at me and I could see in her eyes she was trapped in this world.

She got to her feet and stepped into the shower and started to scrub herself in a way I knew all too well. I hadn't noticed until now the remains of past bruises and broken skin that littered her body. The damage to her body was focused on places that were easy to cover up and hide.

119

"Quick, jump in, Jessica," Louise stepped aside allowing me to step in.

I started to scrub myself remembering what Steve had said. We had just managed to get dried and dressed when we heard the front door open then slam shut.

"We're home," Angie's squeaky voice echoed up the stairs.

"Foods up, get the fuck down here now," Steve's voice bellowed from the hallway.

"I don't want to go back down," I couldn't face them again.

"It will make things worse if we don't. Trust me, come on, we'd better go," Louise pulled me to my feet and opened the door.

Jacob and Paul ran out of Paul's bedroom, they both pretended to have imaginary swords and were locked in some epic battle with each other. Both were none the wiser about what we had just been through. In the kitchen, Susan and Angie had set out KFC.

"So, have you all behaved today?" Susan asked as she looked directly at me.

"Jessica wouldn't play ball at first but, after a while, she did what I asked," Steve answered.

The two men sniggered as they clinked beer bottles.

"Well I suppose you deserve some KFC then but, Jessica, you're not having dessert as you were naughty, to begin with, I hear. Next time you will learn to be good and hopefully, we will not have any more issues," Susan said as she glared at me.

Next time? Was I going to be passed around again to anyone they decided on? Was this now going to be a regular thing? Hang on! What the fuck. Did Susan know what was going on? - my brain went into overdrive.

I could tell from the expression on her face, Susan enjoyed the fact that the penny had just dropped.

Has she really planned this with Shawn and now she wants to taunt me by taking away some shit dessert? - I wondered.

120

I wanted to curl into a ball and die. All four of them sniggered and made remarks without actually saying what they meant. Both my so-called parents had deceived me. I had been lured into this monster's house so that they could have their fun. My stomach churned and fire seemed to burn in my belly with every mouthful. I needed to get away from them.

After dinner, we left the table and returned to the bedroom. Louise seemed to have the answers to some of my questions.

"Louise, how often does it happen?" I probed when we sat down on her bed.

"It happens all the time. Dad's friends turn up and he tells me I have to make them happy. Sometimes Dad watches, sometimes they both get involved," Louise sounded calm and hardened to it all.

Shawn's visits had become my normality and I had become hardened to that but being pulled from pillar to post and made to fuck vile people petrified me.

"Jessica, it's what dads do, you will get used to it," she had such sadness in her voice.

It's what dads do, - the answer that I had been stuck on for months.

This is what dads do and it is our duty as daughters to keep them happy, - my heart sank with this horrible thought.

But, Louise had finally answered my question.

My gut had been wrong; did I have to accept that this was the way things were?

But why do I hate it so much? Is there something wrong with me? - I wondered.

"Louise, do you like it when it happens?" I asked

"Fuck, no!" she replied, surprised by my question. "Sometimes it's not too bad, but no I hate it!"

So, I wasn't the only one that hated it; this was something at least.

Downstairs another party had erupted and I was thankful we were left alone for the rest of the night. I was given another warning from

Steve the next morning before we left and told not to say anything as the fear of God was put into me. We drove home that day and I was lost in thought the entire way, I knew my life was once again going to change. Life would be harder but for some reason, I didn't care, something had broken. My self-worth had vanished and I no longer cared if I lived or died, my body and soul seemed to belong to others. My mind became my personal prison.

Chapter 16

More lies

Ino longer had the option to stay away from school. If the headteacher were to call Susan and tell her I wasn't at school, I would face an unknown punishment. The whole thing scared the shit out of me. The bullies were waiting for me back at school and Shawn was waiting for me if I stayed at home. There wasn't any choice; I just had to deal with whatever came my way.

I had been absent from school for months and, on my first day back, I was surprised when two girls, Kate and Tina, made a point of talking to me. I grabbed at this new found friendship. Rather than sitting in the grubby toilets alone all day or hiding at the back of the class in my invisibility cloak, my day became filled with people. I would still get the odd comment from Johnny and his entourage but it didn't faze me to the same extent. Kate and Tina soon were my new best friends, school became a safer place and I was far away from the dangers at home. I also managed to have a mini relationship with a boy in my year, nothing serious. We just kissed a few times but it didn't worry me when it all fizzled out. Life was on the up.

Christmas came and went and, over the holidays, I spent all my free time with Kate and Tina. They even came to my house for a sleepover and, as the friendship grew, I started to confide in them. I told them about Susan, her drinking and her anger, but not about Shawn. The wall I had built around myself slowly started to come down. I trusted them.

A few weeks after New Year, I came home from school and found Susan crying. I went to investigate and saw a wine glass in front of her. She asked me to sit down and told me she had something important to say.

"Jessica, I really don't know how to tell you this, but I have cancer. The doctor hasn't given me much hope; I'm most likely going to die!" she burst into tears.

I was shocked. I started to cry and sat hugging my mum, I didn't want to lose her. She had taken me to hell and back most of my life but she was still my mum. That night, I sobbed my heart out, convinced I was going to lose her.

Will Shawn toss me and Jacob out onto the street, when she's gone? - I wondered.

Jacob and I had no one else to care for us and nowhere else to go. I went to school the next day and confided in my new best friends. Although they couldn't completely understand, they were heartbroken about my news. As young girls do, they told me everything would be ok and hugged me; in their own way, they were being supportive. I'd never had care or affection from many people; it was such a comforting feeling.

A few days later Kate came into school late. She had injured her knee a few months beforehand and had had a hospital appointment. Before her mum dropped her back to school, she had bought her a couple of bags of Haribo sweets. Kate, Tina and I chatted as we

124

devoured one of the packets together. In a moment of madness, Tina decided she wanted to bunk off school and Kate agreed that this was a great idea.

"Come on Jess, It'll be fun," Tina tried to jolly me along.

"No, I really can't. I wish I could, but I can't," I had to insist. After the last punishment I received involving Steve, I couldn't risk being caught again.

"You're so boring!" Kate added.

"I'm really sorry, I just can't," I wanted to explain why but my defences were still up.

"Well, suit yourself, Jessica. If you're going to be boring can you look after these?" Kate pushed the other packet of Haribo sweets into my hand.

"See ya, enjoy class," Tina threw back at me.

They disappeared out of the gate laughing together. I was alone again for the rest of the day. Totally gutted, I wandered to my science class. Without thinking, I laid my open bag open on my desk. Johnny walked into class, saw the open bag, reached out and grabbed the bag of Haribo sweets. Without a word, he opened the pack and started scoffing the contents.

"For fuck's sake, they're not mine," I snapped at him.

"Don't worry, I'll give you the bag back when I have finished them," he said in jest, placing another sweet in his mouth.

Would I lose my new friends over something as simple as a bag of sweets? I was furious and worried at the same time. Now and again I saved a few coins in my piggy bank so, that night, I raided it. I didn't have quite enough to replace the Haribro sweets Johnny had eaten.

The next day on my way to school, I bought some different chews for Kate. I had managed to divert the possibility of losing my friends and, guarding the now stowed away sweets, I waited for Kate and Tina to arrive. They walked into class with another girl, Emily.

"Hi Kate, someone ate your sweets so I bought you a new packet. I'm really sorry," I explained and handed her the packet of sweets.

"Don't worry, we're cool," Kate replied, almost dismissively.

"Tina, Emily come on, we have maths," she continued.

Both of them turned and walked out of the classroom.

Why is she pissed at me, I replaced the sweets? - I was confused but wandered along to my next class.

At lunchtime, I made my way over to the playing fields where I knew Kate and Tina would be waiting. They were sitting with a group of students and I could hear them bragging about their juice bottles. They had filled them with alcohol.

"Oh, hello Jessica," Tina sneered when she noticed me.

The group spread out and formed a circle around me and Kate. I wasn't comfortable. Other students began to run towards us and, within seconds, it looked as though half the school was gathered. I feared a fight was about to ensue and, if that was the case, Kate had a massive advantage. She was bigger than me and could have done me a lot of damage.

"Are we ok, I replaced the sweets?" I asked in a worried voice.

"No! You're a lying thieving bitch," Kate spat at me.

"What are you on about? I replaced the sweets," I repeated.

"You're a fucking liar! You said your mum had cancer. Well, guess what? I spoke to your mum yesterday and she hasn't got a fucking clue what you're going on about. You're a sick cow! Even your mum thinks you're weird in the head," she screamed at me as the others looked on.

My mum had once again found a way to wreck my life. The sick and twisted part was that I had been worried and heart-broken about Susan and now I was most likely about to get a kicking because of her lies.

"Oh, and to top it off, this little skank stole my sweets," Kate shouted to the ever-growing crowd.

126

"Fight! Fight! Fight!" the crowd that surrounded us chanted.

I stood petrified as she slowly walked towards me.

"Can't even afford a fucking pound," as she spoke, she stared down at me.

"Kate I didn't!" I offered up as I felt my nose explode with pain.

I crashed to the ground and blood gushed out of my nostrils. My eyes started to stream and salty tears stung my eyes. I wasn't sure if I was crying or if I had blood in my eyes. I could hear people cheering and chanting, as I lay on the ground, dazed and barely able to see.

"Kate," I muttered trying to get back on my feet.

This was met by a barrage of painful punches landing on my body.

I'm going to get expelled! - the terrifying thought went round in my head.

Kate then delivered a huge punch and I found myself back on the floor. I heard everyone laugh and cheer. The crowd started to disappear, leaving me on the ground utterly humiliated and in pain until I felt a hand on my shoulder.

"Jess, are you ok?" a soft voice asked.

It was Emily. I had never really spoken to her before but she was the only one in the group who asked if I was ok.

Another trick. Am I about to be humiliated further? - I wondered.

But, she helped me to my feet. I could hardly stand. I was winded and beaten and, as I looked around, almost everyone had reverted to what they had been doing before the fight had broken out.

"Come on, I'll take you to a teacher and get you checked out," Emily said as she placed her arm around me.

We found a teacher but it became apparent he wasn't interested.

"Just go and see the nurse," he said dismissively.

He walked away while looking at his watch.

Just another person that doesn't give a shit! - I thought as he hurried away.

I was in pain and tears and nobody cared. I needed to hide somewhere safe. I took off running even as Emily was calling after me, I ran to the only place I knew I felt safe; the girls' grotty toilets.

"What the fuck are you doing in here, you dirty skank. Come back for more?" Tina glared at me from the toilet door.

Fucking great! Is there nowhere on this planet left to hide? - I asked myself. Looking down at the floor, I tried to hold back the tears.

"Come on, Tina, we have better places to be," Kate snorted.

They barged their way past me and the main door slammed shut. I went into the cubicle, sank onto the toilet seat and burst into tears. Yet again, I had trusted someone and yet again that person had hurt me. Everyone thought I was a liar and thief and my apparent best friend had practically beaten me to a pulp. At that moment, I wished she had finished me off and killed me

What is the point? Life is just too painful and lonely. No one gives a shit about me! - I told myself.

My fucked up life was a disaster. I stood up, calmly took off my school tie and tied a knot around a coat hook on the door. I had no more tears, I was done.

Chapter 17

Waking up

I always thought heaven was meant to be pain-free, so why did my neck and other parts of my body hurt so much? Dizzy and confused, I opened my eyes and found myself in a dimly lit room. *Am I in hell? -* I wondered.

The room seemed familiar as my eyes adjusted to the light. I was in the nurse's office.

I attempt to kill myself and suddenly someone notices! - I scoffed inwardly. Most of my school life had been spent hidden in the girls' toilets and nobody saw I was there. How strange that somebody had noticed after all this time.

Fucking great! I can't even kill myself, I'm such a failure. Why couldn't whoever found me just leave me alone? It was my life, my choice, - my thoughts reeled as the pain spread across my body and neck.

To go through with suicide is a very difficult and extremely painful experience; my body put up a horrendous fight to survive. I had hung myself from the hook on the cubicle door with my homemade noose.

Once it was knotted around my neck, I had simply stepped off the toilet. After that, there was no escape; my feet didn't reach the ground. My body twitched violently as it fought for survival. Without oxygen, my lungs felt as though they were going to explode; it was extremely painful and unpleasant. Then a calmness descended on me and I imagined little lights filling my body. The lights went out one by one and the world went dark. There was nothing.

Lying on the nurse's bed, I felt the little lights coming back on but I also felt unbelievable pain. A sharp stinging sensation throbbed around my neck and the injuries from the fight ached. I had taken a punch to my nose so this forced me to breathe through my mouth. My throat felt like the Sahara desert and, what felt like razor-sharp sand, cut away at my neck with every breath.

"Thank God. Are you ok my dear?" the school nurse burst into the room.

She rushed over to my bedside to check me over.

"My God, are you ok, Jessica?" the headmistress enquired as she took my hand. "Why did you do this?"

Why did I do this? How could I even begin to answer that question? Should I tell her everything and all my reasons why? - I wondered if I had a choice.

Because my attempt to pass away, unnoticed, into another world hadn't quite worked out I was back in the real world and more difficult questions were about to be asked. There was a knock on the door. The headmistress stepped out of the room for a few moments.

"Jessica, the paramedics would like to check you over, would that be ok?" she walked back in.

"If they must," I replied in a croaky and broken voice.

"Ok, Jessica, I'll bring them in," she reassured me by placing a sympathetic hand on my shoulder.

I flinched and she looked confused; I hadn't expected her to do that. She moved to the side and two paramedics appeared in her place. It

130

was as though the paramedics talked in a language I didn't understand. My head was fuzzy and I kept drifting off into my thoughts, while they talked to me.

What will Susan do when she finds out what I did? Is she going to beat me again? Will I be taken to another house to be punished? What does it matter anyway, just another day in my pathetic life! - the thoughts churned in my head.

The paramedics poked and prodded at my injuries.

"Jessica, Jessica," one of them tried to draw my attention.

"Yes, sorry," I struggled to talk.

"I think we should take you to hospital and get you properly checked out," he suggested.

"No! I'm not going," I spoke up but it hurt my throat.

"Jessica, it would be a good idea because we don't know how long you were …," the paramedic paused looking for the right words.

"Hanging?" I replied for him. "No. I just want to go home. I'm not going and you can't make me," I choked as I struggled to force the words out.

"We can't force you to go but if you need us or you start feeling strange, please call us. Promise me?" the paramedic waited for my reply.

I just nodded and lay back on the bed. I turned my head away. They packed their bags and spoke in whispers to the school nurse.

Why do I want to go to hospital? How are they going to make me better? No pill or bandage will heal my life, let's be honest!' - I laughed to myself.

I heard them leave the room and the headmistress coming back in.

"Jessica, can you talk to me? I understand there was some kind of a fight today. Can you tell me what happened?" she asked softly but I didn't answer.

The fight was the final straw but it was minimal compared to what had been going on at home.

If I tell her the truth, will she believe me anyway? No one else did, why would she? - I held onto that thought as my head throbbed.

"Jessica, is this why you did what you did today? I can see you have been badly hurt by someone," she insisted as she studied the other bruises on my body.

Somehow, her words affected me and I burst into tears.

"Everyone hates me! Kate hates me. She punched me and made everyone hate me. Well, they all hated me anyway, so it doesn't really matter. But they all hate me more now, I have no one. What's the point?" A jumbled mass of words exploded out of my mouth.

After I calmed down, we spoke for a while and talked about what had happened. All was going well until Susan burst into the room.

"Jessica, my darling," she spouted out in her overdramatic way.

She pushed the headteacher out of the way and acted like the worried mother. Susan grabbed me and hugged me, something that hurt a lot! This was far from the coldness she had shown me over the past few months. Even while she demanded answers from the headteacher, she blamed the problem on me when, ironically, it was her that had caused this.

Even before I woke up, it had been decided that I would not be going to school the next day. I woke up to an empty house. As usual, Shawn had driven Susan to work and Jacob to school. Eventually, I heard his car pull onto the drive, the front door opened and the familiar sound of footsteps heading towards my bedroom. He walked into my room and sat on my bed beside me.

"Why did you do that?" he asked with a hint of sadness in his voice. "You can talk to me, I know things can be hard with your mother and I know it can be tough at school. I'm always here for you, you know that right?" he continued as he reached out to hug me.

He seemed sincere in what he said and I felt like he was concerned about me; for the first time, I felt I had a dad who cared.

"I could have sorted this out for you, moved you to another school. We could have dealt with this problem. Please just talk to me, Jessica," he went on while holding my hand.

Shawn the man, who had done so many monstrous things to me, was giving a shit about me. His words made me feel wanted; I leant forward and hugged him. Shawn pulled away from my hug but tried to kiss me. I shook my head as I realised how hardened to this way of life I had become.

Fucking brilliant! What a mug I am, affection always comes with a heavy price. I'm nothing more than a punch bag and a sex slave to be kicked to the curb when everyone has had their fun, - I complained to myself as he raped me again!

After he had finished, I went for a shower and scrubbed myself for the next hour, my usual routine, before I went back to my bedroom. Partway through getting dressed, Shawn banged on the door and entered my room.

"Hurry up, come on let's go," he was excited in a childlike way.

"Where are we going?" I asked.

This had become part of the routine; Shawn would do something nice to try and make up for what he had just done.

"Food, silly! Come on, we're eating out," he piped up like an excited puppy.

When the devil went away, it was almost as though the child came out to play. Shawn could act like an adult when he wanted to but, most of the time, he was childlike. He had no real seriousness about him; no job to speak of; he did what he wanted when he wanted. His mum had taken his survival and work responsibilities away from him by handing him bundles of money each week.

We went to McDonald's first then he took me to get some new horse riding clothes; boots, a riding hat and a beautiful pink whip. He upgraded his old phone in the phone shop and handed me his used one. This was different, Susan would normally get his used phones and eventually, I would get it from her when it was battered and almost broken. Shortly after we arrived home, Shawn left to go and pick everyone up from school and work. I was sitting in the kitchen trying to work out Shawn's old, but practically new, phone when they arrived home.

"What the fuck, you promised me that phone," Susan screamed when she saw what I was doing.

I stood up, leaving the phone on the countertop as I tried to escape the situation. I was too late; my face exploded with pain as I hit the hard floor tiles and skidded across them. Susan had hit me with an almighty punch to the face. My face was already black and blue from the day before so another bruise wouldn't have mattered.

"I see how this works while I'm at work all day. What have you and your little tart been up to?" Susan glared at me, I was sure she wanted to finish me off.

I sat huddled up on the hard tiles clutching my face. I watched Susan lunge towards me again.

"Wait I've got you something too," Shawn yelled at Susan.

He jumped in between us and held out a bag that had been gift wrapped. Like a bomb that had just been defused, her mood changed instantly. She opened the bag and found the latest notebook computer and a silver watch with diamonds covering the circumference of the face hanging from the front of the bag. She acted like a giddy school girl as I watched in disbelief. I was still huddled up on the floor with my face in agony. She opened her present.

"Turn it over, turn it over," Shawn squealed.

"Love you forever," Susan read the words inscribed on the back of the watch.

She hugged and kissed him.

"Jessica helped me to choose the watch and computer. Did you think I would treat you differently?" Shawn asked as he held her close to him.

134

It was a total lie. I had no idea he had bought these items. What I did know was that he had bought them to keep her happy and to make up for what he had done to me.

"You are my queen and Jessica is my princess," he offered.

I certainly didn't feel like a princess, I felt more like Cinderella's housemaid. Susan walked over to where I was still huddled on the floor in pain. I winced while I waited for her reaction.

"Thank you, I couldn't have asked for a better daughter," she declared as she helped me to my feet and hugged me.

What the actual fuck! She has just slapped me to the ground and suddenly I am the best daughter in the world? - I was in disbelief while she continued to admire her new gifts.

"Shawn, you're cooking tonight and I'm teaching you," Susan announced, with a big smile on her face.

All was forgotten. I was suddenly forgiven, and everything, as always, was brushed under the carpet.

Chapter 18

Drama therapy

Susan thought it was better for me to stay at home and wait until the injuries to my face and neck had faded. Another chance for everyone to pretend that nothing had happened. The only scars that would ever be left would be the ones buried in my memories. However one person had been called in to account for her actions, Kate had been expelled. The school had done something about what had happened there.

Susan had received a phone call from the school informing her of the expulsion; she seemed pleased about the decision. What Kate had done wasn't any different from the beatings Susan gave me. The only difference was that Susan's beatings were normally focused on my body, not my face. Apart from the last punch she had given me, my face was already black and blue from school so that particular mark could be blamed on Kate. In a way, I felt sorry for Kate because, a few days before, she had been my best friend. Although justice had been served, I felt sadness. I would be going back to school as a loner and branded as a liar, not to mention the one who had tried to take her own life.

I wondered what further impact this would have on the relentless bullying. Apparently, another student had stumbled across me hanging by my school tie; my practically lifeless body slowly going cold. I felt sorry for the student; it probably wasn't nice for them. I never discovered who had found me. The story of what I had done spread like wildfire in a strong wind and Kate's expulsion topped off the scandal. In the modern age of technology and Facebook, one text and boom, everyone knows within an hour. Like a plague, the story spread and it had grown into something more dramatic. I could not think about any of this anymore, the poor little hamster inside my head had injured himself.

Since that afternoon in the toilet then the punch from Susan the following day, my brain seemed to have stopped working. The hamster wheel of thought was broken and I could only focus on small things like a sandwich or a drink of juice. I could not hold a conversation for more than a minute, without totally forgetting how the conversation had started. Simple things like brushing my teeth became tiresome. I would brush my teeth then put the toothbrush down only to pick it back up and repeat the process forgetting I had already brushed them. My short-term memory had been affected.

Another thing I had noticed was that I recognized objects, but they didn't have any meaning at all. A chair was a chair for example. If you had asked me what a chair was used for, it would have taken a long time for me to come up with a reasonable response to the question. Maybe the hamster in my head had died from exhaustion and left a space; my head was no longer filled with questions. Instead, I found myself staring in the mirror. The colours of my broken skin seemed to fascinate me as I watched the many phases of healing.

After one of Shawn's many visits, he arranged for me to look after an eight-year-old loan horse, Polly. A grand gesture to remind me I should stay silent about his actions. I was more than happy to spend the rest of my time off school with Polly. I sat with her and stroked her grey mane, its white patch stretching from the top of her head to the tip of her nose. Polly somehow knew I was broken. She would rest her head on my shoulder and I convinced myself she was telling me it was all going to be ok, she'd be there for me.

I spent hours riding her or talking to her, all Polly wanted from me in return was some fresh hay and the odd apple. She loved being groomed and having her ears tickled. If I had polo mints in my pocket she would always sniff them out. The cheeky monkey took them gently into her large mouth and laughed as she shook her head around. She was the biggest living thing I had ever met and the most gentle. All she wanted was some love; she meant the world to me. I felt she cared about me and gave me the courage to carry on. Polly needed me as much as I needed her.

Humans can communicate with each other and with that ability we can be hurtful but an animal can show so much love without a word. When you think about it, an animal is always happy to see and protect you. They would even give up their own lives for you without hesitation. Not many humans have these qualities. I had heard that even in your darkest hours, the universe can and will give you something that will give you the fire to get back on your feet and face the issues in your life. Maybe Polly was my saviour.

Part of me no longer cared what people thought. I had been ridiculed by everyone, bubble gum stuck in my hair and beaten to a pulp by my best friend. Entire days hiding in a grotty toilet helped me make it through the day. I wondered what else anyone could do to me, that hadn't already been done; rape or murder me. Well, I didn't care about sexual abuse and death; rape, that was a weekly occurrence I had learned to live with and now that I'd had a near-death experience, even that didn't seem so alien to me.

When someone has been broken down so badly to the point they are void of emotions, there's not a lot more anyone else can do or take from them, in fact, nothing, absolutely nothing. Strangely, this knowledge gave me power. I no longer cared what people said or did. A punch would still hurt of course but the accompanying insults would no longer be heard, no longer register, no longer valid. There is an old saying

Sticks and stones may break my bones, but words will never hurt me.

I wasn't convinced of the validity of this statement. Cuts and bruises that heal and disappear may become ancient history but words can leave psychological scars that can never be forgotten. Once you have gotten to the point *words will never hurt you* the damage has already been done. Your brain can no longer register or retain any more hurtful words, it just simply shuts down. The little hamster can no longer run anymore and dies, you lose your spark for life and your fire goes out. Polly had given me my spark back; I just had to find the fire to return to school no matter what awaited me.

The morning of my first day back, I woke up early and rushed to the stables to see Polly. I needed her to give me the courage to get me through the day. Her head poked out of the stable door and she gently rested it on my shoulder.

"I've got to go back to school today. I'm going to miss you. Don't worry, I'll bring you some apples later," I told her and it looked to me like Polly nodded her head.

She seemed to understand, she watched me walk away until I had disappeared out of view.

I must remember to cut some apples up later, to give to Polly, - I reminded myself as I walked to school.

She had given me something to focus on, even if it was just to remember to cut apples. For now, that was enough. Suddenly I was in class, more frighteningly, I wondered how long I had been there. I had been so focused on apples and Polly that I had daydreamed my way to school and into class.

"Jessica, can you come with me please. Jessica!" someone was talking to me.

I looked up to see the headmistress standing in the doorway. The entire class had turned around to look at me but no one laughed or taunted me like before. Even Johnny didn't say a word. I gathered my bag and followed her.

"Jessica, my dear, I hope you are feeling better," she commented while we walked along the corridor.

Another strange question, suicide wasn't exactly an illness that you could get better from, - I thought.

"Someone has come to meet with you today, just to talk. I hope you don't mind?" she asked.

Who was it this time? The police, a doctor or a priest? Maybe a clown, now that would be unexpected, - I didn't say anything.

"We all hope this person might be able to help you," she continued.

She was trying to get a response from me, but I wasn't in the mood. All I needed to do today was to remember Polly's apples.

"Please take a seat," she broke the silence and also broke my daydream.

How on earth did we get here? - I pondered.

It was as though someone had hit the fast-forward button on my life. Ironically, I was in the same room where the police had spoken to me months before. I sat down with my brown bag on my lap and started to consider how on earth I had travelled from one place to another without even remembering how I had gotten there.

"Hi Jessica, I'm Cathy," a voice came from behind me.

I turned my head and watched a woman with short spiky hair in her late 30's almost running into the room. She walked straight past me and landed on a seat opposite. It started to roll away and she tried to steady herself.

"I'm what they call a drama therapist," Cathy threw her hands out as she spoke.

It was almost like she was trying to emphasize the words for a bigger impact.

"You're probably wondering what a drama therapist is?" she enquired.

I didn't respond, I was still wondering how I had gotten into this room.

"Great name isn't it? It has a ring to it, *drama therapist*, it sounds crazy. But I can see you don't want to talk, so we will just sit here in silence. You can go to sleep on the desk if you like. I'm a bit sleepy myself after the entrance I just made," she admitted.

She crossed her arms and pretended to fall asleep on the desk.

What the fuck! Am I asleep or have I gone into one of my daydreams? Have I created an imaginary person? - my mixed up brain was asking.

I knew I was confused and part of me wanted to go over and poke Cathy. As she pretended to be asleep, new questions started to pop into my head.

Is my mind playing tricks on me and is Cathy real or not? I mean really, what the fuck is this all about? - I asked myself.

Cathy pretended to snore softly and we sat in silence for about 10 minutes until I removed my bag from my lap and placed it to the side of my chair.

"These sessions are just for you, Jessica," Cathy spoke softly.

"We can talk or just sit here; it's entirely up to you. This is a safe space," she continued. Her soft voice seemed very different from the original one she had used when she entered the room.

"Can I ask, why are you here?" she lifted her head from the desk.

"I had no choice; I was dragged out of class," I replied.

"Interesting word, dragged," She seemed to ponder over this word.

"If it's ok, can we try something? It's entirely up to you."

I immediately looked down; I could not handle eye contact with anyone.

"Yeah, ok," I almost whispered.

She started to rummage around in her oversized bag and produced some toy figures and six pieces of fabric, all with their unique colour or pattern.

"Jessica, imagine each piece of fabric represents how you feel," she said as she handed me a grey piece of fabric.

"This is a bit weird," I announced, taking the fabric from her. "I don't know, it's grey. I guess it makes me feel cloudy and foggy."

"That's really good. Now, place the fabric on the floor," she instructed as she handed me a red imprinted piece of fabric.

"So how do you feel about this colour?"

"Love, I guess." I studied the material.

Without much thought, my replies came out as each piece of fabric was handed to me until they all had been given a representation of a feeling.

Grey = sort of cloudy and foggy

Red imprinted = love

Bright red = anger

Black netting = imprisoned, trapped trying to get out

Yellow = putting on a brave face

Blue = Sad

Cathy then handed me the small toys one by one and asked me to place each one on the fabrics. Each was to represent a feeling or a person in my life. Strangely, my brain seemed to be working again and my focus was now on each toy. I thought slowly about what each one meant to me before I placed them on a material. Then Cathy asked me to explain what each toy represented. On the blue piece of fabric, I had placed a miniature fence and two small figures, a boy and a girl.

"My brother is the boy and the girl is my sister," I explained.

But my heart sank as I remembered that Jacob was nearly at the age where Susan would be most likely to vent her anger against him. She had turned against Jack, Laura and myself, it was only a matter of time if history was to repeat itself.

"Why have you put a fence around him?" Cathy asked.

I looked at the fabric and realised I had placed the figure of the boy inside the small toy fence.

"To keep him safe, I guess before he gets imprisoned," I answered.

The words just seemed to tumble out of my mouth, no one had asked me questions like this before. We weren't talking about Jacob, just about toys placed bits of fabric.

"What about the little girl, you've put on the fabric?" Cathy asked.

"Oh, that's my sister, I don't really see her much because I don't fit into her world," I replied.

Suddenly. I appreciated how sad and angry I was with my sister.

"Why did you put an eagle on the bright red piece of fabric?" she pointed.

I had placed two toys on this particular piece of fabric.

"The eagle is my brother Jack, he just comes into my life and disappears. He's always angry and never helps me. It doesn't feel like he cares," tears started to well up in my eyes.

"So, what about the T rex?" Cathy went on.

I paused and stared at the T rex; I could feel a wave of anger bubbling inside me.

"My mother," my voice was cold when I spoke.

I didn't realise until that moment how much anger I had towards Susan.

"What about this one, the yellow fabric, Jessica?" I had placed a horse and other animals on it.

"Oh, that's Polly," I said with a beaming smile.

"Who is Polly?" she asked.

"She is my horse, my best friend. I need to get her some apples later," my body flooded with happiness as I talked about Polly.

"What about this one?" Cathy pointed to the black laced fabric.

Two figures were on it; a small man and a little girl.

"That's the devil and that's me," tears leaked out.

"Can we stop now?" I felt slightly overwhelmed.

"Yes, of course, this is your time we can do whatever you like. You have done really well and you should be proud. I'm proud of you," she spoke with sincerity.

An unusual, warm feeling flooded through my body. I couldn't remember a time in my life when anybody had told me that they were proud of me. Also, Cathy had asked me to do something and had not harmed me when I asked her to stop. She stopped but didn't question me as to why I had made the request, this was something I had never experienced before.

"Would you like to see me again? You don't have to, it's your choice," she had given me the option to say yes or no.

I was being treated like a person.

"Yes. I would like that." I smiled at her.

I liked Cathy; she made me feel safe and allowed me to have a voice. The rest of my day was spent lost in thoughts about the session. In just over an hour, Cathy had managed to open up emotions and feelings that I had hidden from the world. I felt she actually gave a shit about me.

I walked to the stables later that day to see Polly, her head was already sticking out of the door when I arrived and, in my mind, she looked happy to see me. I sat with her and told her about my day while I fed her apples. She seemed to listen, her head nudging me for another slice of apple. I was just about to give Polly the last of the apple when I heard someone approached the stable.

"Jessica, Jessica," Susan called out, she sounded out of breath.

What now? Why can't she leave me alone? - I thought, getting to my feet.

"Jessica, there you are. We need to go now," she panted.

"Shawn's gran is not well, we need to go," she repeated.

Despite Susan still being out of breath from the run up the hill, we hurried towards the house I saw Crystal.

"Come on, quickly," Shawn impatiently summoned Susan into the car.

"Look after Jacob, we will be back soon," Susan shouted to Crystal.

The jeep sped off down the driveway but, sadly, later that night, we were told that Shawn's gran had passed away.

Chapter 19

Extended family

School had been uneventful considering it was my first week back. I received a few strange looks and had heard students whisper to their friends as I walked past but, other than that, I had been left alone. My form tutor had informed me that Cathy would be visiting me again; I was looking forward to seeing her. However, a social worker also wanted to see me; I was not looking forward to that. No one at home ever asked me about the visitors that came to my school. It made me wonder if they even knew or if the visitors took second place to the news of Shawn's grandmother who he called Gran.

Shawn was upset by the news of his gran's death. That was the first time I had ever seen him show real emotion. He had always maintained an unemotional, cool, calm and collected manner but I felt sorry for him because I could feel his loss. The house was overtaken by a sense of sadness which lasted a few days as everyone focused on Shawn. Susan rushed around, pandering to his every need and auditioned for the world's best girlfriend role. We were ushered away and told to go and find things to do so that he could be left in peace. When Jacob and I came home from school, Susan and Shawn were, more often than not, focusing on the impending funeral arrangements.

When the weekend arrived, we travelled to meet with Crystal, Shawn's mum. Crystal and Mike were lovely people and always made us feel welcome; I enjoyed visiting them. They lived a short drive away and owned a large house near St Austell. Crystal married Mike after she had broken up with Shawn's biological dad. Mike took Shawn on and gave him his surname.

We pulled onto the start of their driveway only to be met by huge, black gates. Shawn leaned out of the window and pressed the small button, mounted on the wall.

"Hello," Crystal's voice echoed out of the tiny speaker.

"Mum, it's me, open the gate," the gates began to open.

We drove along the driveway and, as on previous visits, I was drawn to how pristine the garden looked. Crystal was already outside her enormous, white house where she welcomed us inside. The house was beautiful and immaculately decorated with every item tastefully placed within the airy space to complement the grandness of the building.

"I'll get the kettle on. There's a slice of cake if anyone wants some," Crystal told us, as she winked at me and Jacob.

"Take a seat," she offered.

She organised a tray with a large pot of tea and some tasty-looking cakes. We sat around the long, dining-room table.

"Jacob, Jessica what would you like?" she asked.

She lifted two mugs from the tray and started to pour from the teapot.

"That cake and a bar of chocolate please," Jacob pointed to the largest cake on the tray.

Crystal laid the sweet fancies on a plate and placed it in front of him.

147

"We need to decide what we are going to do regarding Gran's funeral," Crystal said in a pained voice.

She was devastated by the loss of her mother but was putting on a brave face.

"I don't think this is a suitable conversation. I'm sure the children don't want to be part of this discussion," Mike said by way of a greeting as he entered the room.

He ignored Shawn.

I had seen him do this on several occasions; it was as though he didn't want to acknowledge Shawn's presence in the room. Without making eye contact or extending a welcome to Shawn, he made it clear he didn't want to be anywhere near him. It was evident something was wrong between the two because Mike was normally incredibly friendly and warm-hearted.

"Come on kids, we'll go and find something more interesting to do," Mike announced.

He grabbed treats from the tray and we followed him into his office which would be better described as a man cave. Guitars were placed on stands around the room and picture frames with gold and platinum records hung from the walls. Signed photographs of men with long hair were proudly displayed around the room. I had been in this room quite a few times, in fact, anytime we visited Shawn's mum. Mike usually ushered Jacob and me away from the others so that we could spend time with him. I had grown very fond of Mike. He always had red and white sweets strategically placed on his desk to share with Jacob and me.

"Don't tell Crystal. It's our little secret," he would remind us.

Mike would tell us funny stories about each of the guitars in his collection; it was almost as though the guitars had become his children. The stories were mainly about a band that he had played in; apparently, they had rocked wherever they played. He often joked that he used to have ladies falling at his feet. I loved his stories, especially when he told us about the things they got up to while touring. It sounded like an exciting life and it would seem the band members got into a few dubious situations while on tour. He played his guitars for us and we sang along with him. I have to say, he was a very good guitarist.

"One day you might inherit my guitars. Make sure you get a good price for them, they are famous and worth a lot of money. They are my legacy," he reminded us.

Mike always seemed sad that he had left the band to pursue his business plans. His real love had been with music. The band went on to become one of the biggest UK bands until, unfortunately, their frontman died.

"Freddie was a character," Mike told us.

Mike was the first guitarist in the band known as Queen.

When we returned to the kitchen, the funeral plans had been made and Crystal decided that we should take Gemma for a walk. I was sure Mike wanted to go as well but, whenever Shawn was around, he would opt-out. He made an excuse that he had emails to attend to and disappeared back into his office.

We walked to Carlyon Bay. It was freezing and deserted, the only things visible were wild rabbits running here and there. After our walk, we said our goodbyes and Crystal handed Shawn an envelope filled with money. Mike was friendly to everyone as we left, but when it came to Shawn, once again, he dismissed him.

Over the next few days, Shawn's entire attitude changed. His gran had been extremely wealthy and all he kept talking about was how much money he was about to inherit. She owned the house we were living in and the flat that she had moved into. Shawn had never worked a day in his life and his mother and grandmother had always funded his lavish lifestyle, handing him large amounts of money whenever he asked. The only time he did work was a few months before his gran's death.

At one point, I had jokingly said I wanted to be a TV extra and Shawn suddenly jumped all over this idea. He made his way up to the attic to get his camera and, within 10 minutes, the equipment was set up and I was asked to pose for my apparent portfolio. He chased me around the house with his camera; I wasn't keen on my photo being taken, but it would have been fun to have been on TV. I eventually agreed and we spent the entire afternoon taking photos around the grounds of the house, it was fun.

When Susan came home from work we told her we were both going to be famous. She laughed sarcastically; cracked open a bottle of wine and watched while the would-be photographer continued.

"Jessica, I think we should take some underwear shots," Shawn announced.

He lowered his camera to the side of his leg.

"Sorry. why?" I replied nervously.

"Well, it's what they are going to need if you're going to be a superstar. Isn't that right Susan?" Shawn looked over to Susan.

By this time she was halfway through the bottle of wine.

"I suppose so, well I guess you see them modelling underwear," she agreed.

"Come on, Jessica, it's what they want to see," he cajoled.

His attitude and body language had changed and I knew he was not going to let this drop.

"I'm not really sure if I'm comfortable doing that," I hesitated.

"Just slip your dress off and we'll take some photos," his voice had an impatient tone.

I looked over to Susan and she just stared at me, drinking her wine. They were both making me feel uncomfortable and I didn't know what to do.

Was this what the police were going on about? - I suddenly remembered the brief conversation I had with Racheal and Sharon about photographs of children.

"Jessica, just slip your dress off," Shawn demanded aggressively.

I slipped the two straps off my shoulders and let my dress fall to the floor.

"That's a good girl," Shawn's entire demeanour changed back to playful and happy.

I, however, awkwardly covered myself with my arms.

"Jessica, I can't photograph you standing like that, you need to pose," Shawn said angrily.

I looked over to where Susan had been sitting and somewhere between being asked to lose my dress and me taking it off she had drunk the rest of the bottle of wine. She stood up and walked out of the room taking a fresh bottle with her. Half-dressed and alone with Shawn, I felt uncomfortable.

"Come on, you need to look sexy for the camera," Shawn snapped.

I had no choice; I started to pose for him. He snapped away and asked me to pose in different embarrassing positions.

"Why don't you remove the bra, Jessica? Let's give them some really sexy photos that will definitely get you the part," he suggested excitedly.

"No, I'm not doing that!" I protested.

"Jessica, lose the bra now!" his tone turning aggressive again.

I slowly removed my bra and tried to cover my breasts, this wasn't going to end well for me.

"I told you before standing like that doesn't look cute. Does it?" he remarked with the devil's glint back his eyes.

He made me pose topless with my naked breasts exposed. I was terrified thinking about his next request.

"Remove your knickers," Shawn demanded.

I was scared but he knew I would jump to his every command. If I didn't obey the consequences that followed would be terrifying. After I removed the final item of clothing, he made me pose in all kinds of disgusting positions. If I looked scared or unhappy while he snapped away, he became angry.

"I think that's it, this should make a great portfolio," he finally said.

He let me go that night. I had been expecting a lot worse. Needless to say, I never did get an acting role but, surprisingly, over the next few years, he did. Shawn sent out the photos of himself that I had taken. Somehow he managed to land a walk-on part on Casualty. Well, technically he didn't walk; he was wheeled in on a bed when he played a patient. He thought he was a superstar after that and set up Facebook pages where he claimed he was a professional actor. Additional parts followed and he managed to land himself a part in the Bad Education movie. This was Shawn's entire work history, a few walk-on parts and a healthy inheritance to continue living his lavish lifestyle.

On many occasions, Crystal had threatened to cut him off financially but, because of his inheritance, he no longer needed to worry about money. When payday came and his gran's money passed to him, you could almost see him rub his hands together. He was, not unexpectedly, in a happier mood on the day of his gran's funeral. This made me think that the sadness he had shown when he came home after she had died had been an act too.

Did he just pretend to be upset and distraught? - I wondered.

Maybe he had missed his calling and acting was something he was good at, he certainly had me convinced. Shawn seemed to have the ability to change his mood almost like a switch; at the drop of a hat, his mood could change. People were influenced by his ability to do this, once he had you sucked in, he would switch and the devil would come out. And so, Shawn always got his way.

On the day of his gran's funeral, I witnessed the switch. In the morning he was sad and upset as he talked to the other mourners. Then, when he was called into a room for the will to be read out, his mood switched. The crocodile tears were gone; he came out of the

152

room, smiling. As we left the wake that day, Crystal invited us to spend Christmas with her.

I woke at 4 am on Christmas morning and started to prepare our contribution to Christmas dinner. This was something I had done for a few years, I wanted to make it a special day for Jacob and, selfishly, for myself too. I was determined this year was going to be a good Christmas for everyone. I had carefully wrapped all the food I had prepared before we set off.

Crystal greeted us in her normal friendly manner and as always, Mike was nowhere to be seen when we arrived.

"Jessica, why on earth have you made all this food? I'm meant to be the hostess today. Christmas is meant to be about children; surely this is something your mother should be doing?" Crystal hugged me.

She gave Susan a disapproving look; I wished she hadn't. Susan shot me a look that told me there would be repercussions later. Jacob's eyes lit up when he saw what was in the kitchen; cake stands filled with dozens of cakes and mince pies. A delicious Christmas dinner was already in the oven and, in the lounge, Christmas had arrived.

Jacob and I stopped in the doorway, our mouths practically hitting the floor. The lounge had been turned into a winter wonderland. Around one of the biggest trees I had ever seen, there was a mountain of presents piled high and hundreds of twinkling fairy lights.

Mike appeared in the lounge with another enormous cake stand.

"Ho Ho Ho! Hello everyone," Mike bellowed out his greeting.

He ignored Shawn.

The presents were handed out. That year, my particular favourite gift was a designer bag with a pink pattern. I still cherish it. I had never received this level of generosity from anyone before. After presents, I returned to the kitchen to help Crystal with the cooking.

"Jessica, you really don't have to do this, you are my guest!" she scolded.

"I want to do it, I hope you don't mind," I replied.

It was my way of saying thank you to Crystal and Mike. They had no idea how much their kindness meant to Jacob and me. They had given us a magical Christmas and a sense of being part of a real family. We sat around the table when dinner was ready. Everything was luxurious. Even the crackers had quality gifts inside; worlds apart from the red, paper fish you normally find.

"Blimey, this is better than what you would get in a fancy restaurant. You'll make a great wife someday!" Mike complimented my efforts and winked as he continued, "I'll let you into a little secret. The way to a man's heart is to keep him well fed!"

Mike made me feel like I had finally achieved something and made someone happy. After dinner, we took Gemma for a walk to the highest point on the cliff-top. I sat on a bench and looked out to sea. It was bitterly cold; my scarf danced as the cold wind brushed across my face. I watched the waves crashing against the rocks below and reflected on the past year. Christmas had been so different from the pain and hurt I had been through. It had been a perfect day with no shouting or screaming, pain or tears, even Susan had managed to behave herself. Sadly, what I didn't know, as I sat on that bench and looked out to sea, was that my life was about to change and become even more terrifying and lonely than it had ever been.

Chapter 20

The Dark Web

What does it mean to be a child? Riding a pushbike or climbing a tree perhaps. For Jacob, it was all about zombies on the PlayStation, bouncing up and down on a trampoline or talking to his monkeys. His life seemed simple and full of promise with plenty of friends. Susan and Shawn seemed to treat him differently; Susan was a mother to Jacob. He was mummy's little monkey, the golden child that could do no wrong. If there was an unmade bed or a messy room, she would clear up the chaos he had left behind. The bond between Susan and Jacob was strong,

I never had this with her. For me, a punch to the ribs seemed to be a suitable punishment for any mess that I had left behind. If I left a wet towel on the floor, the result was another bruise to remind me of the seriousness of my crime. My bedroom looked abandoned, as though it had been lost in time waiting for the occupier to return. Nothing was ever moved or left out of place for fear of further beatings. I often wondered if my body would ever be one single colour; shades of red, purple, black and blue and the strangest shades of yellow, the stages of healing, littered coverable areas of my body. My face was used for target practice but saved only for special occasions when, because of the wine, I had pissed her off big time. Susan became so out of control after she drank; her glazed eyes and slurred words led to the most extreme irrational behaviour. Literally, a tea bag could cause world war three!

To me, sober Susan was more of an act; she played the lead role of the loving worried mother for the benefit of watching eyes. She performed for teachers, neighbours and, on the odd occasion, the police when they started to ask questions. I was an annoyance to her and I had also become a threat as far as Shawn was concerned. She feared the man she shared a bed with preferred mine. This poured even more fuel on her already raging, internal fire. But when it came to Jacob, she seemed to have the ability to give her love naturally. I truly longed for her to love me the same way.

When it came to Shawn, the roles were reversed. Jacob increasingly became an annoyance to him. He was the unwanted baggage that came with their relationship. He would get annoyed with Jacob when he had done something wrong but, if I did the same, he didn't seem to care. Shawn almost disregarded him even to the point he sometimes forgot to introduce him when we met new people but he would introduced me and act like a proud father.

Shawn appeared to know everything that was going on in the house, even when he wasn't around; it was almost like he had a sixth sense. For example, if Jacob or I got up during the night and crept to the kitchen to sneak a snack or a drink, Shawn somehow always knew.

"Don't drink my coke again," he would comment to me the following day.

But he would become angry if Jacob did the same. I often wondered if he had marked the bottle in some way as he even knew when a tiny sip had been taken.

When Shawn acted childlike, it would be a good day and he would interact with Jacob and me in a fun way, playing games or running around the garden. However, this childlike state could also manifest itself as a spoiled child and he would huff if he didn't get his way.

Then there was the devil side to him, a side I knew all too well where he would just take whatever he wanted from me even when he was asked not to. He had total disregard for the damage he was causing. This side of Shawn made an appearance more times than I care to remember. The regular bedroom visits that I endured from Shawn were always followed with a gift, but this led to more issues than were obvious. Shawn had no use for Jacob; he was forgotten about therefore there was no need for gifts to flow in his direction. Susan tried her best to keep the balance to make things seem fair, but she simply didn't have the available funds to keep up with Shawn.

Money had no real value for him; he treated it like fun coupons rather than banknotes. I was glad that Shawn didn't take any interest in Jacob, even although it meant that I was rewarded and he was ignored. Jacob wasn't on Shawn's radar; he was safe from the revolting advances and abuse that I had to endure. Jacob was protected from the type of punishment meted out to me and this allowed him to be a little boy with a childhood. Jacob had the chance of a good life.

He looked lost in his own world but happy as he bounced on the trampoline or pretended to be the world wrestling champion when he body-slammed one of his monkeys into submission. I couldn't help myself feeling a bit of a green-eyed monster as I watched him. His carefree childhood was filled with fun and laughter rather than bruises and pain. Any resemblance to a child that was left in me needed to have some fun.

"The next contender to the wrestling ring, Jessica, the bone crusher!" I bellowed.

Running to the trampoline, I joined Jacob in an epic wrestling match. We bounced so high we could see over the top of the trees. My hair blew in the wind and the sun warmed my skin. I felt free as all my problems simply melted away and a sense of happiness came over me. In that moment of freedom with Jacob, I felt like a kid again. It meant more to me than he will ever know.

"Dinner!" Susan yelled from the house.

"Last one in is a rotten egg," Jacob shouted and shrieked with laughter.

He had left the trampoline and was sprinting towards the house.

"Oh you little shit, that's not fair!" I yelled, chasing after him.

"Loser!" Jacob shouted proudly and emphasized his win using his hand to make an L sign upon his forehead.

"You cheated, monkey," I replied to Jacob's clearly unfair win.

Shawn was already sitting at the kitchen table but I took a seat as far away from him as possible.

"What are we having for dinner, Mum?" Jacob asked in his squeaky voice.

"Lasagna," Susan replied.

She seemed proud of her effort. It was the first time she had cooked for a while.

"Oh, can't we have Chinese instead?" I asked.

I was doing a typical fourteen-year-old thing, testing the waters. I didn't want Chinese, I only wanted to see what Shawn's reaction would be.

"I'll just order a takeout," Shawn agreed.

He speed-dialed the Chinese take-out.

"What are you doing? I've just cooked a meal," Susan protested.

"Take out, take out, take out," Jacob chanted.

I had wanted to test a theory but never expected the outcome I witnessed. Shawn's attentive reaction was something I had noticed over the past few months; he was going out of his way to please me, jumping to my command.

"Shawn, put the bloody phone down," Susan roared at him.

The irritation and look of disgust she gave me as she shouted at him told me I would pay a high price for the stunt I had pulled. Causing havoc at the table after Susan had just slaved over a hot stove was probably not the best idea given our family dynamics.

"Don't you want any then, Babe?" Shawn asked Susan, totally oblivious to her fury.

"No, I fucking don't want any!" she screamed back at him.

I was going to pay for this dirty deed, elf duties and bruises would be penciled in for later. Susan slammed a plate of lasagna down in front of Jacob.

"But, Mum ...," Jacob started in protest.

"Eat your dinner, Jacob!" she screeched and slammed her plate down on the table.

She walked into the kitchen and came back with a bottle of wine.

"We'll have the usual please, as quick as you can," Shawn spoke into the phone.

I looked around the table; Jacob was half eating and half playing with his plate of food while Susan gulped down her red wine. She hadn't touched her lasagna. Shawn was engrossed, tapping on his mobile phone. He didn't notice the train wreck that had just happened in front of him.

"Yes!" Shawn suddenly shouted and jumped up.

He made his way over to his computer, his face was beaming.

"What's all the excitement about?" Susan asked with a touch of sarcasm in her voice. "Jessica, do you fancy doing some more modelling photos tonight? I may have something very special lined up for you," he dismissed Susan's question.

The thought of modelling again sickened me. Last time I ended up embarrassed and naked. Shawn, however, miraculously got another walk-on part after my photoshoot. He was filmed as King Arthur in the hit series Merlin.

"I really don't feel like it tonight," I protested.

"Spend some time with your dad, Jessica. We all know how much he enjoys it," Susan said mockingly.

She took a large gulp of wine, picked up the bottle and walked out of the room. Shawn watched her leave; he smiled.

"Can I go and play on the PlayStation?" Jacob asked.

"Yes, of course," Shawn answered.

Jacob ran out too.

"I'm going to go for a shower," I said, trying to remove myself.

There was a knock at the door.

Shit the Chinese, - I thought.

"Can you grab the food?" Shawn asked.

My stupidity had left me with little chance of escape. I dealt with the delivery and returned to the kitchen. Two empty plates sat on the table. Shawn now had me on my own and a chance to pester me into submission once again.

"Jessica, this is exciting, it could be really big for you. Just look at what a small part has done for my career so far," he dropped his five seconds of fame into the conversation.

"I'm really not that bothered about becoming an actor," I argued.

"It's important; the people who are going to be involved in this will make you a star," he said, his excitement building.

But there was little point in arguing with him, he was going to get his way regardless.

"Ok, but please nothing like last time," I begged.

I was deflated and concerned about how the night would end. After we ate, Shawn set up cameras on tripods in the lounge. The more equipment he bought out, the more I felt sick. He brought bags filled with items he had collected.

"All set, your road to fame awaits," he announced.

I sheepishly walked over to where he had set up the equipment and wished the ground would swallow me.

"Let's do some warm-up shots to get you in the mood shall we?" he beckoned me in front of a camera.

Click! A flash of light hurt my eyes. That was the first of many awkward poses.

"Come on, Jessica. Loosen up. Here put some of these on," he threw a bag of clothes at me.

I took a breath, bent down and opened the bag.

"I'm not wearing these!" the horror in my voice was evident.

The bag contained everything from garter lingerie to teddy bodysuits; I was looking at Susan's underwear collection.

"This is what they want to see, they're going to make you a star," his eyes darkened.

"What is this all for anyway and why would I need to wear this stuff?" I asked.

"It's for a very special group of people; important people on the Dark Web," Shawn spoke in an icy voice; the devil had awoken.

"The Dark Web. What's that?" I enquired.

"It's a place where I upload all my special photos and videos for important people to see, people who may want to meet you and make you a star, " he smirked.

The excitement I heard in Shawn's voice that night as he raced over to his computer while the rest of my family sat around the dinner table, will always haunt me. His intention wasn't to make me a star; he proposed to trade his conquest with other disgusting excuses for humans. The next penny that then dropped churns my stomach.

The photos he took of me that night dressed in my mother's lingerie and the other disgusting things he made me do on his camera were swapped. These photos were not only for the perverted enjoyment of other sick-minded individuals, on the Dark Web. He also used the photos he took of me to trade me. The bastard sold me!

Chapter 21

The rapist and my abusers

As I said at the start, this was never meant to be a book. I started to write, to try and untangle the spider's web left inside my head, to try to heal and get rid of my demons. I never realised how much I had locked away. On many occasions, this book has been one right-click away from being deleted, as it became extremely painful to write the tale of my life. I fear that the people I love will judge me and see me differently when they read what has been written.

To write this has become a process and journey and there have been times where I have just wanted to run away, even from my own family. On my journey to learn why they did what they did to me and to unravel the distorted web of lies Shawn and Susan had told me, I have faced distressing moments. It has caused many sleepless nights and I have often wakened up screaming, with cold sweats, as my heart raced due to another nightmare being unlocked.

Sometimes it takes days for the anger to leave after my subconscious accidentally unlocks another memory while I sleep. At one point, this project nearly became too much but I carried on with support from the people who love me. Some of the memories felt like the devil's claws ripping at my soul, as my demons attempted to drag me back down to the pit of hell; the dark place, the pit of depression.

A penny dropped while writing about the Dark Web, so many things suddenly fell into place and anger built up inside me. Suddenly everything made sense and the entire fucking computer almost got launched at the wall. A cuddle with my son was the only thing that helped to calm me down. That cuddle helped me realise the importance of this book. So many kids are abused each year and so many kids are ignored when they ask for help.

The more I wrote the more I realised that this subject is taboo to talk about. It regularly gets brushed under the carpet or people clam up because they are too frightened to listen. The flashbacks and images that have haunted and taunted me for years are something that cannot be simply brushed under the carpet. This is why I decided to tell the graphic details behind my story; it may help others to understand the mental and physical damage these monsters on the Dark Web can cause to a child. It also made me realise that if this book helps even one person, to realise it is not right what these bastards do, then it will have been worth the pain involved, to write this book. This gives me the determination to get my story out there

The night I describe in The Dark Web was central to my understanding of child abuse. Shawn had told me it was a significant place for important people who could make me a star. I was young and very naive at the time; I believed him.

Years later, I found out it is an illegal place on the internet, hidden and not in your average Google search. Some of you will know a lot more about this subject than me. From what I have heard, the Dark Web is a criminal's paradise, hidden from prying eyes where people like Shawn can meet. It's not the topic of conversation you would expect to be brought up over dinner or at the pub. There aren't any Facebook or Instagram groups called, 'Like-minded pedophile friends' group.'

No, these evil bastards use other avenues to connect, where they can view illegal photos and share their conquests, their trophies of abuse. These sick people use the ungoverned Dark Web, a place where rules don't apply. Anything from drugs to human organs can be bought and sold freely. I have been told this by several sources and I have carried out some research on it. There appears to be an element of truth to the stories.

Finding it difficult to put into words and describe the response to Shawn's portrayal of me on the Dark Web. Because he traded me, several abusers appeared in my life and although I can't give names and places, this is my attempt at describing the depraved actions of those who responded.

Twelve Evil Monkeys

There is someone waiting in the shadows ready to pounce on me
You wait and watch and I will never know when or where
I can scream but nobody will hear
when you have me in your lair.

Dressed all in black with a bow tie
Did you find it funny when you made me cry?
Bent over a table or tied to a bed
I started to wish that I was dead.

When you removed your socks it was such a shock
Was your foot put on the chopping block?
With striking vibrant green eyes
Who was this man who ripped apart my insides?

Sideburns man is coming for you
Sorry for the warning but he will turn you blue.
Scared and alone locked in a room

164

He is ready and waiting just to taunt you.

The vimto man made me squirm
The man had something that resembled a worm.
While bubble bath man decided to bathe me
The man dripping in wealth also raped me.

Twelve Evil Monkeys all walking free
One by one you all abused me.
Nobody knows if you really cared
when you all took my innocence without any care.

Was it your brother, dad or a teacher
who took advantage of me?
Strange how a small toy or a trinket
may be enough to tell me who did this to me.

There is still someone waiting in the shadows ready to pounce
I will wait and watch and you will never know when or where.
I will no longer scream like a mouse
as you will never have me again in your lair.

Jessica Harrington

Chapter 22

Twelve evil monkeys

Who would have guessed that the audition photos Shawn took could attract so much attention? Unfortunately, it was not the type of interest one would hope for. Another long week at school was over and when I walked out, I saw Shawn and Susan in the purple Cherokee Jeep parked a few metres away from the school gates. I opened the rear door and climbed in expecting to find my brother in the back.

"Where is Jacob?" I asked.

"He's with his friend, Jack. Anyway, we're going on a shopping trip this weekend," Susan sounded happy as we made our way home.

I had forgotten, but Jacob had mentioned going to Jack's when we were playing on the trampoline a few days before. That evening, we had a nice time. No dramas, no fights, no drinking and no visits from Shawn, just a nice family night in, eating Chinese and watching films. The following morning we set off in the direction of Bristol.

"I've booked us some rooms at a hotel. I thought we could make a proper weekend of it," Shawn announced.

They were both in happy moods and Susan even took his hand while we drove along.

"I've packed some clothes for you, Jessica, and we'll also have a girly day at the shops. How does that sound?" smiling, she looked back at me.

"That sounds good, I'd like that," I returned her smile.

Why are they both being so nice? Has something changed? - I wasn't sure. It took just over two hours before we arrived at a shopping mall in Bristol. We parked up and headed for the shops. Shawn treated us to whatever our hearts desired. New boots, tops, jeans and trainers were only part of our haul; nothing seemed too expensive for him.

After a few hours, Shawn was bored so he handed Susan his bank card. He said he had some phone calls to make and left us to our own devices. I didn't want this day to end. I had craved for time with Susan, a chance to bond and a time to heal some old wounds. Our overdue girlie day helped with this. We were doing the normal things a mother and daughter should do. We bought some giant donuts before we left the mall and I held a donut up to my face.

"Jessica, that's the same size as your head," Susan joked.

Outside, we found Shawn smoking and on his mobile phone.

"It's all in place, don't worry," he reported to whoever was on the other end of the phone and ended the call.

"Did you get everything you wanted? Shall we go to the hotel now?" Shawn asked.

He seemed agitated.

"Yes, I think so," Susan answered.

She smiled and held up some of the bags she was carrying. I struggled to keep up with Shawn; he was racing back to the car.

This was meant to be a relaxing weekend away. Why is he in such a rush all of a sudden? – something was nagging at the back of my mind.

Since leaving the mall, Shawn had been acting as though time was against us, he needed to be somewhere else or we needed to be somewhere else. But I put my thoughts away.

Our impressive hotel was a short journey away. It had high ceilings and enormous pillars that welcomed guests into a spacious reception area. Everything was fresh and well maintained. We walked to the reception desk and discovered that Shawn had booked two rooms, one for himself and one for Susan and me. At thirteen, I was not allowed to have a room to myself. This seemed odd because I saw the hotel also advertised family rooms on the leaflets sitting on the reception desk.

Why wasn't one of these booked instead? - I asked myself.

Susan and I made our way to the room and Shawn made his way to his own private room. We had a beautiful bedroom with an en-suite shower room. I knew we had shared sleeping arrangements when I saw a king-sized bed. I started to lay my new clothes out on the bed. I was particularly careful when I handled my new, soft, silk pyjamas.

"We're going out for some drinks tonight. Will you be ok on your own?" Susan asked.

"Yes, I'll be fine. TV and bed for me tonight, I'm so tired," an evening to myself sounded bliss.

"Do you fancy helping me with my make-up?" Susan asked.

"Yeah, I'd like that," a warm feeling filled my heart.

Susan had asked me to do something with her, a rare occurrence. I went for a shower and found myself singing, something I had not done in a long time. My happiness always brought out singing and it had been a happy day.

Maybe things have changed, - I smiled.

I changed into my new, silk pyjamas before returning to the bedroom to help with the makeup. Susan had already changed into her new clothes ready for her night ahead. She was sitting in front of a mirror. I had almost completed Susan's make-up when Shawn knocked on

168

the door. He had been gone a long time and he had a tray of drinks in his hand.

"A toast to a good day," Shawn grinned.

He handed the drinks out, a beer for himself, wine for Susan and an orange juice for me.

"To us," he raised his glass and drank.

We've only been shopping, a toast seems a bit over the top, - I thought as I gulped my drink.

"We're popping out now. You'll be alright here for a while won't you?" Shawn enquired.

"Yes, I'll be fine. Mum has already told me," I insisted.

With Susan and Shawn hitting the alcohol, it was probably for the best if I wasn't around.

"Ok, well that's settled then. Drink up and I'll take your glass back down with me," he turned to Susan and kissed her hand. "And I'll meet you at reception, my queen."

Shawn seemed eager for me to finish my drink and he didn't wait for Susan so that they could walk out together. I downed the orange juice and handed him the glass in time to catch the devil's smile ripple across his face. Shawn left the room and I went back to help with Susan's make-up. Ten minutes later, she was ready. I was clearing the clothes from the bed when a strange feeling came over me.

"Mum, I feel dizzy," I mumbled.

The room started to twist and turn.

"Don't ruin this for me, Jessica. It's been a long day. Just get into bed, you'll be fine," She was dismissive.

She stood up and picked up her purse.

"You're probably right. I'll just go to bed," was my feeble answer.

I was seeing double by this point, but I didn't want to ruin Susan's mood or her night out. By the time she left, I could hardly stand; everything had become distorted. In the bathroom, I turned on the sink tap. The water I splashed on my face seemed to help slightly, but a feeling of overwhelming tiredness took hold. I stumbled and staggered back to the bed; it seemed like a mile even although it was only about ten paces. I felt around for the bed, my vision was just a mixture of colours and haze. My body felt like it was spinning and I battled to remain upright.

What the hell is going on? Something is seriously wrong! - I finally gathered my thoughts.

I lay on my back and felt my body start to shut down. All feeling was lost. I was totally paralysed and barely conscious as darkness descended. I was barely able to open my eyes but I attempted to look around the room. I could hear something and tried to focus on the silhouette of someone near the bathroom.

"Mum," I thought I had called out yet nothing came out of my mouth.

Everything was distorted and hazy when darkness took hold again. It was impossible to fight it. I started the battle to open my eyes again but could feel the weight of someone pushing down on me. Someone was rubbing their body against my skin.

What's going on? - I silently mouthed.

I finally managed to open my eyes; a stranger was on top of me. I was naked and unable to scream. I felt dead, petrified and a passenger in my own body. The scent of expensive aftershave overwhelmed me. A naked, greying man was using my body for his pleasure but I was a lifeless rag doll. As he gained pace, he leaned back and I could see a massive scar running down his chest.

This evil man has no heart; it has been cut out of his chest, - I fumbled in my head for an explanation.

I could feel everything he was doing to me especially the pain that ripped through my body. He was moving so fast and so deep, I could feel my insides tearing apart. Tears stung my eyes but I could only lie motionless. The nightmare lasted an eternity. I watched and felt everything he did to me, powerless to let out a scream for help.

170

Eventually, the darkness became my friend and freed me from the ordeal and when I woke the monster was gone. I was covered with a blanket and alone in the dark; I still couldn't move.

Little by little, my body started to return to life but my pyjamas were gone. I finally managed to crawl, naked, to the bathroom and reached the toilet. A thick jelly-like substance leaked from me, it had a disgusting odor that made me feel sick. This was no nightmare, the boogie man was real! I had felt this way before, the darkness and the dead feeling. The only difference this time, there was no sharp pain or needle to my neck.

So how did I end up this way, paralysed with the feeling of being dead again? – I asked myself.

I managed into the shower and attempted to scrub this man's smell from me before I sank to the floor and allowed the water to rain down on me.

"Nowhere is safe, nowhere is ever safe!" I repeated out loud.

Tears flowed. I huddled in the shower and a mist clouded my mind as I faded away. I woke later and saw my skin was wrinkled and leathery. Pins and needles spread through my body but I crawled out of the shower and pulled a towel from the radiator. I had to wait for the blood to recirculate around my body before I had enough strength to stand and stumble to the bedroom. I curled up into a ball on an armchair.

There isn't a sharp pain in my neck like before, no needle this time. So, how did I end up this way with a stranger doing what he did? Did Shawn put something in my drink? Has he allowed this man to enter my room? The phone call, he had ended so quickly at the mall 'everything was in place.' Was that about me? Had Shawn known what this man was going to do to me? - I questioned myself.

As dawn broke, the conclusion I came to involved the orange juice. It was the only thing that made any sense. With everything that had happened to me since Shawn entered our lives, my life, anything was possible. The sun streamed in the window marking a new day. I hadn't even realised that Susan had not used our bedroom. She must have stayed with Shawn.

Had she also known what was going to happen to me? - I was confused.

I found my silk pyjamas dumped on the floor beside the bed. Picking them up made me cringe. That evil man must have removed them from me when I had no way of defending myself.

Eventually, a glowing Susan knocked on the door. This was something I never really understood. Whenever Susan had been drinking and no matter how drunk she had been the night before, she always had a glow about her in the morning. She still reeked of alcohol but looked like she had had the best night's sleep ever.

"Mum, someone was in my room last night, someone attacked me!" I sobbed as she came in.

"Don't be so silly, it was just a bad dream. You know you suffer with them, don't ruin a good weekend," I was reminded that anything I said would fall on deaf ears.

Shawn appeared at the door.

"Are we ready to go?" he piped up.

Although he looked at me, he didn't bother to ask why I was crying. We made our way to reception and I felt even more distraught; Susan didn't seem to care about what I had tried to tell her.

A tall, grey-haired man, dressed in an expensive suit and with a gold watch, entered the reception area.

"Hello, mate. How was last night? Did you enjoy yourself?" Shawn asked.

He held his hand out to Shawn and pulled him close, whispering in his ear. Shawn looked like he had just been told off when the man finally released him from his grip.

"This is Susan and my little princess, Jessica," Shawn introduced us. Shawn couldn't hide his worried expression so whatever the man had said had rattled him.

"I really must be getting on," the man remarked as he shook Susan's hand.

He cast his eyes over to me and smiled. The top button of his shirt was undone and I could see the top of a scar. He was the boogie man, the one with no heart and he must have realised I recognized him. His smile turned into a grimace and he abruptly turned and walked away.

"Mum, Mum!" I shouted.

"That was the man! The man from last night who was ..., " but I didn't get the chance to say anymore.

Susan tugged at my arm and dragged me in the direction of the exit.

"Don't make a scene!" she interrupted then whispered in my ear. "He's an important friend of your father."

Sometimes in life there comes a point when you can't dig any deeper, I have tried. Some of my memories are still sealed under lock and key, maybe this rabbit hole just runs too deep. Maybe I would not find the path back from wonderland if I were to dig too deep.

What started as one turned into twelve, twelve evil monkeys, twelve demons, twelve men: twelve attacks that spanned over two years. A so-called family holiday was even invaded by one of the twelve.

Shawn and I walked past a block of many numbered rooms on holiday, a door was opened and I was pulled inside by a man with huge sideburns. It didn't matter how loud I screamed, his hand was so large compared to my face. He just blotted out any sounds that I made, as he pushed harder and covered my airway so I could not breathe.

Even today my partner tells me, I still scream in my sleep.

"No, no, no. Please don't!" I scream, as I frantically use my arms to shield myself from the demons that attack me while I sleep.

This happens most nights. I am told and it is as haunting and harrowing for him, as it is for me. I relive moments of my life in my dreams, twisted images and distorted faces that visit me. Paid-up members of the twelve evil monkeys, still attacking me and never allowing me any peace.

A man with nine toes and another with pinky-red marks covering his face, I named him the vimto man. The colour of his face reminded me of the drink, the disfigured man that made me squirm.

The twelve evil monkeys seemed to be dripping with wealth, expensive Rolex or Breitling watches. They all also smelt of expensive aftershave and most were immaculately dressed. A doctor, hotel owners, a public figure and a teacher, just to name a few. Some treated me rough, some were gentle. But all of them wanted the same thing. One wanted to have a bath with me, he wanted to wash me for some weird reason. I was petrified of what might come next and I actually thanked him as I left. He only wanted to bathe with me, that was his only fetish and he didn't hurt me.

They had one thing in common, they called me Daddy's Princess.

This only dawned on me while writing the previous chapter and I made the connection. Daddy's Princess must have been the name used by Shawn to advertise me. A sick place on the Dark Web hidden from prying eyes, where bids and trades are made. But not for stocks or shares, the deal that was made was for me! The scary part about all this, I often wondered what Shawn got in return.

I was fourteen years old and Shawn allowed me to be taken so brutally by these men; he might have been given other girls as a trade for his perverted pleasure or maybe he was simply paid in cash.

The thought and reality of this truly sicken me and it has knocked me sideways. There are most likely others that went through the same as I did and most likely still are. I do know some of these men still walk free and have never paid for their crimes. Twelve evil monkeys, twelve demons, twelve men, Twelve attacks but one of you left something behind.

Chapter 23

Caught on camera

My life had changed and things were becoming more difficult. It was scary knowing that strange things could happen to me therefore nowhere felt safe. Polly, my horse gave my life some purpose, she needed me and I needed her. I had completed a few more sessions with Cathy and had managed to talk to her. I would tell her about a friend of mine who had some problems and ask for advice on how to help my imaginary friend. This worked for me; it was easier to talk about a third person rather than myself. I knew she couldn't act on anything I said or prove that I was talking about myself. Every week we would meet up and have hot chocolate, a time for Cathy to listen to me without judgment. If she asked a question I didn't want to answer, she would allow me to avoid it without any pressure. She had become the only person in my life who gave me a chance to talk and have an opinion. Slowly my trust started to build during the sessions and I concluded that my entire life had been filled with lies.

I was asking questions about my life that had confused me for years, I wanted to know how other families acted towards each other. My childhood had been so fucked up; I didn't know what was right or wrong. This had caused me to be at war with myself. When I felt something was wrong, I didn't have an opinion. I was always bullied into thinking it was right.

It's just what dads do. I had learned to accept what Shawn was doing and dealt with it in my own way, even though deep down I knew it was wrong. I started to wonder why other kids seemed so happy if their dads were doing the same thing to them.

Is there something wrong with me? Why am I so different? - I often thought.

I had a million questions about my life and since the mysterious attacks by unknown men, I had a million more. I had been drugged and forced into situations that terrified me, my life had become petrifying.

When I look back, I must not forget I was a child at the time. I was a total loner and had no one in my life to talk to, everyone told me lies. After years of abuse, it just became my life, it became normal. But, Cathy was skilled and broke down what she wanted to pull out into manageable parts During her visits, she brought out doubts that had plagued me for years and helped me realise that what Shawn and Susan did was far from being right or normal. She had a massive web to unravel and it was going to take a long time to get to the bottom of my story.

I realised people had lied to me when Cathy opened my eyes; she found ways where I could divulge things that had haunted me. The fabrics and other methods she used gave me the freedom to express myself without actually verbalizing how I felt. The only sparse fabric was the red imprinted one. This was usually empty apart from the little boy or the toy horse. That's when we would talk about Jacob and Polly. The emptiness from that gave me clues; I had very little love in my life and it didn't feel as though my family loved me. All I craved from life was someone to adore me and now that I had some insight, it bothered me.

I loved Polly and I knew she loved me but this was different, Polly had been bought and she would have loved anyone who gave her apples. If she had been bought for another girl, Polly would have loved her instead. I severely lacked unconditional love.

Would I ever experience this? Am I actually capable of loving someone? Will anyone ever love me? - I mulled over these questions.

I was fourteen years old and everyone I had loved had walked out on me, beaten me, ridiculed me or taken advantage of me. My entire life was filled with false love made up of lies. My head was filled with so many questions, the hamster wheel started to turn again. The little guy was alive and running for me only this time the wheel was spinning in the opposite direction. I was re-addressing questions that I thought I had already answered.

A social worker visited me at school. I had been taken into the meeting room which was fast becoming my personal office. I didn't take to the social worker; she asked a string of questions and jotted my responses down onto her notepad. She had questioned me about Shawn but I refused to answer her. I walked out of the meeting.

Everyone seemed to want to rip my family apart, telling me they could take me to a safe place, but what they didn't know was that I had found my safe place; my silence. If I went to their safe place, I would no longer be the target but Jacob would be left in danger. Susan's drinking was out of control and, practically every night, Shawn was trying to protect me. I couldn't bear to think that Jacob would suffer the same as me.

Over the years despite what Shawn did to me, I had developed a bond with him. It had become normal in a strange way. But, because I had accepted years of constant sexual abuse, certainly didn't mean I liked or wanted it.

When I asked for Cathy's advice on behalf of my imaginary friend, she told me this was wrong, but Cathy was like the stranger telling me the sky was blue when all along I had believed it was pink. After a while, she got through to me and I would spend the entire week thinking about our sessions. This led to many sleepless nights as the hamster ran upon his wheel inside my head.

One night I could not sleep and decided to go for a smoke, it was late and everyone had already gone to bed. I crept out of my bedroom and made my way to the lounge and out of the French doors. Once outside, I realised that I had left my lighter in my bedroom. I didn't want to risk waking anybody up then I remembered Shawn kept lighters in his desk drawer. I found a lighter and when I closed the drawer, his computer screen lit up and my bedroom appeared on the screen. My empty bed and all my possessions were being recorded. Horrified, I sat down only to discover it wasn't only my bedroom that was being recorded. I clicked on the small squares beside the main screen and saw Susan and Shawn sleeping in their bed followed by Jacob curled up in his bed. The entire house was being filmed and suddenly, the penny dropped.

I always thought Shawn had some kind of sixth sense, he always seemed to know what was happening in the house even when he was out. He had been recording everything the entire time and he was recording me. It was as though a bell had chimed in my head. I moved the mouse to the drop-down menu where I found a file marked Jessica.

Oh God, do I really want to know? - I thought to myself.

Deep down, I knew what was there. I clicked the mouse on the file and a new screen opened. There were hundreds of little boxes with a play sign covering each image. I clicked one at random and a new screen popped up. The computer made a loud sound as it started to play. I nearly jumped out of my skin, so I paused the video and turned the volume down. I pressed play again and watched myself

178

walk into my room wrapped in a towel. I took the towel off and started to dry myself.

What the actual fuck! - I thought.

I clicked on another video and a new screen popped up. I pressed play and this time the camera was from a lower point of my bedroom, it faced directly towards my bed. Shawn walked into my bedroom and undressed; then I watched him rape me. Vomit started to rise in my mouth. I stopped the video while I composed myself. I took a deep breath before clicking on another video.

This one was different; it started with the camera being picked up and positioned to face another angle of my bed. I came into view sprawled out naked on my bed; I seemed to be awake but unconscious at the same time. The camera zoomed in on my vagina and someone's fingers were inserted into me. I fast-forwarded the video to a point where the camera was filming my lifeless body moving up and down. Then it zoomed in on my vagina again and focused on a penis moving in and out of me. I was in shock at what I had just witnessed so I turned the video off. Suddenly I heard a bedroom door open.

"Shit!" I muttered almost under my breath.

I hurriedly closed the pages and got the image of my bedroom back up. I heard someone shuffle towards the kitchen while the bloody screen was still lit up.

"Fuck!" I mumbled.

There was nothing I could do to close it down. I grabbed the lighter and crossed the lounge to the French doors. With shaking hands, I lit my cigarette, opened the door and stepped outside. Shawn switched the kitchen light on then made his way to the fridge. His computer screen was still lit but he hadn't noticed. He opened a bottle of coke and stood at the fridge drinking it. My heart was thumping and I could feel my throat and mouth going dry. He closed the fridge door and made his way into the lounge. The screen was still lit up; my heart was jumping. He walked straight past his desk and headed towards the balcony door where I was standing outside.

"Oh blimey, you made me jump what are you doing up?" he asked, as he placed a cigarette in his mouth and searched his pockets for a lighter.

"I couldn't sleep," I offered.

I watched the glimmer from the computer screen disappear.

"Have you got a light?" Shawn asked.

My head screamed; all I had was Shawn's lighter. It was only a disposable lighter but it had a recognizable pattern on it.

"Yes," I replied nervously.

I handed him the lighter. He lit up and took a long drag, then paused and looked at the lighter before handing it back to me.

Does he realise it's his lighter? - I started to tremble,

"It's freezing out here, I'm off to bed," I said, as I stubbed my own cigarette out.

"Night, sleep well," he replied.

I could almost feel his eyes burning into the back of my head as I hurried across the lounge and disappeared down the corridor. Once inside my bedroom, I jumped into bed and pulled the covers up over my head.

Shit, did he realise I had been at his desk? Fuck! Is he watching me now? - I wondered.

The hamster was sprinting again. The images I had seen on his computer started to fill my head, my lifeless body, my naked body filmed for his pleasure sickened me.

Is this what fucking dads do as well! - I thought as a rage built inside me. I had got annoyed before but this further invasion of my life angered me. I heard Shawn shuffle up the corridor then his bedroom door opened and shut. I pulled the covers from my head and turned my night light on. In the top corner of my room, a small box looked down on me; I had believed it was part of the alarm system. I have no idea

180

how I never noticed this camera before, it looked so obvious. I switched off the light and pulled the covers back over my head.

What the fuck do I do? If I rip the camera out, he'll know that I know. If he finds out I know, what will he do? Will he kick me out? - I was worried.

The thought of living in a cardboard box, cold hungry and living out of bins scared the shit out of me.

If I go to the police, will I be pulled away from my family and never be able to see Jacob again? What will happen to him? Where would he end up? Would he be left with Susan and Shawn? Would he then be destined to take the beatings or worse, visits from Shawn? However, if I say nothing, I will have to live a life where I know I'm being filmed! - I cried as sadness overwhelmed me.

Every escape plan or option I thought of carried a huge consequence, each with its horrors and each option scared the shit out of me. There was no way of escaping this and nowhere to run to either, I was royally fucked! That night, the hamster ran a marathon inside my head. I cried my heart out. I had no idea what to do anymore.

The next morning I got out of bed and went into the bathroom and only brushed my teeth. *Does he also have a hidden camera in the bathroom? If I was to pee will he be filming that too?* - I suddenly thought. I got dressed in the corner of my bedroom where I knew the angle of the camera angle didn't reach.

Chapter 24

Monster

Every corner hid a monster; even as I slept, a monster was watching. What I had learnt about the cameras was probably the most terrifying in a lot of ways; I had no privacy at all. Every single painful and terrifying moment caught on little fucking cameras and filmed for Shawn's own perverted personal pleasure.

He had already told me that he uploaded his special videos and photos for important people to see, on the Dark Web. This was most likely for the evil twelve monkeys and others like them. I wondered if they had watched me sleep at night then being raped by Shawn. It was one thing to be raped but the horror was stepped up when I found out he had broadcast it for others to see. Any victim would be sickened by this.

But, I was also feeling a different kind of sickness and nauseous and I often found myself vomiting. My body also felt different for some weird reason. Despite being sick, I was incredibly hungry most of the time. My body felt swollen and tingly. Susan heard me one morning as I vomited in the bathroom.

"Are you ok?" she asked.

"Yeah. I think I have a tummy bug, I've been sick every day this week," I explained.

She looked at me a second too long then walked into her bedroom. Moments later she handed me a small plastic pot.

"What's this for?" I asked.

"Pee in it and I'll take it to the doctor and find out if you are ok," she told me.

This seemed an odd request. Susan followed me as I walked back into the bathroom.

"Mum, I can't pee with you standing there," I announced through my embarrassment.

"Just pee, I am your mum for goodness sake," she scolded.

Eventually, I managed to do what she asked and Susan took the plastic pot from my hand.

"I'll take this to the doctor today. Now, get ready for school," she ordered.

That was odd, - I thought.

I dismissed the whole thing, got ready for school and left. When I came home, I saw an empty wine bottle. Susan had started to drink early so I quietly disappeared into my bedroom to avoid her. About half an hour later, I was getting changed when she appeared at my bedroom door.

"Look at you, you disgust me," I heard pure hatred in her voice.

Her top lip was curled and the slur was back in her voice, her face looked distorted.

"Mum, I'm just getting changed, that's all," I announced.

I knew only too well where this was going to lead and I was petrified.

"You think you are better than me, don't you? A little whore, that's all you are," her venomous words cut through me like a knife as saliva spat from her mouth.

"Mum, I don't ...," I was interrupted as the breath was taken from my body.

She had punched me full pelt in the stomach, this wasn't going to end well for me. I buckled over, winded from the punch as another almighty blow connected with my kidneys.

"You dirty little slag!" Susan screamed

I fell on my hands and knees and gasped for air. Hunched over on all fours, my body lifted with such force I spun on to my back. Susan had kicked me as hard as she could in my stomach. I was already gasping for air from the first rein of punches; her fierce kick left me unable to breathe. A tremendous pain ripped across the midsection of my body and hot pokers stabbed at my lungs.

"Get up, you little fucking tart! Get up!" she continued yelling.

She stood over me but she was not finished yet, even although I was down on the ground she still wanted more. I tried to get back up on my feet, but the pain was excruciating and I could only breathe in short gulps of air, enough to stop me from passing out.

"Whose is it!" she shrieked.

"Mum! What ... are ... you ... going ... on ... about?" I attempted to reply between each breath.

"You're a fucking liar," she screamed as another punch connected with my stomach.

I fell to the floor again but this time I huddled up into a ball. I gasped for air like a small fish out of water.

Another hit from her might just finish me off altogether, - I thought as I lay on the ground.

I looked up at her. She stared deep into my eyes as I watched the anger drift from her face. She looked confused, ashamed even. She turned and walked out of my room with her hand covering her

184

mouth. The mid-section of my body was on fire but I continued to lie on the floor, unable to breathe.

Why did she do that? What have I done wrong this time and what does she mean by whose is it? - I thought as I slowly crawled to the bathroom.

I locked the door and pulled my clothes off before I crawled into the shower and turned the taps on. The hot water stung my battered body. I watched a steady stream of blood disappear down the drain. Susan had done some very serious damage to me this time, the blood leaked from my vagina.

Over the next few days, I could not move and my entire stomach had gone dark with bruises. I was bedridden. I had no choice but to lie on towels otherwise my bed would have become saturated. The blood and small balls, like plum seeds, continued to flow from my body. My stomach had the worst cramps I have ever experienced in my life and I thought I was going to die. Susan would not take me to the hospital. There's no doubt she would have been asked about the cause of my horrendous bruising. Instead, she became my nurse and played the part of a worried mother. The biggest mind fuck I have ever experienced was when she nursed me back to health. She told me that I had had a very bad period and tried to convince me that the period had caused all the bruises too.

Does she really believe that I just had a bad period? - I wondered.

It was like she had created a fantasy world in her head and she wanted me to do the same.

Susan had beaten me so badly that day I believe she had caused a miscarriage. She had once told me that Shawn was unable to have kids, I don't know why he couldn't; she never told me the reason. Shawn had never gotten me pregnant before, even after years of abuse from him so there probably was some truth to what she had told me. The only other person who could have been the father was one of the twelve evil monkeys. The grey-haired man from the hotel to be exact; the boogie man with no heart. This dirty man had left me with an innocent child growing inside me, after what he did. That was until Susan murdered it!

Chapter 25

A family affair

It took nearly four weeks for me to recover. The bruises still surrounded my belly and strange shades of yellow had replaced the black and purple. My stomach pains and cramps had also eased. Susan had beaten me on many occasions before but never so violently. I truly believed that she would have killed me that day if she had carried on.

I had always been very wary of her but, after that day, I was scared of her. I think she even scared herself that day. Her attitude towards me changed and she began to act like a mother who loved her child. This was a total head fuck! Maybe she felt guilty for what she had done and how far she had taken it that day. That was not the only thing that started to change in the house.

Shawn was changing as well. He appeared to be tired of Susan's drinking and her outbursts. When arguments erupted or Susan was being irrational, he just gave up and walked away. He no longer tried to put his point across or to calm her down. He also changed towards me, rather than being an abuser all the time, he started to act more like a dad, helping me with the cooking and protecting me from Susan's drunken rages. Even though he was still visiting me, he gave me the impression he was bored of me. Maybe I was no longer a challenge, maybe I was broken. He had smashed me into unrepairable pieces and maybe this took the excitement away.

Because he was acting like a dad, a different bond developed between us. Strangely, I felt safer with Shawn than I did with Susan. His visits continued, although they were less frequent and, on two occasions, Jacob caught him in the act. He ran away to tell Susan that Shawn was hurting me but she just ignored him and told him to stop being silly. At almost seven years old, Jacob was still too young to understand, but I know the memories of what he saw still haunt him today. He has questioned me about it as he tries to deal with his demons.

My life was harrowing in so many ways, the twelve evil monkeys and the cameras dotted around the house were always a concern. I spent my life looking over my shoulder and trying to work out ways to avoid being filmed. Maybe this added to Shawn's boredom; he no longer got the footage that he once did; he no longer got the thrill he once had.

Five or six months had passed since Susan had practically beaten me to a pulp. I returned home from school one day and, for some reason, I was later than normal. Jacob was at his friend's house and Shawn had already ordered take out by the time I had got home. He seemed annoyed that I had arrived home so late and Susan was in the lounge chatting with two men.

"Eat your dinner," Shawn snapped at me.

"I'm not hungry," I replied.

Whenever other people were around I tried to avoid food and drink.

"Eat it!" he became impatient.

I sat down and took a few mouthfuls before I got up to go to the bathroom. With two other men in the house, the quicker I was behind a locked door the better. I hoped the men would leave and I was prepared to wait in the bathroom until they did. I spent about half an hour sitting on the bathroom floor reading a magazine before I decided to have a shower to pass some more time. I stripped naked and stepped in, as the water hit me I started to feel dizzy and my body felt heavy. A feeling I had felt before although certainly not as powerful

Bang! Bang! Someone was knocking on the bathroom door.

"I'm in the shower," I shouted out.

"Oh, Jessica, open the door," a voice I did not recognise shouted back.

I didn't reply. I stood in the shower petrified looking at the door.

Bang! A loud thud against the door and the entire door vibrated.

"Oh my God, please no!" I muttered to myself.

By now, my body was trembling and I felt as though I was about to fall. Bang! The door vibrated again as I backed myself to the corner of the shower. I had nowhere to hide. I was trapped, naked, in the bathroom with only a tiny lock to protect me. Bang! The lock gave and the door burst open. Two men stood at the doorway as I screamed. They barged their way into the bathroom and one of them tried to pull me from the shower. I swung to punch him but my arms were weak. I slipped and fell on the shower tray. As I hit the hard surface with a thud, the first man grabbed my ankle and dragged me out of the shower. I tried my best to grab hold of anything I could but everything was slippery. I landed on the tiled floor.

The skin on my back was cut open as I was tugged across the mottled surface of the tiles. A thin trail of blood was left behind. I managed to grab the architraves that surrounded the door to prevent the man from hauling me further. The second man prised each of my fingers from the door frame and, as soon as my first hand lost its grip, so did the other. I found myself being dragged along the corridor and into the lounge. The first man grabbed my wrists and together they lifted me onto the sofa. I tried my hardest to wriggle free but the darkness was starting to take hold and they succeeded in pinning me down. The first man who had grabbed me by my ankles started to undo his jeans while the other held my arms above my head.

Susan was sitting upright on the opposite chair and stared at me with dead eyes.

"Mum!" I screamed frantically but she just continued to stare and didn't say a word.

"She can't hear you, Princess," the creepy man pinning me down said.

I looked over to Shawn who was sitting on his desk chair.

He was sipping on a bottle of Budweiser beer, watching me but not saying a word.

"Dad, please help me!" I pleaded.

He did nothing but carried on watching what was unfolding in front of him. The man who had dragged me then dropped his jeans and started to rub himself against me. He took over pinning my wrists to the sofa so the other one let go and walked over to Susan. He started to undress her but she didn't move or even blink.

"Mum!" I screamed out again.

She still didn't respond, she continued to stare at me with dead eyes. The man carried on rubbing himself against me despite me trying to wriggle free. He laughed at me. The other one had stripped naked and picked Susan up. She looked like a rag doll as he placed her on the floor. He then stepped back and stared at Susan. He came over to where I was being pinned down.

"Look they have the same fannies," he joked and all three of them burst out laughing.

Both men repeatedly raped me and Susan that evening while Shawn watched and drank his beer. Susan didn't make a sound; her dead eyes stared straight ahead. Her eyes and the look on her face that night will never leave me. Her dead eyes seemed to watch me while

I watched her. We were both repeatedly brutally raped by these sick men and Shawn just let it happen.

The next day Susan seemed odd and was unaware of what had happened to her. It was obvious she had been heavily drugged. I had been under the influence too but the dosage didn't knock me out, it wasn't enough to save me from the ordeal. I was aware of every detail and the pain and terror. My body was cut to shreds by the flooring tiles that left thousands of paper type cuts across my back. One of the worst things about this entire ordeal was that I knew one of the attackers well and would have to see him again.

Chapter 26

Making a deal with the Devil

The rest of the week, everything was different. Although I wanted to talk to her about what happened, Susan seemed locked in her thoughts. It was difficult to tell if she had any idea what had happened to her that night and I was scared of her reaction if I was to hint at it. There was the risk that somehow it would all become my fault if she didn't believe me. I could not take a chance of another kicking from her, so I didn't say anything. What was the point?

The devil had left Shawn and he was back to acting like a dad. But that night, although he hadn't got involved, he watched, drank beer, laughed and gave instructions to the two men about what they were or were not allowed to do. I knew one of the men, he was well known public figure and every time I bumped into him, I felt his stare on me. I had never felt anger towards someone like this before, I was furious and my blood boiled whenever he was around. I desperately wanted to tell someone what he had done but the thought of people knowing that he had touched me, sickened me. This man's breath was the worst I had ever smelt, it was as though someone had taken a shit in his mouth.

When I walked to school each morning, that's the time I would encounter him. I prayed that he would disappear and I wouldn't have to see him. But he didn't and, like my other abusers, I had to learn how to face the situation. As a young schoolgirl, this was extremely difficult to deal with and caused untold anxiety.

I returned to school and tried my best to stay away from the house as much as possible. I was still furious about everything that had happened, I took my normal place at the back of the classroom. The first and second periods came and went and I have no idea what I was meant to be learning. Visions of what I had seen that night stuck on the forefront of my mind, there was no shaking it. Susan's dead eyes and everything they did to us kept flashing into my mind. During the third period, one of the ambassadors came into my class and handed me a note. An ambassador's job was the same as a prefect but, in our school, those from first year were used as ambassadors to help with reception duties.

'Jessica please meet your mother in town at the coffee shop after school today instead of going home,' the note read.

Instead of going home. Why was I not allowed to go home? - I wondered.

I became concerned. Susan had never sent a note to the school before, not one like this anyway.

Was I getting kicked out? What else can it be? Am I going to be tossed out onto the street, homeless with nowhere else to go? Susan must be wanting to meet me in town to hand me a bag of clothes. I bet she'll be happy about that. It's quite clear that she doesn't want me around. She never has a nice word to say about me. - I thought to myself, as the poor hamster was back on his wheel, running as fast as he could.

Where will I sleep, where will I get food? – my thoughts were running wild.

My mind tried to come up with a plan before the inevitable happened.

The bell rang to signal the end of the third period and I felt the hamster fall on his little wheel from the shock of the bell ringing. I snapped out of my frantic thoughts and looked around the room; the other students were gathering their belongings and filing out of the classroom.

Why can't I just be like them, normal with normal families? - I wondered. They seemed happy, laughing and joking with their friends, leaving me feeling alone and unnoticed. I gathered my belongings and left the classroom but I didn't join the others, I headed back to the only place I felt safe, the girls' toilets. The bell for the fourth period rang but I continued sitting in the cubical. It was as though I was frozen in time. I was unable to face people again. All I could do was think about my fate that lay ahead. The final bell of the day rang, the bell I had been dreading since I was handed the note. I waited for the noise in the hallways to dampen down and the school to fall into an eerie silence.

"Well, I had better get this over with then," I muttered.

I picked up my bag from the floor and made my way out of the toilets, into the corridor and out into the cold air.

The town was about 45 minutes away by foot and I found myself jogging most of the way, part of me wanted to know what this was about and part of me didn't. However, I knew the earlier I got this over with, the quicker I could work out what I was going to do. Eventually, I arrived at the edge of Truro town centre, took my mobile out of my pocket and sent a simple text to Susan.

'I'm here, where do you want to meet?'

'We're at the coffee shop.'

I spied Susan and Jacob sitting in the corner of the coffee shop when I walked through the door. Three large hot chocolates were waiting on the table and three suitcases were also sitting on the floor.

194

It isn't just me getting kicked out, it's all of us, - I thought.

I could see Susan had been crying.

"We have to move Jessica, I need to protect the both of you," Susan announced as I sat down.

Protect us, this is new, - I scoffed inwardly.

"Why what's happened?" I asked.

I looked over at Jacob who was already using his finger to eat the cream from the top of his drink.

"It doesn't matter!" she replied sharply. "I just need to make sure you are safe."

Susan looked me straight in the eye.

Safe? She's never cared before, why now? - I wondered.

I took a sip of my hot drink.

"I've spoken to Jasmine and we're going to stay with her for a few days," Susan sniffed as tears welled in her eyes.

When we lived in our council house, Jasmine had lived on the same street. I got on well with her brother, Carl; we grew up together. Jasmine had become good friends with Laura before Susan had kicked her out of the house. Alcohol issues had also dominated their family life and, ironically, Jasmine and Carl had spent a lot of time at our house when they were looking for a place of safety. Susan had given them somewhere to stay when things got difficult. She had comforted them both and Jasmine had come to see Susan as a mother figure. She had no idea that Susan was just the same; a rotten drunk.

"Jasmine only has a one-bedroomed flat, how are we all going to fit in there?" I asked. "We will have to make do, now drink your drink," Susan started tapping away on her mobile phone.

Her lips formed a little smirk appeared which told me she was texting Shawn. The entire situation was quite surreal and not what I had expected. We sat quietly and I took another sip of my hot chocolate.

"Drink up. Jasmine should be home soon," Susan said, breaking the silence before gulping down the remainder of her drink.

"Oh, Jacob, for God's sake," Susan cried out in frustration.

I looked over at Jacob; the contents of his mug were everywhere. Not only did he have chocolate and cream all over his face but also his top was splattered with the runny mixture. He had a silly grin on his face which broke the tension and made me laugh

"Jessica, sort him out," Susan demanded.

She couldn't hide the irritation in her voice as she handed me some baby wipes.

We left the coffee shop and began the walk to Jasmine's, Susan marched in front of us at breakneck speed. Jacob and I could barely keep up. Eventually, we arrived and Susan rang the bell.

"Come in! You all must be freezing," Jasmine said when she opened the door

She welcomed us into her home.

Jasmine was in her late twenties, she had long, blond, flowing hair, large blue eyes and a pretty face. But her best feature was her smile; it always seemed so warm-hearted. Her flat was tiny with a combined kitchen and living room. It was clean and well-kept but hardly big enough for four people to live in.

"Make yourself comfy. Jessica and Jacob, you guys can have the bed and we will have to make do with the sofa," Jasmine pointed in the direction of the bedroom.

Jacob and I walked into the bedroom and found a double bed and a small dressing table. This wasn't going to be a long-term solution and I suddenly missed my bedroom. I would have to share a room and a bed with monkey boy.

"I'm just going to pop to the shop to get some wine," Susan announced.

We had hardly been there five minutes and already she wanted to hit the bottle.

"Well, let's get you settled in," Jasmine said as soon as Susan had left the flat.

196

I thought I detected a slightly irritated tone.

Jacob and I stayed in the bedroom most of the night. I could hear Susan slurring her words as she complained to Jasmine about Shawn. Jasmine came into the bedroom to check on us and I could tell this was an excuse to get a breather from Susan's six-hour ramble.

For the next three weeks, this became our life. Jacob and I went to school then spent the evening in the bedroom. Susan got drunk and talked to Jasmine about Shawn for hours. Jasmine tried to busy herself or make excuses to leave Susan in the living room, her resolve was weakening. Her home had been invaded and Susan was drunk every day.

This living arrangement was becoming a struggle for everyone, arguments started to break out over the smallest of things. The once tidy flat became messy, it was cramped and nobody had any private space. This arrangement had a sell-by date and we were already well past it. Susan was stuck in a bubble, drowning her sorrows. She hadn't done anything to try and sort out our latest dilemma. Our current situation was going to dissolve.

I couldn't see a way out so I begged Shawn to take her back. As I saw it, this was the only option we had left although I was sure what the consequences would be. He was our only lifeline because Susan had already given up her council house when we moved in with him. I used to text Shawn each night to explain our dilemma; sometimes he would reply but, in the main, he ignored me. This was hurting. He had been in my life for a long time and, even although he was the devil incarnate, I had learned to accept him. He had broken me to the point where I was accepting of his evil ways. I did not enjoy anything he put me through but I had become used to his ways.

I likened it to a prisoner being released after ten years. His dream had come true but, once outside, the difficulties involved in adjusting to a new life would be overwhelming and the place he was freed from became the very place he now craved. The sudden change in our circumstances made me want the life we once had. Shawn had become a big part of my life and, now that we were struggling, it didn't seem to matter what was right or wrong anymore. I missed my bedroom, my belongings, my personal space and Polly. We were now living under pressure and it was only a matter of time before something was going to give. It was inevitable.

One afternoon, I returned home after school only to discover that the first casualty of this situation was Jasmine. She had opted to move out of her own home and find sanctuary somewhere else. This meant only one thing, Susan was the only adult in the house and she was drinking heavily. It didn't take a rocket scientist to work out that Susan would turn violent again. Daily, I watched her anger grow.

In the weeks since we had moved in, Susan had managed to hide her anger from Jasmine. If I walked into the lounge, Susan would look at me in disgust but she was able to control what would have normally been the accompanying snide comment. Jasmine noticed this and would give Susan and me confused looks as the room fell into silence. With Jasmine gone, Susan had no reason to contain herself anymore. I would soon fall victim to Susan's rages once again; major chinks were appearing in her armour. A few days after Jasmine had left, I was wakened by Susan. I could smell alcohol on her breath.

"Jessica, can you go and get my jeans from the washing line?" she asked.

I was to walk less than ten yards to the small garden to get her jeans, there were levels of laziness but this was taking the piss!

"Can you not get them yourself?" I asked sleepily.

"No, you go and get them!" Susan screamed at me.

"Just wear my jeans, they're over there. I'm trying to sleep," I suggested.

The anger in my voice was because of the stupidity of Susan's demand. It probably took more effort to wake me than it would have done if she'd gotten the jeans herself.

"You lazy slag!" Susan yelled aggressively.

She turned and walked out of the bedroom. She didn't want her jeans at all, she only wanted an argument and stupidly I had been too tired to realise what was going on. I leapt out of bed and began to put my clothes on. I knew this was not over yet. I could hear Susan mumbling to herself in the lounge, her rage was building.

"Fucking ungrateful slut, you can't even be arsed to do the smallest of things," she shouted at me from the lounge

Susan would wind herself up to the point where the anger that had been building for weeks would explode. No one else was around to intervene this time, I was about to take the full brunt of her rage. For all I knew, a pending missile was about to head directly towards me so I needed to remove myself fast. I hurried to pull on my trainer but it was as though I suddenly had two left feet. My damn trainer was refusing to go on. Finally, it did and I grabbed my phone, but it was too late. Susan appeared at the doorway and blocked my exit. She looked like a raging bull and I may as well have been dressed all in red.

"You are a dirty little slag! You can't do anything right can you! Why is it everyone wants you and not me!" Susan pointed in my face as spit flew out of her mouth.

"Mum, please just let me go," I begged.

I could not handle another beating.

"Let's face it, you fucking slag, you stole Shawn and ruined my fucking life," she yelled accusingly.

"Mum, I didn't steal anything, it's not my fault," I pleaded with her.

By this time, I was backed against the bedroom wall and I couldn't move.

"Why the fuck do you think we left? You fucking idiot, he only wants you not me!" her eyes were locked firmly on mine.

As an active volcano does, she was about to erupt.

"Oh, and Jasmine left a note. She wants me to leave but guess what? She's happy for you to stay. Everyone wants you and not me. Let's ring your new boyfriend, shall we? Get him to pick up his little tart," she screeched.

She reached into her pocket, pulled out her mobile phone and dialed Shawn.

"Hello," Shawn's voice echoed through the speaker.

"You had better come and get your dirty little slag, I'll have her ready for you," she snapped.

With the call ended and her phone back into her pocket, I took the chance to run. I slipped past her and made a bolt for the door. I wasn't quick enough. I felt her hand grabbing my hair before I was yanked back. Then, with full force, my head was slammed into the bedroom mirror hanging on the wall. The mirror shattered into thousands of pieces and I fell to the floor. My head was ringing and everything had gone hazy. I could hear Susan shouting behind me but I couldn't make out what she was saying. A warm trickle of blood ran from my forehead and down my left cheek. I reached up and pressed my finger into the thick, red fluid. I could feel fury building inside me, a fury like I had never felt before.

Fight back! - a voice inside my head screamed at me, enough was enough.

In a flash, my senses returned to me as my body took over from my brain. I was just a passenger along for the ride. I got back up on my feet much to Susan's surprise. I grabbed her hair and smashed her head into the broken mirror. She fell to the floor and the remaining shards drizzled down on her. I stood over her only to find the fury that had taken over my body, had faded.

What have I done? - I stood back.

The realization of what I had just done started to set in. Susan didn't appear to be moving and neither was she making any noise.

Oh fuck, have I just killed her? - I wondered

200

A feeling of guilt clouded my soul.

Why do I feel guilty? - I asked myself.

Instead of saving me from her perverted boyfriend, she believed I had stolen him.

Stolen him! The man who was meant to be my father figure, the man she made me call dad! She brought him into my life, she allowed him to drug and rape me repeatedly and allowed his so-called friends to do the same. I'm still a child! I've neither asked for this life that she's given me nor asked Shawn to do the things he does to me. She knows what he's been doing all along, yet she still blames me for her actions and then has the fucking cheek to ring him. Just to hand me back! I'm just a piece of shit, I mean nothing to her! - I justified my actions.

She deserved this. What I had done was nothing compared to the things that she had inflicted upon me. During the commotion, Jacob had wakened and was sitting up in bed. He stared at me as Susan lay on the ground. I heard Susan moan and she started to move again. I was thankful she wasn't dead.

What will she do to me after what I've just done to her? - I suddenly thought.

I couldn't leave Jacob here with her but at the same time, I needed to get out of this situation fast.

"Jacob, get your shoes on quickly," I said softly as I started to make my way back into the bedroom.

Without warning, my hair was yanked again and I felt chunks ripping from my scalp. I screamed out in pain. Susan pulled me across the room backwards by my hair and opened the front door. The next thing I knew I was thrown out onto the pavement, the door was slammed shut and my face dampened with a steady stream of blood.

"Jacob," I shouted, as I got my feet and banged on the door.

I heard other doors slam shut inside and the flat fell into silence. I didn't know what to do next, homeless again and this time I had nowhere else to go. My biggest fear had just become a reality. Laura was not an option anymore and, as for Jack, God knows where he was. My head pounded and tried to wipe the blood away as it ran into my stinging eyes. I was up shit creek without a paddle and the only familiar place I thought of was school. I still felt safe there.

I turned into the next street and, on the opposite side, I saw Shawn's purple Cherokee Jeep parked up. An overwhelming sense of relief washed over me. Here was someone who could help me, even if it was the devil. I opened the car door and jumped in. Through my tears, I tried to tell him what had just happened.

"Mum has just done it again. She hates me," I sobbed.

He reached over and cuddled me.

"It's ok, I've got you now," he reassured me.

He told me that I could go back to live with him but I had to wait a couple of hours because he had a friend at the house who was in the process of leaving. He promised he would come back to meet me outside my school as soon as he had dealt with his friend. He gave me some money and baccy and I watched the jeep drive away. I had been saved by the devil. Even as I wondered what the cost would be, I knew that, without him, I would be eating from bins and sleeping on the streets. I started walking to my school and, along the way, I kept going over what had just happened.

How has my life come to this? Is this really the best idea, going to live with Shawn? - I wondered but I had no other options.

No one else was going to take me in. The adrenaline had worn off and the pain from my injuries started to hurt, my head was a mess.

Will he act like a dad or will I be expected to do other things? - I began to worry.

I reached the school gates but, because it was a Sunday, they were closed. I slumped down on the ground and rolled a cigarette.

Have I just sold my soul for food and shelter? Does this make me a bad person?' – my thoughts were going wild again.

202

It seems difficult to imagine, no one but my rapist to care for me. I wondered if I should have gone to the police but I didn't trust them. They had already let me down and sent me back to Susan. I couldn't see how it would be different this time. I had little to no confidence and I didn't blend in well with society. I probably would only have lasted a week living rough on the streets before some ordeal would have consumed me. I already knew monsters were real and Shawn was the devil that I already knew.

I watched the purple Cherokee Jeep pull up to the curb in front of me and, as I stepped into the car, I realized I had made a deal with the devil.

Chapter 27

Nowhere is safe

Michelle Branch quietly singing Everywhere on the car radio broke the eerie silence on the fifteen-minute journey to Shawn's house. I felt the music was following me, it was everywhere, reminding me that Shawn's evil presence filled the place I once called home.

What does this deal hold for me, - I wondered.

I put on a brave face but inwardly I was petrified. The trees lining the driveway stared at me, judging and accusing. The lifeless leaves littering Jacob's trampoline signalled a warning of decay and destruction.

The car headlights lit up the driveway, giving it a sensation of mystery. In the semi-darkness, the house looked abandoned and sinister; gloom replaced its once fresh appearance. I looked out at the kind of house found in horror movies. The place that people avoided, not daring to approach on Halloween because of the demonic stories associated with it.

We only moved out a few weeks ago. How can everything have changed so much? - I asked myself.

Every fibre in my body told me this was no longer my home; things felt wrong and distorted. Immediately Shawn pulled on the handbrake, I wanted to run from the bad vibes. He killed the engine and my stomach retched.

"Are you ready? Shall we go in?" Shawn turned to show me his childlike grin.

"I suppose so," I covered my anxiety by bending down to pick up my baccy.

Shawn stepped out and, by the time I looked up, he was opening my door.

Why did he do that? He's never done that for me before, - I was confused.

In the past, I had watched from the bedroom window as he opened the car door for Susan. Now I sensed he was treating me like her, but I wasn't comfortable with his simple act; he had become a nervous stranger.

I followed him to the front door. It swung open to reveal the dark, uninviting entrance. When the hallway lit up, it was familiar but somehow different. We headed through to the kitchen. Dirty coffee cups and plates filled the sink; empty beer bottles and takeaway boxes littered the worktops. The once clean and tidy kitchen smelled of rotting food.

"I'm sorry. I've been really busy and haven't had time to sort this out," Shawn explained by way of an apology.

Busy? Shawn never really did anything, did he mean lazy? - I laughed to myself.

He attempted to get some semblance of order by moving a couple of beer bottles and stacking a few empty pizza boxes. I glanced around and noticed an empty shot glass with a child's watch inside. It was pretty, a girl's watch.

"Whose watch is that?" I asked pointing at the glass.

"I don't know, I thought it was yours," Shawn replied.

"No, it's not mine," I said.

"Oh, I don't know then. I found it lying around," he shrugged his shoulders. "Why don't you have a shower while I sort this mess out? I'll order some food, how does that sound?" I sensed he was trying to change the subject.

He averted his eyes and threw beer bottles into the bin.

"Is it ok to get some clothes from my room?" I asked in the hope that my belongings were still there.

"Yes, of course. It's your room, it's how you left it," he reminded me. I tentatively opened the bedroom door. The wardrobe door lay open revealing a row of empty hangers. Susan had grabbed my clothes the day she left. Everything else had been left undisturbed as though waiting patiently for my homecoming. Now that I had returned, I felt like an infiltrator.

I picked up a towel from the end of my bed and closed the bedroom door behind me and headed to the shower. A chill rushed down my spine when I realized I couldn't lock the bathroom door. The broken snib sparked memories of that fateful night. But, I was momentarily distracted by grubby, wet towels strewn across the floor; someone had used the shower.

Traces of yellow pee covered the toilet seat. Shower gel bottles and a toothbrush I didn't recognize, lay on the sink. I cringed. The bathroom felt foreign to me. I wiped down the toilet seat, flushed the chain then placed the used towels in the washing basket. A quick clean to the shower meant I was ready to undress and step in.

The luxury of warm water sprinkling over my body and easing the pain from Susan's punches was amazing. The stream of blood trickling down the drain was nothing new to me and didn't detract from the comfort of the shower cubicle. Reluctantly, I turned off the taps and stepped out. I wiped the steamed-up mirror and looked at my reflection.

A different Jessica stared back; I was fourteen years old but my look failed to disguise my harrowing story. My tired, pain-filled eyes sat deep set on my pale, lined face. I had aged. I had seen the same look on Louise when I met her at Steve and Angie's house and had wondered why, I now understood. By the time I returned to the kitchen, Shawn had cleaned up and was in the middle of making some tea.

"How was your shower?" he asked.

"Yeah, it was good thanks. I really needed it," I smiled.

"Food should be here soon."

I felt weak and, without hesitation, sat down at the breakfast bar.

"I'm starving, it's ages since I ate," I wished for a plate of food to immediately appear in front of me.

"I've ordered your favourite sweet and sour chicken," he announced, placing a mug of hot tea in front of me.

The delivery arrived and, as Shawn went to the door, I glanced around the kitchen. The glass with the watch was now a shelf, it looked like a trophy on display.

Where did that watch come from? Why does he have it?' - I asked myself.

For a split second, I wondered if the watch was a trophy, one that had belonged to some other poor young girl. Shawn took a seat beside me and began to serve the food. As I ate, my weakness dissipated

"So, what's been happening?" he placed his fork down on his empty plate.

"Mum's drinking has gotten worse," I admitted.

There was no need to explain about the beatings; Shawn could see my bruises. The only real common ground we shared, related to Susan's drinking episodes how they ended up.

"Yes, I certainly don't miss that," he looked down at the kitchen worktop.

"I do miss your mum and I miss you though. This place has not been the same since you all left," I heard his words and wondered if he was about to break down.

"It's been really bad. I feel like I have been pushed from pillar to post. I never feel safe or secure," I surprised myself with my admission.

I sensed we shared similar pain and sadness which encouraged me to open up. We were both casualties of the aftermath of Susan's war. The only hint of sadness I had seen in Shawn before was when his gran passed away. But, I wasn't sure if that had been a true emotion. His sadness evaporated once he inherited the money from her estate. This was different, I detected a real sadness and loss; he seemed lonely.

I rarely felt safe with Shawn but that night I didn't dread his company. The monster I had witnessed had been replaced by an understanding and comforting individual. The change in him encouraged me to talk for hours.

"Jessica, you're bleeding!" Shawn interrupted our conversation.

I hadn't noticed the thin trickle of blood from a gash winding its way down my cheek. Shawn found a first aid kit and a small, black pouch. Carefully, he wiped away the blood and dressed the cut then picked up the pouch and opened it to reveal a small pot of clear liquid and a syringe.

"Why do you have that?" I jumped up.

Whatever was in the syringe was not going near me.

"Just something to take the edge off," he muttered.

He grabbed my arm.

"No! Get that away from me!" I protested.

But, I was too late; Shawn had already thrust the needle into my neck. Almost instantly, the room started to spin and I felt my body numbing over. I disappeared into unconsciousness. My disorientation meant I could feel the weight of someone on me although they seemed far away. It felt as though my eyelids had been taped shut and my body had sunk into the ground. I managed to open my eyes slightly and, through my distorted vision, I made out an unknown, hazy figure moving around on top of me before I lapsed back into unconsciousness.

When I opened my eyes again, the clock facing me read 02.35 am, the blue, digital glow showed me I was no longer in the kitchen. Dizziness took hold again until I saw 04.47 am displayed. I knew by the red silk bedding I was in Shawn's bed. Lying there, naked, his overweight, nude body sprawled out next to me.

What has he given me and what has he done to me? - my head reeled.

My body began to shut down again, I had lost control.

It was 7 o'clock before I could finally move. Sunlight beamed across the room and dust danced in the light. Although still heavy, my body and my mind were coming back to life. Physical movement was lagging behind a mental drive, but I managed to roll onto my side. Once my feet felt solid ground, I pulled myself up to a seated position. When I had the balance to stand, I left the snoring Shawn behind me. Fighting to hold back the vomit that had gathered in my throat and mouth, I made it to the bathroom and emptied my stomach.

"How could I have been so stupid," I scolded myself.

I only had myself to blame; the moment I stepped into his car I knew something like this could happen.

Does this make me a slut? Have I really just traded my body for food and shelter? Am I a bad person? What else am I meant to do? - questions flew around in my head.

Ashamed, dirty and disgusted, I stepped into the shower and let the hot water mix with my tears. In my bedroom, I dressed but not for school, this was my first day of work experience in a local hotel.

God, how am I going to get to work on time? - I asked myself as I gathered the few things I needed.

Through his bedroom door, I saw Shawn was already awake and pulling a t-shirt over his head

"I need a lift to work," I said as coldly as I could muster.

"Sure," he replied.

While he continued dressing, I moved into the kitchen where the plates from the take-out still sat on the breakfast bar. I stared at the empty syringe and wondered if it was the same one from the day on the balcony.

"Are you ready?" Shawn called out, interrupting me as I contemplated how much my life had changed since then.

Shawn had already started the jeep and, judging by the speed of his actions, he needed me out of the way. My dull mood was mocked by the bright sunlight which illuminated the outside world. I screwed up my eyes against its dazzle and jumped into the jeep.

"So, do you want me to pick you up tonight?" Shawn asked as we sped off in the direction of Newquay.

"Yeah, I suppose so."

I was homeless and didn't have any money.

What am I going to do? - I wondered again.

My only option came with a heavy price; food and shelter for sexual favours.

Could I really live like this? - I asked inwardly.

I was distracted when we pulled up outside the hotel. Shawn leaned over to kiss me but I turned so his lips only touched my cheek before I jumped out.

"Good luck," he called after me.

I closed the car door and watched him speed away.

Get your shit together, Jessica, - I told myself.

I looked at the grey smoke from my cigarette as it drifted away and my nerves started to settle. The beautiful building I was looking at held both happy and sad memories for me. The Headland Hotel oozed with palatial magnificence. Perched on the cliff's edge, it proudly overlooked the beach below. The grand, gothic entrance was dwarfed by castle towers which disappeared into the blue sky.

I walked up the stone steps and pushed the door open. The sheer size of the banqueting hall overwhelmed my tiny, insignificant figure. Even the highly polished grand piano looked trivial as it melted into a corner where gold-leaf framed paintings of regal faces hung from the walls. The plush pile of the carpet on the sweeping staircase was secured by beaming, brass bars, finishing off the luxurious look. In an adjoining room, a few smartly dressed people sat on large, leather loungers, reading newspapers; their flip flops and beachwear abandoned for the moment. In an adjoining room, the high ceiling sheltered the pastel-painted dining room where white table cloths and shining silverware adorned the dining tables.

"Can I help you, madam?" a soft voice broke my trance. "Madam?" As there was no one else around; it seemed the smartly dressed lady behind the antique reception desk was addressing me.

"Madam, can I help you?" she repeated.

"Yes, sorry," I walked towards her. "Hi, I'm Jessica. I'm here for work experience."

"Yes, yes. We've been expecting you, Jessica. That door leads to the kitchen, you should report to the chef," the receptionist instructed.

"Ok, thanks," I replied.

With a final glance and a smile, she began tapping on her keyboard. Inside the kitchen, square, white tiles on walls and stainless-steel worktops were in stark contrast to the muted colours of the area I had just passed through. Pots and pans bubbled and the people cooking, chopping and cleaning created a buzz. An older man was shouting something at a girl in her twenties.

"Yes, Chef," she shouted back once he had finished.

A feeling of panic told me to turn on my heel.

"Who are you?" the man I know knew as Chef stood in front of me.

"Urm, I'm Jessica, work experience," I stuttered.

"Well, Jessica work experience, do you know what a potato is?" he narrowed his eyes.

Towering above me, he oozed superiority.

"Urm, yes." I continued stammering.

"Yes what?" he barked.

"Yes, Chef," I offered

If the staff weren't staring then, they must have been sniggering.

"That's better. Right, put this on and follow me," Chef instructed

I took the apron, hairnet and white hat and followed him as he turned on his heel and snaked towards the food preparation counter. Without help, I struggled with my new outfit.

"That looks shit! Do it again!" Chef bellowed at one of the workers.

I almost fell over Chef as he stopped to pick up a box of potatoes. He picked one out and held it close to my face.

"Jessica work experience! This is a potato, this is a potato peeler and that's a pile of potatoes that need peeling. Do you understand?" his demeanour was as intimidating as his height.

"Yes, Chef." I nodded.

His job was done; the pile of potatoes and one petty peeler were now mine.

"What are you doing? For fuck's sake!" he screamed, marching off towards his next victim.

Jessica work experience! Does he think that's my name or is he just being funny? - I started to peel the potato.

After twenty minutes and a few peels under my belt, I took the opportunity to look up at the buzzing kitchen. I had enjoyed my mind-numbing task; it blotted out thoughts of my life.

Chef's kitchen ran like clockwork; bad work deserved a scolding but good work merited a compliment.

"That is to die for!" became his usual accolade.

Chef's invitation to sample a successful dish was praise in itself. His passion was food and the way it was made. Two hours later, I peeled my last potato and proudly popped it onto the gigantic pile. My hands were cold, but I was pleased with myself.

"Well done, Jessica work experience!" Chef bellowed.

He was everywhere at once.

"This is a carrot," he said mockingly then proceeded to peel it.

"I want it cut equally like this," he demonstrated as, in a flash, he made a pile of exact sized, square shapes.

"Can you do that?" he stared at me.

"Yes, Chef," I answered with wary confidence.

A large sack of carrots and two plastic containers appeared before me. Such were my tasks for the rest of my day. The mundane jobs gave me a chance to switch off from the dilemmas I was facing at home. My trance was broken the moment I finished chopping another pile of vegetables and Chef's voice sounded behind me.

"Well done, Jessica. Yes, you've done well today so I hope you'll be back tomorrow?" he declared by way of a question.

"Thanks, Chef," he had praised me and I was beaming.

The day had disappeared. Part of me wanted to stay but I hung my apron and hat up and left the kitchen. Now my sinking heart had to think about reality.

What's in store for me tonight? Where will I be staying and who will I be staying with? More importantly what'll be expected of me? - I speculated as I made my way into the main hotel area.

"Jessica, there's a taxi waiting for you," the lady at reception called to me.

She pointed to a minicab parked up just outside the door.

"Oh, thank you," I acknowledged her despite being confused.

This is odd. Who's sent a taxi? Shawn has a car. Why would he do that? - I asked myself.

Susan! Maybe she's sent it, - I tried to answer my own question.

I hoped not. I had honestly felt my life with her was over; I couldn't deal with her anymore. She would never stop drinking and she would always be violent towards me. I needed to get out of her life and start afresh.

But who, other than Susan. would have called a taxi for me? - I couldn't get my head straight.

"Taxi for Jessica?" the driver poked his head out of the window.

"Yes," I nodded.

I opened the rear door and climbed in.

Chapter 28

Brainwashed

The taxi driver pulled away but I didn't want to sound stupid and ask who had ordered my cab. He seemed to know where we were going which was in the opposite direction from Shawn's. We were heading towards Jasmine's.

"Breathe, Jessica, breathe," I mumbled to myself

My fingernails uncontrollably dug into the palms of my hands. I could not release my grip. My fists clenched together and my knuckles started to turn white as I sat with my eyes closed, letting the wind from the open window chill my face. My tension started to release. I tried to concentrate on the sway of the car and my body and mind calmed down. Slowly, my fists relaxed and I looked down at my palms. Each hand had four indentations and I had drawn blood where my fingernails had dug into my hands. I was right, the cab driver eventually pulled up outside Jasmine's house.

"Do I need to give you some money?" I asked the driver.

I was slightly worried, as I didn't have any money to give him.

"No. no, the cab is already paid for," he replied.

Thank God for that,- I breathed a sigh of relief.

I thanked the driver and stepped out. Pulling my baccy from my pocket, I rolled a cigarette and watched until the cab had driven away before I slumped against the wall.

I can't stay here, not with Susan not again, I can't keep going through this with her. I'm done with that life, - I lit my cigarette and took a large drag.

"Jessica, thank God, I've been so worried," Jasmine called out.

She ran towards me and hugged me to the point where I could hardly breathe.

"Where did you go? Where have you been?" she looked at me.

We sat on the steps to her flat and I explained what had happened. I told her about Susan's drinking and the fight that had taken place. Jasmine told me that she had returned to find glass all over the floor then told Susan she had to leave. She said that Jacob could stay and, not surprisingly, Susan had gotten angry so she packed all her belongings and disappeared with Jacob.

"Jacob, is he ok? Where have they gone?" I wanted to know.

"I have no idea but he seemed ok when they left," Jasmine assured me.

"After they left I tried to find you. I have been so worried but thankfully, I managed to find out where you were working today. I rang the hotel and found out what time you were finishing and arranged the cab for you," Jasmine explained.

"So, what happens now?" I asked.

"Well, you are welcome to stay here," Jasmine told me. "Susan has gone, you will be safe now."

Safe now! Jasmine's words somehow made me relax and a calm feeling overwhelmed my body. A weight had been lifted from my shoulders and I started to cry. Jasmine hugged me and let me cry. No words were spoken.

"Cuppa? Shall I make some food too?" Jasmine eventually asked.

216

"That sounds amazing," I wiped away my tears.

We spent the rest of the night talking about things that had happened and the topic of conversation soon turned to Shawn. I didn't know what my feelings towards him were, even though he had done so many terrible things to me. He disgusted me, but I had developed some feelings towards him. When he wasn't visiting me during the night, somehow he had managed to become my dad. When I needed a shoulder to cry on, he was there for me or laughed with me when something was funny. In a way, he had protected me from Susan.

However the sexual side of my relationship with him had been happening for years, my virginity had been stolen so brutally by him. I had not been given a choice because the abuse had started when I was 10 years old. By the time I was in my teens, I had become so hardened to Shawn in a sexual way. Sex meant nothing to me, it was just something that was expected from me and I had no choice but to give it or have it taken from me.

I had always longed for a father figure in my life and I had learned to love him as my dad, I had missed him since we had moved out of the house. When he acted like my dad, I saw him as someone who could protect me and I had grown to love that side of him. I guess this was why I felt I needed to protect him. For this reason, I didn't tell Jasmine about the sexual activities that had been going on between us. I had been well trained in protecting him.

Jasmine asked lots of questions about him; she fished for information to find out if he had ever crossed the line with me. He had certainly crossed the line in so many ways; he was so past the line now, it may as well have been in another country. But I still felt that I should protect him and not tell Jasmine about the devil he truly was.

Has he got his hooks into me so much that I actually care about him? Or am I just clutching on to a life that I once had, a family life that included him. Maybe I'm just scared to be on my own? - I wondered.

Jasmine told me that I could stay with her as long as Susan was out of the picture. That was fine by me and for the time being, I was out of harm's way. This gave me time to gather my thoughts and to sort out my feelings, rather than rushing around worried that I might not have a roof over my head and making bad decisions.

But like everything else in my life, these decisions were outside my control. Something new and frightening was always waiting around the corner for me; I never knew what that might be.

As that night drew to a close, I checked my phone and found several messages from Shawn.

'Where are you?'

'I'm waiting for you.'

'What's going on?'

'I'm getting worried now.'

I hadn't let him know I had gone to Jasmine's so I text him back.

'Hey sorry, Jasmine got a cab for me after work and I'm staying at her house.'

I read through all his messages again and their tone implied that Shawn did care about me. He genuinely seemed worried so I dismissed what had happened the previous night with him. It's what dads do. It's a normal part of life. No one else ever seemed to bring up similar experiences they had gone through with their parents. They only ever talked about boyfriends or girlfriends, never their dads. I had noticed that people around me had started to talk about sex; it had become the most talked about topic of conversation of late. The kids at school and even the people I worked with all talked about sex. I didn't get involved with the conversations, I listened instead.

I wanted to see if anyone would mention what their parents may or may not have done to them, I wanted someone to finally confirm whether or not my life had been built on lies. But, the more I listened, the more I realised the sky that I had always thought was pink was actually blue. My entire life had been built on lies.

So why do I still feel so compelled to keep everything a secret and protect Shawn? - I began to question my motives.

Shawn's method of control had been to give me warnings after raping and sexually assaulting me as had the others who had abused me. I was told that bad things would happen to me if I were to tell anyone. Steve, Louise's dad had told me he would fucking kill me if I was ever to breathe a word. It was special and normal, Shawn had told me, it was just what dads and daughters did. We had a special relationship and I was his princess. I had been told never to speak of it to another living soul; that was etched onto my brain.

Years had passed since Shawn had forced himself upon me after drugging me and the abuse turned into an almost daily, if not weekly, occurrence. My mother seemed to think this kind of behaviour was acceptable, this was a lot for a young mind to understand and handle. I had hated Shawn with a passion when I had first met him and thought he was gross and weird. He had made me sick to my stomach whenever he touched me and he had been so cruel and violent, so how the fuck had I developed feelings for him? I still wanted to see him after everything he had done and I missed him.

How was this possible? - I wondered

Here was a man who had put me through the most degrading and painful experiences of my life.

What does this mean? Why do I feel this way? - I thought to myself.

When Susan had been violent, Shawn had protected me and he was the only other person that I could talk to about her. He understood how bad she could be and, although from a different perspective, had also tried to teach me how to defend myself when the bullies at school had beat me. If I was upset, he would take time out of his day to speak to me and talk me through my problems when no one else seemed to care. When the police and social workers told me that I would be taken to a safe place, I had worried. Not just because of Susan's warning, but also because the many adults who had entered my life had raped and abused me. I thought I might be better off with the devil I knew, Shawn.

What if these new adults in this safe place did the same? What if they were like Steve? Would I be sent to someone like him, if I was taken to a safe place? - additional worries for me.

Susan had told me that the safe place was horrible; I had already seen some horrible places.

How much worse than these places could the safe place be? - I would often think.

I still believed that what Shawn did to me was normal and every parent did the same to their child. I had also witnessed Louise's dad do what he did to her, while he did the same to me. Here was another father who had a special relationship with his daughter.

"That's my girl!" Steve had said as he slapped her on her arse.

I had spent my entire life never really knowing what was real, right or wrong and I always felt confused with no one to ask.

Over the years Shawn had become my dad and he seemed like the only person who looked out for me, I wanted a dad and I wanted my family back. After my sell-by date would inevitably come to an end with Jasmine, who would take me on then? There wasn't anyone else, Shawn was my only hope and the only person that I had left in the world. He wanted me in his life when my mother didn't.

'Are we ok? I've been so worried.'

Another message from Shawn popped up on my phone.

Is he really worried about me or worried I will tell someone what he had been doing? - I debated.

I had been cold towards him when he drove me to work that morning.

'Why have you been worried?'

'You disappeared today, I didn't know if you were ok or not. Can we meet Friday? We could go swimming at the Headland. Would be fun like old times.'

There will be people around at the hotel, maybe he just wants to spend some time with me, time with his daughter? - I hoped.

'Ok, I finish at 4 pm on Friday.'

'Be in the pool waiting for you x. PS if you want to talk it might be best to contact me by email from now on, I'll explain later.'

'Ok, see you Friday.'

I put my phone on my bed and let my mind turn over again.

'What does he need to explain later? That seems a bit strange,' - I shook my head.

I looked around the bedroom that I had once shared with Jacob. I missed him massively, but having a bed to myself that night seemed like heaven. Jasmine had given me the bedroom and taken the sofa again. I was grateful as it had been a very hard couple of days. I was asleep before my head even hit the pillow that night.

Chapter 29

Strange places, stranger thoughts

At the end of each night, Shawn emailed me. We would have a short conversation which would always end with a pleasantry.

'Nite, Princess, see you Friday x.'

Shawn had said in his emails that he still wanted to be my dad and for some reason, this made me happy, no one else in my family seemed to want me.

On Friday morning, Jasmine woke me for my work experience and I told her that I would be late home as I was meeting some friends after work to go swimming. I hated lying to her but I could tell she wasn't keen on Shawn. She had asked so many questions about him, bringing his name up in conversation while we chatted at night. She must have known there was more to my story than I was letting on. She was like a dog with a bone, as she searched for the truth. But I didn't want to spill the beans, I believed there was a chance for my family to somehow repair and, even after everything Shawn had done, I felt I had to protect him.

Before I left that morning, Jasmine checked that I had enough money for food and drinks and told me to have fun with my friends. As the taxi driver took me to work, I immediately felt guilty for fibbing to her about who I was meeting. Life had changed so much in such a short space of time and for some reason, I felt like I had to lie and pretend that I didn't speak to Shawn anymore. He had been openly known as my dad and now he seemed to be a dirty little secret. There were clandestine emails and secret rendezvous with a person I once shared a family home with and strangely, all the secrecy made it feel exciting to meet with the man I called Dad.

We pulled up outside the hotel and I thanked the taxi driver. I closed the door and pulled one of my pre-rolled cigarettes from my pocket. I needed to compose myself before entering the hotel; there was something about this place that I just could not put my finger on. It felt like my mind was hiding something from me, something from my past that happened here. I extinguished my cigarette and calmly walked into the hotel. I greeted the receptionist as I walked past.

I had learned so much during the time I spent working in the kitchen and I enjoyed the tasks that had been set out for me. Chef showed me an entirely new dimension to cooking which made me want to excel. I felt as though I had achieved something and had become part of a team, this was something I had not experienced before. No one knew anything about me and this gave me the chance to reinvent myself instead of blending in and becoming the invisible person.

That day, I was given a new task; I was to prepare desserts. I didn't appreciate I could make good cakes and puddings until I had finished. Chef let me try some of the desserts I had prepared, they tasted truly amazing. He complimented me on how wonderful they were and once again, he made me proud of myself. When I left the kitchen that day, I had a big smile on my face. I was excited to tell Shawn about my week and what I had achieved. I wanted him to be proud of me too.

A staircase led down to the hotel spa where the grand feeling of the hotel shifted in style. The base level of the building was modern with oversized, white floor tiles, low ceilings and modern furniture. Soft music played in the background. A large circular desk stood at the bottom of the stairs and had been finished with small, glass mosaic tiles. A woman dressed in white with neatly tied back hair wearing bright, red lipstick, stood behind the desk.

"Welcome to the spa, how can I help?" she said politely.

"Hi, I have been working upstairs and I was told it would be ok to use the pool today," I ventured.

"Yes, of course, just go through that way," she pointed to a door situated between some glass shelves.

A large, golden Budda looked down from one of the shelves and joss sticks burned either side of him. Although the smell was nice, it made my nose tingle.

I walked to the door and it suddenly buzzed. Like a bolt from the blue, a memory popped into my head. Jacob and I had waited at this door before when we were a lot younger.

Maybe it was just deja vu, - I tugged at the door.

Inside the pool room, the heat hit me. The movement of the water in the pool made the tiles on the walls shimmer and dance, the entire place seemed magical. Then I remembered that Jacob and I had played in this pool before. I could see a cave-like area that had a jacuzzi, sauna and steam room. I looked past the pool and another memory flashed then disappeared as my recollections were interrupted.

"You made it then," Shawn spluttered, appearing from the water.

I had not seen him swim over and he made me jump.

"Yes, I'll just go to get changed," I said but something familiar drew my gaze back to the cave area.

"Hurry up, the water is really nice," he swam away, rolling over playfully.

224

I walked to the ladies changing room and put my bikini on. Luckily, Susan had packed my swimwear despite her haste to leave Shawn's. My pink bikini with bows that tied up either side of the knickers had been scrunched up among the bundle of clothes. I became conscious that my boobs had grown again and were attempting to escape from the bra. After I loosened the straps, it fitted.

That will have to do, - I convinced myself.

I wrapped a towel around my body and walked along the pool edge. Shawn swam alongside me.

"Come on hurry up," he said.

I placed my towel down on a chair. Shawn was in the middle of the pool and watched my every move. I headed for the steps to climb into the pool. He looked at me in a way that could have been mistaken for a permanent fixture. The only movement was his eyes; he stood so still. Like a new centerpiece, he watched me with an ever-growing intensity while I made my way down the steps.

"Are you ok?" I asked self-consciously.

"Yes, I have really missed you," he smiled.

"Oh, ok. I've missed you too," I volunteered naively.

We spent the afternoon messing around; we tried to do underwater handstands and splashed around in the pool. As the pool area emptied, we decided to go for a sauna in the cave area. Curved pebbled walls surrounded a jacuzzi which had been placed in the middle of two doors. Shawn opened the left-hand door and we walked into a room where the intense heat hit us. There were two levels of wooden seating in the room and as I sat down on the wood, I burnt my bottom. Shawn laughed and poured some water from a large wooden bucket onto the bench.

"There you go, that should be better now," he invited me to sit down again.

Shawn had a fun side to him that was difficult not to like, I felt as though I was just out for a swim with my dad and enjoying the time I could spend with him.

"You look much better," he complimented me.

"Yes, I'm feeling better. I have had a really good week," I told him.

I told him about my work experience and what I had learned. He listened and I rambled on about everything I had been up to. The room heated up more and I could see my skin glisten; beads of water ran down my body.

Suddenly, another flash of a memory, my skin had glistened like this before. But in my memory, I was in pain and I felt an urge to get out. "It's really hot in here; shall we go in the jacuzzi instead?" I stood up quickly.

Shawn nodded and we left the room.

I stepped into the hot bubbly water filled with salts and sat down; the water covered my entire body. The bubbles hit me in the face but I continued to tell him about my work experience.

The door to the right of the jacuzzi opened and a couple stepped out of the steam room. I turned to look at them and noticed small black cameras dotted around this area. The steam rising from the open door jogged another memory. A room filled with steam and someone's hand covering my face. I winced. The couple showered then joined Shawn and me in the jacuzzi. Shawn shifted closer to me when they got in despite there being plenty of room. The couple said hello then sat down to continue their conversation.

I felt Shawn's hand touch my thigh and I tried to brush his hand away, this, unfortunately, made his advances worse. He quickly moved his hand under my bikini bottoms and started to rub me.

"Please stop," I whispered to him and tried to remove his hand.

The couple glanced at me; maybe they had heard what I had said. My protest had made him more determined. He forced his fingers inside me. I gasped and held my breath; the force was painful.

226

"Relax. You don't want them to know, do you?" he whispered in my ear with a sneer in his voice.

No. I don't want them knowing, I don't want the embarrassment and I don't want you doing this either! Why not just be my dad? - I couldn't think straight.

He continued to force his fingers in and out of my vagina. He became excited and the water started to splash around more because of his movements. It must have become obvious to the couple. They looked at us, whispered to each other then left the jacuzzi. I was horrified and unhappy. I was a fourteen year old child and, if Shawn's actions were so obvious, they had ignored them and walked away.

Why didn't they say something? - I questioned inwardly.

I tried to stop him. This just made him more strong-minded and, only after he watched the couple walk past again and leave the pool area, did he eventually stop. They had glanced over and whispered to each other again before they left, this meant the pool area was deserted.

"All this talk of food is making me hungry. Shall we get out and get some?" Shawn asked.

It was as though I had been in the middle of describing the food that I had made while at work.

I followed him to the changing rooms and walked into the ladies while Shawn walked into the men's. The ladies was deserted so I stripped off my bikini and wrapped a towel around myself. I was walking towards the shower when the changing room door burst open and Shawn strode in.

"What are you doing in here?" I looked around indicating that there could be other females there.

I covered myself with my towel but he ripped it away, leaving me naked. Anyone could walk in and this big secret that I had been told to guard with my life, would no longer be a secret. He didn't care. He turned me around and pushed me hard against the vanity unit next to the shower and bent me over the sink. I could see in the mirror that he had already dropped his swim shorts. My hands gripped the sides of the sink. He looked directly into my eyes in the reflection of the mirror and, when he noticed my eyes had caught his, he rammed himself into me. He wasn't Shawn the dad anymore; his eyes were dark and the look of evil was heightened by the pure wickedness that had shot across his face. He enjoyed the pain he was causing me; the playful dad figure who had listened to me and splashed around in the pool had left the building. Instead, the devil stood behind me digging his claws into my hips. I could tell that he was desperate and no longer cared about the consequences if he were to be caught, it added to his thrill. This was the thing about Shawn, he loved the buzz of excitement.

I had no choice but to escape into the secret crevices of my mind when, without warning, memories came flooding back. This wasn't the first time that he had attacked me at this hotel, in fact, I could remember twice it had happened. Susan and Jacob had been playing in the pool when Shawn had taken me to the sauna where he abused me. The next time he did it, it was in the steam room.

I had been between eleven and twelve years old and scared to death. Somehow, until the moment I drifted away in my mind with Shawn behind me in the changing room, my memory had blocked out the experience. My brain had tried to protect me and leave me with a happy memory of playing in the pool with Jacob, rather than the horror of what had happened. Shawn had gotten off on the thrill of perhaps being discovered, just as he was now.

He had grown bored of me when I started to avoid his cameras; he had to escalate things.. The danger and thrill seemed to be what he got off on. He was prepared to risk it all and it didn't matter if he was caught in the ladies changing room. The drug of excitement was what he craved and he needed to feed his addiction.

But I too had a craving. Shawn had stayed in contact with me when I needed him and I had latched on to that. Everyone else had

228

abandoned me. To be wanted by someone had become my addiction. I desperately wanted Shawn to be my dad, instead, I was bent over the vanity unit with my so-called dad's penis inserted into me. This may have been thrilling for him but it was heartbreaking for me.

Susan had accused me of stealing Shawn away from her, maybe she was right. Had I unintentionally stolen him by wanting a dad? - I posed an important question.

Shawn seemed to be the only person Susan truly cared about and wanted yet she had handed me back to him like I had no value or worth.

"He wants you not me," she had screamed.

No wonder she hated me so much; my need had become my drug.

I was brought back into the present when Shawn finished with a judder and pulled his swim shorts back up.

"I had better get out of here. We can grab some McDonald's on the way back," he said on his way out.

The door closed behind him but I was still bent over the vanity unit staring into the mirror and wondering what I had become. I picked up my towel from the floor and walked into the shower and started to scrub away the evidence of what had just happened. I would normally be in tears while I cleaned myself, but I wasn't and this worried me.

I have allowed Shawn back into my life, I have no real reason to see him anymore. I knew what meeting with him would most likely involve. Yet, I agreed to meet with him anyway. Why?' - I wondered.

The answer was simple. Shawn fed my addiction; he was the only person that seemed to ever want me in his life.

Since the day I was born, no one had ever loved me. My real father had never been in my life and my mother, well need I say more about that? If I wasn't being bullied at school, I was being beaten and abused at home. I had spent my entire life looking over my shoulder and no one wanted to be my friend. I never knew if I would have a roof over my head from one week to the next and I trusted no one. Nothing was a constant; I had always lacked any form of stability. Even Jasmine, I was sure her kindness was temporary and would one day come to an end. She would no longer want me; it was only a matter of time, as the invisible clock ticked away, my time would run out. Then I would then be left with adult problems, without a clue what the fuck to do next. The only person I could rely on was Shawn, he had, without fail, always come to my rescue in my hour of need.

My sudden shift in my emotions towards Shawn was very confusing and had taken me by surprise. The devil had somehow wormed his way in and, despite what he did to me, I had grown to care for him. I was angry at the world and at the situations I had been forced to endure, I was angry at my family for deserting me and at Susan for her drinking. I had nowhere to call my own or even somewhere to call home. I was angry at myself because I never felt safe. Ironically, I was no longer angry with Shawn for one reason. He wanted me!

After we left the spa and drove to Mcdonald's, we both seemed lost in our thoughts. The radio played in the background. Shawn ordered some food and we parked at the far corner of the car park.

"Some people came to visit me, they told me I wasn't allowed to see you unless it was supervised. But there is a chance I won't be allowed to see you at all," Shawn explained.

"Who came?" I enquired.

"Look, it's complicated. This is why I asked you to email me from now on. It just stops people from asking questions. It's safer that way," he assured me.

"So, I'm not allowed to see you anymore?" I said with a heavy heart.

"It's important we keep everything a secret from now on. You do want to see me still, right?" he looked at me with a puppy dog eye expression on his face.

"I have no one else left," tears threatened to brim over.

"Everything will be ok. I will always be here for you."

230

Shawn took my hand, pulled me towards him and cuddled me. He confirmed that his visitors had been from social services. I felt as though the hands of the invisible clock had ticked again towards my greatest fear, I would soon be totally on my own. It didn't matter how reassuring he tried to be from that point on, I was already shattered. I was scared of what my future might hold. Any hopes I had left of our family being magically reunited had been destroyed and I knew, as Shawn drove me back to Jasmine's that night, she would not be able to keep me forever.

Chapter 30

Taken

The following week, a social worker came to visit me at Jasmine's and I was told that I would no longer be allowed to see Shawn. The stranger told me that I was not allowed to see the person I had called my dad. I was furious; this decision made me want to see him more. A few weeks later, Jasmine caught me talking to Shawn on my phone; she snatched the phone from my hand and confiscated it for a week.

When I had lived with Shawn, no one seemed to care what was going on. I wondered why people cared now. It didn't make sense to me but Jasmine told me he was dangerous and I should not talk to him.

Why is Shawn dangerous? Has he hurt someone?' - I couldn't understand.

I didn't see him as a dangerous person. To me, dangerous people were murderers or gang members. I had never seen a film or read a book about people like Shawn, the taboo subject that people try to avoid.

The phone was given to my social worker so s/he could look through the emails and messages Shawn had sent me. Thinking back, social work would have seen the suggestive messages he had sent. When Jasmine finally returned my phone, I contacted Shawn to let him know what had happened. My passwords had been changed so I could no longer email him. He told me we could neither talk nor see each other for a while.

Had he also found his own way to get rid of me, does he no longer want me? – my heart skipped a beat.

Everyone was making decisions for me and no one would tell me the reasons why. They were happy to ask me adult questions about my life, yet they treated me like a child. I never felt like I had control of my own life, I was left to suffer the consequences of the decisions made by other people. No one ever explained why Shawn was dangerous, so how could I understand that the decisions made by others were to protect me?

A couple of weeks had passed since I had any contact with Shawn; I felt lonely and depressed. Jasmine was the only person left in my life. I could talk to her but I was careful with what I said and changed the subject if she tried fishing for information again.

Work experience finished and I reverted to the invisible girl at school. I still had visits from my drama therapist, Cathy. Although I enjoyed these sessions, she also tried to get into my head. We talked about the issues my imaginary friend had rather than me telling her that these were my problems. I felt as though I had to be on my guard. She was more than aware that I was talking about myself, not that she could prove anything. Two social workers had visited the school and attempted to talk to me about my situation, my living arrangement and of course Shawn. They asked more difficult questions about my life but I didn't want to talk to them.

"How are you feeling?" I didn't know how to answer that question?

"Yeah, I'm peachy thanks."

I didn't know how I felt about anything anymore, my life made no sense to me.

My entire family had deserted me and the only person left, albeit he was my abuser was forbidden to see you by a total stranger. There seemed no sense to the outcome.

The only other person left in my life was Jasmine. She had notified the school of my current situation which ultimately led to the visits from more strangers and questions about my family. I had been prepared and trained for years just for this moment; I answered the questions automatically without giving anything away. I still felt compelled to protect Susan and Shawn, so I explained that nothing was wrong; we were a family going through a bad patch.

All these strangers wanted to do was to remove me from everything I knew and whisk me away to some unknown place, what they called a safe place, wherever that may be. I knew it was only a matter of time until even Jasmine would be removed from my life. Then I would truly have no one. The invisible clock ticked away.

School ended for the summer holidays and I hoped for at least the next six weeks that I would be left alone. I knew I didn't have a lot to do over the summer so my days were spent around the house. I didn't have friends to visit or money to entertain myself. The only excitement I had was cooking a meal for Jasmine.

On my fifteenth birthday, I woke up feeling depressed. I knew no one would bother with me. Months had passed without any word from my family. My day would most likely be spent doing the same thing as I had done the day before. However, to my surprise, Jasmine didn't go to work that day.

"Happy birthday, Jess," she beamed.

In the lounge, she handed me a card and present. She had remembered my birthday and I was over the moon as I opened the card.

To Jessica,

I hope you have a great birthday
ps. you will get your main birthday pressie later on tonight.

Love,
Your big sis Jasmine x x x

"Right, I have a girls' day out planned. How does swimming sound? Then we can grab a Chinese before you find out what your main prezzie is," she jumped up and down waving her arms around with a massive smile on her face.

I had no idea what this big surprise was but Jasmine was very excited.

"That sounds amazing. Thank you so much," I hugged her.

She had managed to make me happy for the first time in so long and I was grateful to her. The fact that she had remembered was one thing but, as for the present, that was amazing.

We jumped on a train to Plymouth and spent the day at the pavilion swimming before returning to Truro. We got ready at Jasmine's and then went to her mum's house for a Chinese meal.

After dinner, we travelled to Falmouth. I still didn't have a clue what the big surprise was but we walked towards a giant marquee where hundreds of people were waiting to go in.

"What are we doing here?" I was curious.

"You'll find out," she smiled and text someone.

A few minutes later Carl appeared from the crowds of people, dressed in a security uniform.

"Happy birthday, Jess," he greeted me.

He gave me a big hug and handed me a card. Inside were two tickets.

> *Fazor supported by the Mend, Britain's Got Talent finalists live in Falmouth.*

"Oh, my God! Are you serious?" I was shocked by what they had both arranged.

"Yep, you might need these as well," Carl pulled VIP backstage passes from his pocket.

I jumped up and down in excitement and gave Carl a massive hug. Tears of emotion formed in my eyes. Jasmine and Carl had gone to so much effort and showed such kindness towards me, I was overwhelmed.

The concert was fantastic. We were in the front row watching the performances and, after they had finished, we were invited backstage. I was given kisses on the cheeks from everyone and Chris from the Mend signed his baseball cap before he gave it to me. He got everyone to sing happy birthday and, although that part was embarrassing, I had a fantastic birthday and one that I will always cherish.

Over the next few weeks, things began to look up for me and I felt content. I found fresh confidence within myself and I managed to make some new friends during the holidays. Although we had never spoken before, Lisa, Chloe and Alice went to the same school as me. I spent my days hanging out with them or doing chores around the house to help Jasmine. She paid me for the work I did but, even though I would have done the chores for free, I was grateful for the money.

My life was improving and, by the end of the holidays, I felt like a different person. I would be returning to school no longer the invisible girl, I finally had some friends. School was also a happier place for me after the holidays, life had become strangely uncomplicated. I wondered what the next drama would be; I think I was scared of being happy. Happiness had been short-lived for me and was usually followed by something dreadful.

A few weeks after term started, I returned home to find Carl, Jasmine's brother, but no Jasmine at the house. He asked me to go and do some homework or read a book. He hardly spoke to or looked at me. I had always gotten along very well with him and I had never seen him act this way before, he was not his usual chatty, friendly self. He was keen to keep me occupied.

I heard a knock on the door that was about to destroy my happiness, my world was ready to spiral into an entirely new direction. The invisible clock had chimed and my time had run out. Carl opened the door but looked as white as a ghost when returned to the lounge. A lady I recognized appeared behind him.

Michelle had visited the school before the summer holidays and probed me about my family. I found her very direct when she spoke to me. I did not like the questions she had asked and, when I refused to answer them, she became annoyed with me. I had taken an instant dislike to her then and it dawned on me why Carl had been acting differently. I was about to be taken away, taken to the safe place that had always terrified me.

"Jessica, today you will be coming with me," there was no sugar coating.

"Where are we going?" I felt my hands start to shake.

"There is no time to talk, now go and grab your bag. Let's go!" she snapped back at me.

Michelle seemed to have more important things to do; she kept looking at her watch. I was an inconvenience to her day. She couldn't even take time to explain things; I was only another kid she was collecting to drop off, God knows where. This was my life but that didn't matter to her, she was about to rip me away from all I had left.

"Can I grab some things at least?" my eyes filled with tears.

I glanced over at Carl who was sheepishly staring at his shoes. I could tell he hated the fact that he was the one who had allowed this woman into the house.

"You have five minutes," she replied, consulting her watch again.

In the bedroom, I threw my worldly possessions into some bin bags I had grabbed. Floods of tears streamed down my cheeks as I rushed around.

Am I jinxed? Am I not allowed to find some form of happiness? Is this why this is happening? What have I done that is so wrong? Am I really so bad that no one wanted me? - my heart broke.

I packed the last of my belongings. I took one final look around the bedroom, walked into the hallway and dropped the two bin liners by the front door.

Michelle was talking to Carl quietly in the lounge.

"Why am I being taken away? Does Jasmine no longer want me?" I asked no one in particular, wiping my tears.

"Jasmine has been taken into hospital, she is sick Jess. She can't look after you anymore," Carl explained.

He gave me a massive hug.

"Everything will be ok, I am so sorry," he whispered in my ear and then kissed me on the forehead.

"Right come along, people are waiting," Michelle ordered, ushering me out.

I glanced back at Carl before he closed the front door; he looked devastated.

Michelle's car was parked nearby. I had hoped it would be parked further away because I needed time for a cigarette. Then I realized I had forgotten my tobacco. Michelle placed my two bin liners into the boot of her car.

"I forgot my baccy, can I go and grab it quickly?" I asked.

"No, get in the car," Michelle insisted.

I opened the door and climbed into the car as tears flowed again.

"Please, can we stop and get some?" I pleaded.

"No, you are under age you should not be smoking anyway," she started the car.

I sat silently sobbing and took one final look back at Jasmine's flat as we drove away.

I'm totally on my own for real this time, - I was terrified.

Michelle stopped the car outside a shop.

Have we arrived at the safe place? Is it a shop? This seems a bit odd, - my thoughts were all over the place.

Michelle came out of the shop holding a packet of baccy and a lighter, she opened the car door and handed them to me.

"Don't dare tell anyone. We are not allowed to do this, have one quickly and we will be on our way," she said with a softer tone

My God, this woman does have a heart! - I smiled inwardly.

I rolled a cigarette and stepped out of the car. A sense of calm came over me as I lit up and watched the grey smoke drift away.

I had been pushed from pillar to post my entire life and I was about to join a new family who didn't know anything about me. They couldn't pretend to call me one of their own, I was not a baby and that meant I would always be the outsider living in someone else's house. I also knew that at any point, Michelle or someone else like her could come and collect me again and I would be forced into another unknown situation. My life had become two bin liners and nowhere that I recognized as home. That was my future until I became eighteen years old and was no longer of concern to social services.

What will happen then? - I pondered.

"We had better go," Michelle called from her car, interrupting my train of thought.

I stubbed my cigarette out and we drove for about five minutes until we turned onto a side road in a small village. Michelle stopped outside a nice-looking house made of brown bricks. There was a garage with a brown door. The front door opened and a woman appeared on the driveway. She waved as she walked towards the car. My chest felt tight and my skin became sweaty. The woman opened my door but I felt as though my personal space had been invaded.

"Hi, I'm Carol," she said, smiling.

Carol was a rounded lady with red hair cut into a bob, her skin was pale.

"Everything will be ok," she beckoned me out of the car.

"Shall we go inside? I can give you a tour and we can get to know each other," she continued as I got out of the car.

I had seemed to have lost the ability to speak but I walked up the driveway.

What is the point in getting to know this person and having the grand tour of this home only to be rejected and unwanted when the invisible clock decides to run out on me again, - my thoughts were depressing.

The social system had control of my life and I could be moved on again at any point.

I followed Carol into the house and Michelle followed us carrying my two miserable-looking black bin liners. They could have easily been mistaken for bags of rubbish. Carol's house was spotless, everything had its place and I could tell she was very house proud. Photos of a young girl hung from the walls and told her life story. They ranged from baby photos to past holidays; I was sure this was Carol's daughter.

"This is my daughter, Alison, she will be home soon," she pointed to an up-to-date photo.

She walked me around her house; each room downstairs was spotless.

Why do people insist on giving the grand tour of their homes? - I was being critical.

My life had just been turned upside down and I suddenly felt like I was on an episode of through the keyhole.

Why would I want to be shown happy family photos, when I have just been ripped away from everything I know, - I winced.

It felt like salt had just been rubbed into my wounds. It sounds mean but it's how I felt, Carol was kind enough to take me under her roof but why? Was it because she wanted me or was it about money?

I was shown the upstairs areas and finally the room I would be staying in. It was painted cream with a window that looked out onto the road. A computer desk sat in the corner and a small grey TV was bolted to the wall. The entire room looked more like a basic hotel room, rather than a child's bedroom. Just what you need and nothing else, a purple wardrobe and a metal single bed.

Michelle placed my two bin liners on the floor and told me to get settled in. She thanked Carol and left the house.

"I'll let you get settled in," Carol announced.

She also left the room. So, this was the safe place, a place where I was feeling more alone than I have ever felt in my life. The reality of everything that had happened flooded in thick and fast; I sank to the floor and started to cry. I must have sat in the same spot for over an hour in tears. I thought over my entire life and the chain of events that had finally led me to this place filled with strangers. The experience of foster care is one of being an infiltrator; unwanted and uninvited.

"Jessica, can you come down please?" Carol asked from the bottom of the stairs.

I took a deep breath, wiped the tears from my eyes and walked towards the sound of her voice.

"Would you like some food?" she asked before I had put my foot on the top step.

I didn't want to accept food from someone I didn't know, it didn't seem right.

"It's made and on the dining room table waiting for you," she told me, walking out of view.

I stood at the top of the stairs debating what I was going to do. I was hungry; I needed to eat. Like a timid cat trying not to make a sound, I slowly walked down the stairs and into the dining room. I found a single place had been made up for me at the table, a plate of food and a glass of water in an empty room. I sat down and began to eat. I looked at the happy family photos hanging proudly on the walls. The rest of the family were not at the table eating with me, I was an outsider within their house. I could hear them eating in the living room together in front of the TV.

I had my own family once upon a time, - I remembered.

I stared into space, alone and scared.

Why does no one want me? What did I do to deserve this? - I burst into tears.

I didn't want to be in this cruel world anymore! Everything I knew had vanished and I was anxious about putting roots down with Carol because I didn't know if I would be staying or going. But, I knew I should appreciate what was there for me because it could be taken away and there was no telling what would unfold. The uncertainty of everything was worst feeling in the world

Chapter 31

The boy who saved me

My life in foster care continued the same as it started, alone except for people I didn't know. I would go to school, go back to Carol's then straight to my bedroom. I sat alone until I was called down for dinner. I would eat alone before going back to the bedroom for the remainder of the night. This was only ever going to be a temporary fix and I never left the bedroom except to wash or have a cigarette. I didn't see any point in trying to get to know anyone else because I knew, at some point, I would be collected and moved again.

One of the problems with foster care is that no one really wants a teenager. Babies or children under five stand a better chance of a new home as they can be moulded into a family with relative ease. Teenagers bring baggage and seem to have little hope of integrating, they are left wherever there is space until they are moved on. It was awkward trying to get to know a family and feel at home, only to be told you would have to leave again. My life was incredibly lonely, I was afraid to accept happiness only for it to be snapped away from me. Besides, any happiness was short-lived as it was usually followed by a devastating, traumatic experience.

A few weeks passed and the routine of life in foster care had not gone unnoticed by others in my class. Social services paid for a taxi to take me on the thirty-minute journey from St Stephens to school each day. Johnny and his mates saw this started to taunt me again; he made it his new mission to find out about my life. Inevitably, he discovered the truth and he made my life a living hell. Comments about nobody wanting me and new nicknames kept coming.

I returned to Carol's at the end of each day and ran straight to the bedroom where I sobbed my heart out. When Carol would call me for dinner, she could see that I had been crying. She would ask if I was ok and I would tell her that I had been watching a sad film. She left me to eat alone while they watched Countdown on TV in the other room.

All I had left in my life were my new best friends, Lisa, Chloe and Alice. They had become my lifeline at school; they were the only people I had left to keep me going. Somehow during all the dramas that had happened to me that year, the four of us had been given the role of prefects. The ambassador's role was designed for the younger years but we were in our final year where prefects reigned. I was very proud of myself when I was handed my prefect badge. A few weeks later we were sitting in the girls' toilets. Lisa, Chloe and Alice were chatting and sat on the worktop near the hand basins. I was in a cubical.

"Wouldn't it be nice to have a day off school?" Chloe put out the feelers.

The conversation quickly turned to how it would be possible to force the school to close for the day. What had started as an innocent conversation rapidly turned into a plan to flood the school. I have no idea how and why this conversation escalated so fast but we attempted to flood the school. We stuffed toilet tissue down all the

244

toilets and sinks then flushed the chains. We also left the taps running. The toilets overflowed, the basins filled and water spilled onto the floor. Sure enough, the girls' toilets area flooded and we found ourselves standing in a large puddle of water. The realization that we had achieved our goal set in. We ran from the toilets in an attempt to get as far away from the crime scene as possible; we had to avoid being caught. Once we stopped running, we burst out laughing and talked over what we had done. We thought it was hysterical until the next day when, sadly, school was open.

The toilets had been cleaned and were back in working order, our plan had failed. We returned to our classes that morning and shortly after, I was called to Mr Evans' office. Mr Evans was one of the Head Teachers at our school. I arrived to find my accomplices waiting outside, I immediately knew why we were there and we were in trouble. Mr Evans door opened and we were called inside.

"Right girls, I take it you all know why you are here? The CCTV footage we have is quite compelling evidence," Mr Evans said sternly.

I looked at my friends, we had forgotten about the cameras in the school corridors.

"It was all Jessica's idea, Sir!" Lisa blurted out.

Chloe and Alice nodded in agreement with what she had said.

Fucking great, my mates have just blamed me for everything. It had been Chloe's idea, not mine, - I was gutted.

I looked at each of my so-called friends.

How could I have been so stupid? I allowed more people into my life and now they've turned on me, - my thoughts stunned me.

It wasn't fair that I should take all the blame.

"Sir, that's not exactly true," I said quietly, trying to contain my anger.

"You were all recorded running from the bathroom and not one of you came forward to explain what had happened. So, as far as the school is concerned, you are all equally responsible," Mr Evans made the situation clear.

I felt slightly better; he had been fair and we were all going to be in trouble, not just me.

"Being a prefect has a level of responsibility and none of you seem to have conducted yourselves in a responsible manner, so please hand me your badges and you are excused," he held his hand out while we surrendered our prefect badges.

I watched as my so-called friends unpinned their badges and placed them in Mr Evans' hand then left the office. I slowly unpinned my own and stared down at it, I was about to hand over something that I had worked so very hard to obtain. My friends had given me the strength to carry on but they had betrayed me. I had lost the last lifeline I had. Without knowing it, they were the ones who had gotten me through the past few weeks when I had been in foster care; all they had had to do was be there for me. That's all I had needed.

I placed the badge in Mr Evans' hand and left his office. Once I reached the corridor, my friends were nowhere to be seen,

Typical, so that's the way it is then, dumped again and not even an apology for what they've done, - I wandered slowly back to class.

I opened the classroom door, made my way to the back of the room and took my seat.

"What was it this time, some second-hand clothes?" Johnny whispered to me.

He laughed with his mates.

Why is my life this way? Is there something wrong with me?' - my eyes filled up.

My friends were nowhere to be seen for the rest of the day and when the final bell rang, I wandered out of school alone and got into the taxi that was waiting at the gate. Back at Carol's, I went to the bedroom and cried. No one wanted me, not one member of my family had contacted me. Susan, Laura, Jack and even Shawn had all disappeared. Jacob was still young, he was nine years old and I worried about him. No one had told me anything about him, where he was or if he was safe. I had, however, been told that when the social services had asked Laura to help out with me, she had refused. This added to the feeling of being unwanted. Everyone was gone and loneliness, as I had never felt before, swept over me. The feeling grew stronger and stronger in the pit of my stomach, for the next three weeks.

I would get up in the morning and go to school but Lisa Chloe and Alice would go out of their way to avoid me. Johnny made nasty comments each day so that, during my breaks, the toilets, once again, became my only sanctuary. Avoiding everyone was the only way I could protect myself from more hurt and pain.

When the bell rang to mark the end of school, I would get back into my taxi. I waited in my bedroom to be called for dinner then ate alone before returning to the bedroom for the rest of the evening. One time, the eating situation got too much for me and I was curious. I went down early for dinner and waited in the lounge, just to see if it was something I was doing that had caused them to eat separately from me. My dinner was served to me in the lounge but I was told to not touch the remote. They moved into the dining room where I usually ate and sat together at the table. I guess this was their time together and I was the outsider, not part of the family.

Eat, sleep and repeat without a soul in the world to call family or a friend or talk to. I spent night after night staring at my mobile phone, wishing someone would text or call. But no one did, there was little point in having the phone. I spent my nights scrolling through Facebook, I would read other people's stories and wondered why they had the lives they had and mine was so horrendous.

A random stranger would occasionally friend request me, but that was all they were, strangers, and no one I knew or cared about. I spent every night in tears, crying myself to sleep. This was my life and there was no way out. There was nothing left in my life; happiness was always taken away from me in some cruel way.

This went on for weeks until one day I arrived back from school after another day of torment from Johnny. Something had broken inside and I couldn't take anymore, I was done! I walked into my bedroom and sat at the end of the bed waiting for Carol to call me for dinner. As usual, I sat by myself while everyone else watched TV in the lounge. I was never invited to join them.

I cleared my plates away and went straight back up to my room, I knew I would not be disturbed for the rest of the evening. I picked up my school tie, lifted the mattress up from the bed and tied my tie around one of the metal bed slats and dropped the mattress back down onto the bed. I placed the other end of the tie around my neck and stood by the headboard. There weren't any tears rolling down my cheeks. I took a deep breath before freeing my lungs of air. I could feel the tension around my neck as the tie took the weight of my body falling to the floor. Pins and needles gather and I fought against the natural desire to stand up.

I was locked in a battle with myself to stop the inevitable. I told my body not to react and the pain would be over soon. I could feel my arms and legs flinching. Life was being sucked out of them and my head became cloudy. The pain started to disappear and I could finally feel myself slipping away.

Something doesn't feel right, what is that vibration? – flitted through my head.

Without warning, my arms pushed down hard on the floor and lifted my body, causing my airways to suddenly reopen. I was immediately sent into a coughing fit; my body gasped for the air it so desperately craved. I loosened the tie from my neck, sat back down on the floor and wept. I had failed again.

Soon after, I remembered that there had been a vibration that had caused my body to act in the way it had. I reached into my pocket and retrieved my phone. I unlocked it and there it was, a text message from a boy called Sam.

'Hey, how are you doing?' the text read.

What the fuck am I meant to write back to that question? - I wondered.

Hi, I'm all good, I was just trying to hang myself. So thanks for the interruption! - I wondered what the reply might have been if I had sent him that text?

'I'm good, thank you.'

I put my phone down and slowly got to my feet, my neck throbbed and my mouth felt dry. My phone vibrated again, I picked it up and there was another text from Sam.

'Yeah, I'm good. I just thought I would say hi. Your Facebook profile said you were close by.'

I thought this was a little strange that Sam had randomly text me and I was also annoyed that he had interrupted what I was doing.

'Why, where are you then?'

I put my phone back down and it immediately vibrated again.

'St Denis, but I used to live in St Stephens. I was in foster care there a while back.'

This completely threw me; I had never actually met anyone else that was in the same position as me.

What if this is a joke? Is someone playing a cruel joke on me? - I asked myself.

'Foster care, what was that like?'

A few moments later there was another message. Sam explained by text that his dad was very ill and his mum had walked out on them. She only returned when she needed money and as a result, he had ended up in foster care. He then went on to say he had lived with a foster carer called Carol who lived in St Stephens.

What the hell, this has to be someone joking around. - I smirked

St Stephens isn't a big place and Sam's description of Carol's house was too exact not to be untrue. He even described the bed that I was

249

sitting on, how the slats squeaked when the metal rubbed together. Sam had somehow saved me by sending me his random texts, a few moments later and I would have been dead. I found myself locked in a conversation with him; we continued chatting well into the night. He had managed to take my mind off things and over the next few days, I spent a lot of time texting Sam. We mainly talked about his life because I tried not to give away much about my own life. As he talked, I found myself relating to what he was saying. I was in the same situation that he had been in and he quickly became my new lifeline. He must have felt the same as me, disjointed from a world where I craved the most basic form of human emotion, love.

Chapter 32

Sam

How ironic life can be. I waited weeks without contact from anyone, then like two buses that turn up at the same time when it is cold and wet, I was in demand.

Shawn decided to text.

'Hi really sorry I haven't been in contact. Hope you are ok. PS I miss you x.'

I arranged to meet him.

I waited until Carol and the rest of the family went to bed before I snuck out to find Shawn parked at the end of the road. We talked for a few hours and I begged him to try and get our family back together. He said he would think of something to help then he dropped me back at Carol's. Things developed and I ended up sneaking out to see him a few times a week. We would go for a drive and chat which normally ended up at McDonald's. Shawn cared about my situation and was pleased that I had met my new friend.

Not only had Shawn shown a renewed interest in what I was doing but also Sam asked to meet me and I instantly found myself with butterflies in my belly. It was one thing to talk by text where Sam could not judge me or hurt me but it was a different ball game to meet in person. I wondered if he would like me so, to be on the safe side, I made a couple of excuses.

The hamster ran for his life once again, as my mind jumped from one question to the next when Sam had asked to meet.

Is this really a good idea? Is he really real and is he being truthful? Should I take the risk and meet a total stranger? What if he isn't who he said he is? What if I don't like him? - questions kept flying around my head.

He was my only friend and I wanted to believe he was genuine. But my biggest worry was that I might lose him once he met me. I had felt comfortable talking to Sam by text, he seemed to understand me even although he had no clue that I was also in foster care. He asked a few more times to meet and after talking it over with Shawn, I eventually agreed.

I found myself running out of school towards the taxi the next day after the school bell rang. I could not wait to get back to Carol's, I could not wait to meet Sam.

"Are you ok?" the taxi driver asked.

I realised that I didn't know the taxi driver's name, even although she had picked me up every day for the past couple of months. Now and again, she had tried to make conversation with me but I had responded with one-word answers, looked out of the window lost in my thoughts and practically ignored her. She must have known something was different when I opened the car door that day; I had a smile on my face.

"Yes, I'm ok, thank you," I replied, as she drove off in the direction of Carol's.

"Did you have a good day at school?" she asked.

"It was ok. I'm meeting a friend later and I'm a little bit nervous," I replied.

"Why are you nervous?" she asked.

"Cos it's a boy," I replied sheepishly.

"Sweetheart, you have nothing to worry about. He would be a fool not to like you," she announced.

I could see in the rearview mirror she had a warm-hearted smile on her face.

"I'm Jane, by the way," she told me.

"Nice to meet you, Jane, I'm Jessica," I answered as we pulled up outside Carol's and for the first time, I thanked her.

I got out of the taxi and ran to the front door and once, inside the house, I flew up the stairs towards my bedroom to get changed.

My phone vibrated, it was Sam.

'I'm nearly at the park.'

My smile became a beacon.

'I've just gotta have some dinner and I will be there.'

'Ok see you in a bit.'

The call for dinner came. I ran down the stairs and ate faster than normal

"What's the rush," Carol asked as I ran out of the kitchen.

"I'm just meeting a friend," I announced and hurriedly left the house.

"Ok, make sure you are back by 10 o'clock," she shouted after me

My stomach was churning and my legs were shaking. The short walk to the park was full of apprehension. Then I saw Sam leaning against some railings. He was tall and skinny, wearing a tracksuit and trainers; he looked slightly scruffy.

"Hey," he said.

"Hi," I replied like a giddy school girl.

"Shall we go for a walk around the park?" I nodded with a stupid grin on my face.

We walked slowly along the path and the awkwardness disappeared as the conversation flowed. Sam was easy to talk to and I felt relaxed in his company. I started to tell him about the bullies that I had to deal with at school. He listened then asked about my family. I had been asked so much about my family over the past few months; I didn't want to talk about them with him in case he would judge me in some way. I quickly changed the subject and Sam seemed to understand that I didn't want to talk about them. He kindly started to talk about something else.

"So where do you actually live?" he asked instead.

I had still not told him that I was in care and lived with Carol. I was ever cautious that this might be a setup and maybe someone at school had put him up to this. I had learned the hard way when it came to trusting. Johnny had been extremely keen to find out where I was living with my foster family and, at the back of my mind, I thought it possible he had put Sam up to this. Johnny would have used his new knowledge to torment me. In my life, anything was possible.

"Just up the road, Creakavose Park," I replied.

"No way, I used to live on that road with Carol when I was in foster care," he told me then probed deeper. "So which house?"

What do I say now? – but it was too late

I had just described Carol's house.

"That's Carol's house," Sam looked at me. "She has a daughter called Alison?"

"Yes, she is my sister," I answered too quickly, not knowing what else to say.

Why did I just lie to him? - my cheeks started to feel very hot.

I suddenly found myself firefighting as I tried to create a plausible back story to cover the lie I had just told him.

"We have different dads. I normally live with him," I was hoping to give him a reason why we had never met before.

"Oh, ok," Sam shrugged his shoulders and changed the subject again.

254

He knew that I had just lied to him and I found myself wanting to run away from him and my fib, I was embarrassed and felt stupid. He hadn't long begun to explain his childhood when I interrupted him.

"It's getting late, I had better go," I stopped him in his tracks.

I had thrown him. He looked forlorn but I left the park and walked back to Carol's.

Why did I lie? Have I just fucked up and lost the only friend I have? - I was furious with myself.

I liked Sam and enjoyed talking to him, but I needed to protect myself from getting hurt. Somehow, I was brilliant at hurting myself.

My phone vibrated and I nearly dropped it as I rescued it from my pocket.

'Hey, I had a really good time. Hope you did too.'

I found myself reading his simple text over and over as my sadness quickly turned to relief.

'So did I, it was fun. x'

'See you soon, I hope? x'

He had added a kiss too.

A content smile rippled across my face, Sam had managed to make me smile once again with something as insignificant as a simple text. The next day Sam asked if we could meet again and I agreed instantly.

'How has he made me so happy?' – a warm feeling filled my body.

Where there had been darkness in my life, there was colour; everything was brighter.

Chapter 33

Love is blind

My mission was to spend time with Sam. Despite hardly knowing him, my life was more bearable; I wished my days away waiting to see him again. The last bell of school day couldn't come quick enough and by now I was sprinting towards Jane in the waiting taxi. The journey was eternal but after she had dropped me off at Carol's, I found new energy. Mulling over what I should wear, I brimmed over with happiness.

"There is someone at the door for you, Jessica," Carol called from the hallway.

'The only people who ever call on me are the social services.' - I thought, as I ran out of my room and skidded to a stop at the top of the landing. Sam was standing at the front door with Carol. I ran downstairs, grabbed Sam by the arm and whisked him away from the house.

"Be back by ten," Carol yelled after us.

In foster care, a curfew is of utmost importance. To be late means mountains of problems ensue. A police search is triggered, a description of what occurred goes to social services, a report is written on file and future placements can be affected.

"Bye, Carol," Sam shouted back.

He tried to find his balance while I pulled him along. Once we were out of Carol's earshot, he turned with an amused expression on his face,

"What was all that about?" Sam screwed up his eyebrows.

"Oh, nothing," I mumbled once I had caught my breath.

It was then I saw a guy in the driver's seat of a car parked nearby. He was staring at us.

"Who's that?" I asked.

"Oh, that's my cousin, Jamie," Sam announced. "He gave me a lift here. Do you fancy coming back to mine?"

I hesitated. I didn't really know Sam and I was wary about going to a house, especially with two guys. But, I trusted Sam for some reason; he'd lived in foster care and Carol knew him. I threw caution to the wind and agreed to go with them.

Jamie was slightly older than Sam. He was skinny and scruffy with straw-like hair that could have done with a brush.

"Hey," Jamie chirped as I got into the back.

We drove off in the direction of St Dennis, arriving at Sam's dad's house soon after. Sam and I climbed out but Jamie wasn't coming in; he promised he would be back later. He revved the engine, spun the wheels and zipped away leaving us standing in a cloud of tyre smoke.

The new aspect of the house belied what lay inside. The stench of cigarette smoke filled the air; overflowing ashtrays lay on every surface while used cups and plates littered the worktops. Two guys sharing equalled no one cleaning up. After Sam introduced his dad, he asked if I wanted to go up to his room. It was no better than the rest of the house; bundles of unwashed clothes were strewn across the floor and the unmade bed signaled a typical boy's bedroom. He seemed embarrassed and attempted to fix his bed before inviting me to sit down.

"So, I guess you know that I'm in foster care then?" I ventured.

He bundled up his dirty washing and chucked it into a corner.

"Yes, why didn't you say anything?" he sat down next to me.

"I was embarrassed, I guess. I feel stupid that I had tried to lie about it," I admitted.

"Yeah, I get that, I felt like that too. I tried to hide it. It's hard for people to understand what it is like; they always end up judging you when they find out," Sam's somber tone tugged at my heart.

"Tell them to go fuck themselves, that's what I do. Anyway, how was school today?" and instantly, Sam had changed the subject.

He understood why foster care was difficult to talk about. His attitude made me feel comfortable so we talked for hours that night. I told him about my mum and how I had ended up in foster care. I spoke a little about Shawn, but I didn't tell him what had been done to me. I was not ready to tell that side of my story to anyone. The evening was flying by until we heard Jamie's car screech to a stop outside.

Over the next few weeks, I had plenty of company. If I wasn't with Sam, I would meet with Shawn in secret after everyone had gone to sleep. Sam and I would hang out in the park or, if Jamie was about, we'd get a lift to Sam's. His life was entertaining; the situations he had been involved in made good storytelling. I guess he was a bit of a bad boy, always up to mischief and often in trouble. His hilarious life made me forget my problems and, over time, I started to develop feelings for him. I was becoming happy again and this scared the shit out of me. I knew happiness meant something bad was about to happen. It only a matter of time; the invisible clock still ticked.

Two weeks later at Sam's house, the sound of Jamie's car, marked the end of our evening together. Sam was not joining us on the journey back to Carol's; Jamie needed to be somewhere else after he dropped me off. I kissed Sam goodbye and made my way out of the house to the car. I had gotten to know Jamie; he seemed ok. In Jamie's preferred driving style, the car roared off. Screeching around tight corners, I held on for grim death but still managed a light-hearted conversation about Sam. Suddenly, the car skidded to a halt in a layby. Jamie killed the engine and turned off the lights.

"Urm, what are you doing? I've got to get back before ten!" I nervously reminded him.

"It's ok, we have time. I find you really beautiful," he looked at me with a half-smile on his face.

His manner was intimidating.

"Thank you, but you know I'm with Sam right?" I was worried.

"I've seen you smile at me," he muttered, leaning over to kiss me.

"What the fuck are you doing?" I screamed and pushed him away.

He smelt of burger king, disgusting. I wiped my mouth with the sleeve of my jacket.

"I won't tell you if you don't," he leaned in again for a second attempt.

This time he used his weight to pin me against the car seat. I felt one of his hands between my legs as the other pulled my hand towards his crotch. I was frozen. Here was someone else, bigger and stronger, getting the better of me. The old feeling of being powerless washed over me. Although ingrained, I had not felt this way for a while.

Jamie suddenly stopped what he was doing and slumped back into his seat; he started the car and sped off up the road. I used my sleeve again to wipe the saliva Jamie had left all over my face and straightened my clothes. A few minutes later we pulled up outside Carol's. I moved to open the car door when Jamie grabbed my arm, pushing it down onto his crotch again.

"Let me go!" I yelled, pulling my arm away.

"Oh, come on, we could have a quickie. I don't take long," this time he grabbed me with more force.

His hand was rubbing the inside of my thigh but I found it difficult to struggle free from his vice-like grip.

"Stop, leave me alone!" by this time I was yelling.

At that moment, another car pulled up in front of Carol's house; this caused Jamie to stop. I looked up to see Mark, Carol's husband, had arrived home. Thankfully, this allowed me to escape from Jamie. Mark and I hadn't had much of an interaction. I guessed there were some issues in the marriage because Mark slept in the spare bedroom.

"Is everything ok, Jessica?" Mark enquired.

He glanced at Jamie sheepishly winding up his window.

"Yes, I'm fine," I offered.

"It's late, I suggest you get yourself inside it's past 10 o'clock," Mark reminded me.

I sighed at the sound of Jamie's car speeding away.

Mark had just saved me from God knows what but, instead of thanking him, I ran to the bedroom and burst into tears. My world was crashing down again.

Why does this keep happening to me? Do I have Please Attack Me written on my forehead or something? - I sobbed.

The vibration of my phone interrupted my thoughts, it was Sam.

What the fuck will I do? Will I tell him what Jamie has just done? Will he even believe me? – I was at a loss.

After all, Jamie was part of his family.

How can I keep this to myself if I still want to see Sam? That'll mean I'll have to see Jamie again. – I debated.

Jamie had left me with a huge dilemma. My happiness was about to be destroyed, and the price to be paid was Sam. The invisible clock was about to chime.

My phone vibrated again, this time it was Jamie.

'Please don't tell Sam, I'm sorry. I didn't mean to do that.'

Unbelievable! – I thought.

Another vibration.

260

'Hey babe, do you fancy seeing me again tomorrow? x'

It was Sam.

What the fuck am I meant to do now? - I wondered.

I was becoming angry at Sam, a defence mechanism. It was easier to be mad with him before he walked away from me.

'No, sorry, I'm busy tomorrow.'

I omitted the usual kiss at the end.

'What about Friday then?'

'Nope sorry, busy,'

I slammed my phone down on the bed before it vibrated.

'Hey, Princess, do you want to meet up later? x'

It was Shawn. My phone was shining like Christmas lights on a tree. Another text then arrived.

'Ok, what the fuck has Jamie done? x'

This time it was Sam. I had to give him credit where credit was due, Sam had read between the lines from my standoffish texts.

But how does he know Jamie has done something? - I wondered.

My phone went off again.

'Please don't say anything, I am really sorry.'

It was Jamie. Anger was building as I read his text. Next, my phone started to ring. It was Sam.

"What!" I almost screamed into the phone.

"Talk to me, what has my cousin done this time?" he sounded worried.

What's he done this time? Is this a regular thing? - I asked myself

"What do you think he's done?" I replied curiously.

"Well it seems like whenever I get a girlfriend and Jamie has time alone with them, I never hear from them again," Sam told me.

Girlfriend, did he actually just call me his girlfriend? – a grin appeared on my face.

This was new, I had never been called someone's girlfriend before; I liked it.

"Jamie tried it on with me, if it wasn't for Mark, fuck knows what would have happened," I explained.

He didn't say anything, there was a long pause.

"I'll fucking kill him," Sam growled through gritted teeth.

"Just leave it," I suggested.

"Look, meet me tomorrow please," Sam pleaded.

"Ok, I will," I ended the call.

Why is my life so complicated? Am I cursed or something? - I sat down on the bed.

My phone flashed again.

'Are you ok?'

Shawn's text needed to be answered and finally arranged to meet with him that night. We drove around, I chatted and he listened. I had needed someone to calm me down; I had needed a dad.

The next day was Saturday, no school. I didn't have to wait the entire day before seeing Sam. There were five messages from Jamie but I didn't bother reading them. Sam had probably already had a go at him so I didn't want to read what might be nasty texts from Jamie. I wanted to get the conversation with Sam done and dusted. I needed him to believe what had happened; he had become a big part of my life and gave me a reason to carry on. Sam was outside waiting for me as Carol and I pulled up. After she left, he ushered me up to his bedroom.

"Tell me exactly what happened," Sam demanded.

I sat down on his bed and explained the events involving Jamie. I wasn't sure if Sam was annoyed at me or Jamie. He silently stared at the floor leaving me feeling uncomfortable.

"Look if you don't believe me, here's my phone and the messages that he sent me last night," I handed it over.

As Sam read through the messages, the muscles on his face tightened.

"Wait here," he handed me my phone and walked out of the room.

262

I was beginning to think that Sam was taking a long time to come back when I heard a car pull up outside. Car doors opened and slammed and people were arguing. I went to the window to see what the commotion was. An expensive-looking car was parked outside; a man and woman were shouting at each other. As they walked towards the house, Sam stepped out of the car.

"What the fuck!" Sam had not only walked out of the room, but he had also walked out of the house.

I pulled my trainers on and raced downstairs in time to see the front door open and the man and the woman walk in. Sam was there too, his face covered in cuts and bruises and his clothes were dishevelled; he had been in a fight with someone.

"You must be Jessica," the woman asked when I reached the bottom step.

She was well-spoken and immaculately dressed without a hair out of place; a well-heeled lady.

"Yes, why?" I answered nervously.

"Nice to meet you, do you mind if we have a chat?" she asked politely.

Her tone indicated it was more of an order than an ask; she held the lounge door open for me. I looked at Sam; he smiled, revealing blood-stained teeth.

What on earth has he done? - I wondered.

Sam's dad had been asleep in his armchair. When he woke up, he shook his head at the number of people in the room.

"Sam has just attacked our son, Jamie. As far as we can gather apparently it was over you, Jessica," she looked at me.

What the fuck! - I mouthed to Sam.

With a shrug of his shoulders, he smiled again.

"We need to get to the bottom of this. I am not having my son being accused of ridiculous allegations," she continued.

So, her golden boy could do no wrong in her eyes.

"Ridiculous allegation? He's a dirty perv. Why do you think I hit the twat?" Sam scoffed.

He seemed to be proud that he had defended my honour.

"That's enough Sam, we are aware of your opinion. I would like to hear Jessica's side of the story," her tone sharp.

I was interrogated by her for the next hour. She asked questions about what Jamie did that night but found excuses for his actions and developed arguments to shift the blame onto me. However, I was comforted by the knowledge that Sam's dad believed me. By the time the couple left, a rift had split the families and I felt like a homewrecker. I wished I had kept quiet about the incident. I made my way up to Sam's bedroom to gather my belongings. I was embarrassed by the entire situation and thought I had better leave, but Sam followed me and begged me not to go.

"What about your family? I don't want to cause any problems," I countered his pleas.

"Well, if they want to stand by Jamie after what he did. Fuck them! Jess, I actually love you and won't let anyone hurt you," Sam held my hand.

He was the first person who had fought for me and, in his own way, protected me. He was also the first person that had ever told me that they loved me, just for being me.

I guess at that moment, I realised that I had fallen for him too.

Chapter 34

Dilemmas

Sam and I were inseparable during the run-up to Christmas and what had happened with Jamie brought us closer. The happiness that I had found in Sam had other positive effects on my life too. I had managed to rekindle my friendship with my old friends. Lisa, Chloe, Alice and Naomi. The three girls involved in the flooding incident apologised to me and I was happy to have them back in my life. It made a huge difference at school. The bullying stopped and life became less complicated.

I was getting back to my version of normality. But, life could hardly be called normal; my mother had been AWOL for months and I had no idea if Jacob was safe. I was still sneaking out late at night to spend time with Shawn, although that had become fun. Instead of attacking me, he taught me how to drive. We ate burgers while chatting and, once again, I felt as though I had a real dad.

Unfortunately, the festive season was about to highlight just how far from normal my life was. I had to decide where I would spend

Christmas, but the decision was never mine to make. Christmas is meant to be about families, but in foster care, this is not the case. It is quite clear that the foster child is not part of a family and, during the holidays, kids who are in care are often asked to leave their foster families. This is so that the foster carers can have a reprieve and spend time with their own families. Unwanted kids at Christmas would be sent to residential children's homes. However, if you had another family member, a grandparent or a sibling over the age of eighteen, you can spend time with them instead.

Carol had asked for family time at Christmas. I didn't know if I had any grandparents and Shawn and Susan were out of the equation. I had no idea where Jack was so my only chance of staying out of a children's home for Christmas was Laura. I asked my social worker to contact her to ask, thankfully Laura agreed. I hadn't seen her for months; I was excited yet nervous.

Carol drove me to Laura's house on 23rd December and as I was about to leave her, she handed me a Christmas stocking filled with presents.

"Happy Christmas, Jessica," her face beamed.

"Who is this from?" I shook my head.

I was more than taken back that I had been handed the stocking. I wondered if Susan might have sent it, after all, she was still my mum.

"It's your Christmas presents from Mark and me," she continued smiling.

I was overwhelmed by the gesture and thanked her more than once.

Over the holidays, there was still no word from Susan or Jacob, Laura tried to make the time special but I could tell I was in the way. Naturally, their Christmas focused on baby Susan because I had been a last-minute surprise. I was thankful to Laura but also happy when Carol came to collect me. I couldn't wait to spend time with Sam but I had arranged to meet Shawn first. I asked how his Christmas had been and we talked over old times. I found myself wishing I could wind the clock back to the year we spent with Crystal and Mike.

The holidays passed quickly and the school term restarted, it was our final year at secondary and school it was different. I was invited out to different places by old and new friends. Not only was school different, but I also detected a change in Sam. He wasn't happy when I spent time with my other friends. He turned up at the school gates and wanted to know who I had been talking to. His lack of trust meant he became controlling.

I had been back at school for a month and, at the end of the day, I found Sam at the gate. He looked nervous and, as I approached with my friends, he got down on one knee.

"Jess, will you marry me?" he opened a small box containing a ring.

I was fifteen years old. We had only known each other for a few months and yes, I loved him, but this was too much. Other students gathered around us and, before I knew it, half the school was staring at Sam as he waited for my reply. I wanted the ground to swallow me, I was so embarrassed.

Like most girls, I had grown up watching Disney movies and I believed that one day Prince Charming would sweep me off my feet and make me his princess. The proposal would happen in some magical setting with fireworks in the background. My grand proposal was at the school gates while I was dressed in my school uniform. I loved Sam, but I could not see him as my future husband or Prince Charming for that matter. Images flashed across my mind; me, dressed in a stunning wedding dress, walking down the aisle where Sam, dressed in tracksuit and trainers, was waiting for me.

Sam waited patiently for my answer while he held out the ring for everyone to see.

"Urm, I don't know," I didn't know what else to say.

"I thought you might have more of an answer than that," he was getting the message.

Sweat began to gather on his forehead.

"Say yes, say yes!" the crowd chanted.

Sam was not the only one feeling the heat of the situation; I also needed this madness to stop.

My life had been spent trying to be the invisible girl and now I was the centre of attention.

"Ok," came out of my mouth involuntarily.

The chants turned to claps and cheers; Sam jumped up and placed the ring on my finger. I had agreed to his mad proposal. I looked down at the ring on my finger; it felt wrong. Instead of feeling happy I felt sad. I could not imagine spending the rest of my life with him. I had always wanted someone to love me and Sam did, but this felt more like he was pissing up a tree and marking his territory.

'Did he do this just to make it known to everyone else that I'm his? - I began to wonder.

The moment Sam had placed the ring on my finger; a crack appeared in our relationship, one that would never heal.

I had said yes, not because I wanted to, but because I needed to get out of the situation he had put me in. Although I had Sam, I felt alone. I started to think about the people I no longer had in my life, my real dad was never going to walk me down the aisle and Shawn was banned from having any contact. My mum would not take me dress shopping or help with planning my big day. None of them would be at my wedding. I shuddered at the thought and my sadness grew. I was never going to have the Disney wedding I had dreamed about, the magical day that the rest of the world would enjoy. Sam's proposal had added to my already complicated life.

Weeks passed without knowing how to tell him that I loved him but didn't want to marry him; I was scared he would leave me. The tiny ring he had given me was meant to bring joy; instead, it had brought dilemmas and sadness. I found myself keeping the ring in my bag when Sam wasn't around, until one day I lost the bloody thing. I frantically searched everywhere for it, but it was gone. When I finally plucked up the courage to tell Sam what had happened, of course, he was furious.

"Why the fuck did you take it off?" he yelled.

"I didn't want to damage it or to lose it. I thought it would be safer in my bag," I was digging for answers.

"Well, that's fucking helpful. You lost it anyway," he shouted with a hint of sarcasm in his voice.

Eventually, he calmed down after he had worn a pathway into the carpet and smoked a few cigarettes. He insisted that he would save up for a replacement ring. I may have plucked up the courage to tell him about the ring, but after the reaction he had, how could I admit I didn't want to marry him?

Chapter 35

Prom

My network of friends grew as rapidly as the cracks widened in my relationship with Sam. Fortunately, we both had other things to focus on, especially when Sam's younger brother was given permission from social services to return to the family home. Luke was a year younger than Sam; he was tall and skinny with intense brown eyes. Sam was over the moon that his brother was back and he didn't lose any time in introducing Luke to everyone we knew. That included my friend Naomi and, not surprisingly, a relationship blossomed between her and Luke.

Their new liaison helped ease some of the pressure between Sam and me. We became a foursome. This was until Luke decided that he had taken a shine to Alice instead of Naomi. A major rift developed between Naomi and Alice and my friendship group split in two. While Naomi and Alice refused to talk to each other, the rest of the senior year was distracted by the upcoming prom.

Cupid was shooting his little love arrows everywhere I looked and students partnered up with each other in preparation for the big day. As arrows hit the rest of my friends, they were asked to prom but I knew I would be going alone. Sam was two years older than me and would not be allowed to attend.

Despite the arguments within our friends' group, we agreed to go to the prom together. Alice was in the same situation as me so we decided to meet up with Sam and Luke after prom had finished. Once this decision was made the only thing left to do, was to find the perfect outfits.

I found a lovely pair of pink high heel shoes then a beautiful dress. The dress was dark grey; it had a heart-shaped bodice outlined with imitation diamonds. When I tried it on, I looked so different and, for the first time, I felt beautiful. However, it wasn't as easy as that. I couldn't buy the dress and shoes, I had to make a note of the items along with their cost and hope the social services would agree to pay for them.

Sadness overcame me as I watched proud mums and dads shopping with their daughters, searching for the perfect prom dresses. Their dresses would be bought and paid for by a loving parent, while I had to go through the embarrassment of applying to social services. Since Sam's proposal, emptiness had been growing inside me more than ever, every single life event or milestone in my life was the same. There would be no one to wish me luck or give me away, no proud grandparents if I was to ever have my own family one day. I walked out of the shop thinking if there had been a sobriety coin for abandonment, I would have clutched it and called my sponsor.

At that moment, I began to understand why people with alcohol addictions struggle to go about their day. Alcohol is everywhere, in supermarkets, restaurants and even the petrol station so the temptation for what they crave is in their face. The only difference was, I craved to be wanted, for someone to be full of pride for me and, unfortunately, I was surrounded by reminders that I was unwanted and no one was proud of me. I would love to have heard that I had grown into a beautiful young lady.

I left for the evening ahead but this empty feeling had grown to such a point, where I *needed* not *wanted* a mum or dad. I suppose this was the reason why I called Shawn; I guess he had become my sponsor. He was someone that I recognised as my dad even though I knew that he could not be around to take photos of the prom for the family album. Although he was banned from seeing me, he could still play a part in my big day and as our phone call ended, I felt excited.

So much had happened at school since I first arrived. I had been bullied and beaten up and I had lost my family. School had been a place of safety and a place of danger for me. I had been the unnoticed girl for a long time but things had changed in my final few months at school. When the morning of prom finally arrived, our entire year group was buzzing with excitement in anticipation of the night ahead. Another chapter was about to end in my life and, when the final bell rang that day, I didn't want to leave.

I met up with Naomi and we headed to the hairdresser. Carol and Shawn had given me some money so that I could get my hair done after school. The stylist cut and styled my thick bushy mane into beautiful curls which were then clipped back to reveal my neck and shoulders. I felt older and more confident as we checked out our new hairstyles in the mirror. Afterwards, we made our way to Naomi's house to get ready for the evening ahead. Naomi's mum had arranged for a friend of hers to do our makeup and nails before we got changed.

Before I slipped on my prom dress, I sprayed myself with Kylie Minogue perfume and I instantly felt emotional. This was one of the only things I had left from my mum. When Susan had left Jasmine's, she had forgotten to take her favorite perfume with her and when Michelle had come for me, I had packed it into my bin liners. Susan would wear the perfume on special occasions and smelling the fragrance of her again was another reminder of how much I had lost. This little bottle of perfume bought back another memory of a happier time too. Together, Susan and I had painted her bedroom at our council house, grey paint had dripped onto the black lid of the bottle and it was never cleaned off. I kept the perfume with the grey paint drip on the lid. My mum was not going to see me today and tell me I looked beautiful but, in a strange way, by wearing the perfume, I felt like she would be part of my day.

I slipped into my prom dress and my beautiful, pink shoes and, as I stared in the mirror, I saw how revealing my dress was. It hugged my body and showed off my assets, my boobs looked larger than normal making me self-conscious. I had always tried to hide my body away from everyone at school and now I was going to the prom where my entire year would see me like this.

I can't do this, they are all going to make fun of me and laugh at me, - I started to panic. Then Naomi joined me in the mirror.

"You have to admit it, Jess, we look good!" Naomi wiggled to straighten her dress.

"Do you really think so?" I asked.

"Are you kidding? You look stunning," she assured me.

Her compliment gave me the confidence I needed.

I'm going to the prom and I couldn't give a shit what people think of me, - I reminded myself.

Naomi and I broke out into a celebration dance before we made our way downstairs. Tears formed in Naomi's mum's eyes when she caught sight of her daughter in her dress for the first time. She placed her hand over her mouth and began to cry.

"You look so beautiful, I am so proud, " she pulled Naomi into her arms.

I looked over to the front door and wished that my mum would walk through the door, hug me and tell me she was proud of me.

Does she even know it's my prom today? - I wondered.

While photos were being taken of Naomi in her dress and with her mum, the doorbell rang and my heart skipped a beat. Naomi's mum answered it and, to my surprise, Cathy, my drama therapist appeared in the hallway. I was in shock that she had turned up at Naomi's house but I was delighted to see her.

"My goodness, Jessica, you look like a princess," she chuckled. "Well, do a twirl then."

I stood up and spun around.

"Do you think I look silly?" my uneasiness about what my dress revealed emerged.

"You look stunning, you really do," Cathy said as tears formed in her eyes.

She handed me a beautiful bunch of pink roses.

"Jessica, I know you're nervous, but just think how far you have come. Do you remember the first time we met?" she asked.

"Yes," I nodded.

"I walked in that room and you looked so scared sitting with your bag on your lap, your shoulders looked ridged and you were frightened of the world. You told me you were only there because you were dragged. Do you remember that?" she asked.

"Yes, I remember," I said.

"You have come so far since that day, I am so proud of you," a tear dripped down her cheek.

Cathy was right. The first meeting with her now seemed so long ago and loads had changed. I had changed; I was stronger than I was back then.

"Oh, I see you managed to get the pink fuchsia shoes you talked about," she admired my shoes.

"Yep, I finally got them," the smile on my face said it all

274

Since I was a little girl, I'd always wanted pink, high-heeled shoes and I remembered telling Cathy about my dream that had now come true.

"If you get nervous Jess, just think of this moment and your pink shoes, they will give you a disguise when you need one," Cathy said. She always had an interesting way of using objects to draw strength from.

"Thank you for everything you have done for me, you don't know how much it means to me that you are here," I choked back the tears.

"You are a lot tougher than you think," she said with a hug.

The doorbell rang again and Carol appeared. I was shocked that two people who had no real reason to bother with me, had both managed to make me feel special. Our friends started to arrive with their proud parents and more photos were taken. I watched from the hallway.

"Girls, take a look outside," Carol raised her voice through the melee. We gathered outside in time to see a white, monster truck limousine pull up.

"Are you serious?" I shouted excitedly.

I turned around to see both Cathy and Carol grinning at us.

"Well, I couldn't have you arriving in a beaten up, old taxi now could I?" Carol's cheeky smile widened.

I could not believe she had done this for us all. I hugged her again.

The monster truck was mental; leather sofas curved around the inside while base speakers boomed out music that made our bodies vibrate. There was a disco ball and I could not help but beam as I watched the excitement on my friends' faces when we pulled away and headed to the hotel for our prom night. I felt like Cinderella, the princess finally going to her ball.

By the time we reached the hotel, none of us wanted to leave the limousine. The short drive went too quickly. I had been enjoying the luxury of our private party but now my nerves started to twitch.

I can do this - I told myself.

I smiled down at my pink shoes before stepping out of the car.

The hotel entrance was grand and a red carpet had been laid out for us. A photographer stood waiting. I felt like a celebrity as I walked up the red carpet and had my photo taken. The doors to the hotel opened to reveal a large room that had been draped with balloons and banners. Beautifully decorated tables were scattered around the dance floor. A mix of colours danced around the room from the soft lighting; it felt magical. Most of my year had already arrived and were standing, immaculately dressed, in groups. Everyone looked fantastic; there wasn't a school tie in sight.

I took a deep breath as I walked into the ballroom; my heart started to thump. People were staring at me and I wanted to turn and run.

No, be brave, Jessica. You are never gonna see these people again - I looked down at my pink shoes and remembered what Cathy had said.

As if by magic, my head lifted and my back straightened, my shoes had given me the confidence boost I needed and I walked confidently into the crowd of people.

"Blimey, small fry, you scrub up well," I heard a voice shout out.

I turned around. Johnny, the boy who had taunted me my entire school life, was standing in front of me.

"Really, is that going to be followed with an insult?" I asked curiously.

"No, honestly you look really nice," he insisted.

"Oh, thank you," I said slightly confused.

This was the nicest comment he had ever made to me.

"Have a good evening," he said before he turned back to talk to his friends.

Did I just dream what he said? - I asked myself.

When I arrived at our assigned table, I saw my name neatly written on a place card between Naomi's and Alice's. Once everyone had arrived, a three-course meal was served. Speeches were read out and it was as though we were guests of honour at a music award ceremony. The entire evening was lovely; a perfect time that sadly had to come to an end.

Alice and I made our way to the exit and once outside, the headteacher asked who was picking us up.

"We're getting a taxi," I said quietly.

"I thought we were …," I interrupted Alice by grabbing her arm.

I dragged her away and headed towards a taxi that Naomi was getting into.

"Where too?" the driver asked.

"Can you just drop us at the bottom of the road please?" I handed Naomi a five-pound note for our share before the taxi stopped and we got out.

"Jess, what's going on?" Alice asked.

"We are meeting my dad," I explained as the taxi drove away.

Each parent I had watched over the past few weeks had given their kids the same look. They were now seeing young adults rather than children. I longed for someone to recognize this in me; I wanted the same look. An overwhelming need to feel normal and wanted led me to this point.

The day I bought my dress and shoes, I had called Shawn to ask if he would drive me home from the prom. He said that he would be honoured. Yes, he was a monster, but he was a monster that had saved me in many other ways over years. Since I had been in care, he had become more of a dad to me than ever before. He had listened to my problems and reassured me everything would be ok; he had even taught me how to drive. When Sam asked me to marry him and I envisaged my wedding, Shawn was probably the only person that I could have relied on to make the effort and turn up for me. I had even pictured him walking me down the aisle. After all the pain and hurt that he had caused me, Shawn had somehow managed to become my dad.

I had dreamt about a fairy tale ending to my perfect night, where a parent would tell me they were proud of me and give me the same look that I had seen on so many faces. It made me realise how much I missed my family, but this was only ever going to be a dream, as the clock struck twelve.

An eerie thick Cornish mist had gathered across the road as the dark clouds floated over the moon. Our hair danced in the wind as we walked towards a purple Cherokee Jeep. We were blinded by the strong glow from the headlights but Shawn suddenly stepped into view. The proud father I was excited to see wasn't standing in front of me; instead taking his place was the devil with his eyes firmly fixed on Alice and me.

Letters

Cathy,

You once said to me, if you could help just one child your work would be complete. I was that one child. You will never know how much you helped to save my life.

The Girl in the Pink Fuschia Shoes, the manuscript you wrote about me has helped me to write my book and understand myself a little bit better.

Thank you so much for everything, it meant the world to me.

Jessica xx

Mike,

Although you will never have the opportunity to read this, thank you for the time you spent with me. It meant a lot to me, you were always so kind.

RIP.

Jessica xx

Louise.

I hope Steve paid for his crimes against you and the others he undoubtedly abused. If you ever read this, Louise. I really hope you made it out and you have a peaceful life full of love! Jessica xx

Epilogue

Have you ever wondered what a guilty man in the dock looks like as the penny drops and he realises there will be no get-out-of-jail free card for him this time? He might be a blubbering mess, pleading for forgiveness. Maybe he repents while waiting to be told his fate. Perhaps that's how it should be.

For me, as I watched Shawn, my rapist and abuser, in court, it was as though he didn't have a care in the world. The system meant nothing to him; prison appeared to be nothing more than an inconvenience. It was a game, a total joke to him. Shawn, the devil himself, rocked backwards and forwards on his chair. All he needed was a bag of popcorn and his slippers and he could have been at home chilling, watching *Netflix*. Maybe inside there was some form of remorse from a frightened and regretful man, but I couldn't detect it.

It was mental torture watching him. I felt numb and scared, as we waited for the verdict to be read out; it all came down to this moment and twelve strangers in a small room. People I had never met were debating the fate of Shawn, my stepfather. He was yet another member of my family who was about to be, justifiably, ripped away from me, all I could do was sit and wait.

The police only managed to convict my stepfather for a small portion of his crimes. There was a much bigger story that was never told. I didn't disclose the full truth at the time of the court case. The judge and jury had merely heard part of my story; I was too frightened and ashamed to give all the facts. The things he did to me were too horrific; I could not bring myself to talk about what happened.

The only other person in the room who knew the truth was Shawn. His lawyers had attempted to discredit me and made me as though I was the one on trial. Some of the questions they asked revealed the most embarrassing and personal details of my life in front of a room filled with strangers.

Throughout the trial, alarm bells had been ringing loudly in my head, as I remembered the threats that had been made on my life. Threats were given by Shawn and the others he had tricked me into visiting and who, ultimately, participated in sexual abuse. However, this man who I had called Dad, had been there for me when no one else seemed to care, he was the only person in my life that had come close to being a father figure. I cared for him in a father-daughter type of way, but sadly he lost my trust when he abused me.

Some are born with a silver spoon in their mouths, some are born less fortunate! - I silently reminded myself.